Praise for *Geography of the Soul*...

"An extraordinary read! *Geography of the Soul* is arduous and gentle, challenging and provocative, as Dr. Fitts takes the reader on a true pilgrimage across the Ridgeway Trail in England, 100 miles on foot. I predict, just like Cheryl Strayed's *Wild* sent record numbers of people out of their comfort zones to walk the Pacific Crest Trail, people will soon be out in droves to the *Ridgeway Trail* to walk in Royce's adventurous footsteps. As a woman, I wondered if I'd be able to relate to Royce's story. I'm surprised and delighted to report that I not only related but felt he was peering into my soul as he was revealing his. *Geography of the Soul* turns out to be a book for anyone with a soul and a dream, and the willingness to find magic in unexpected places.

Kelly Sullivan Walden,
Dream Expert, Media Personality, & International
Bestselling Author of *A Crisis Is A Terrible Thing to Waste*

"Royce takes you on a non-linear journey into the inner and outer landscapes of his life. His stravage, as he describes it—
'...engaging in a defiant walk, a decision to stray without limits...'—invites you to see beyond your conceived notions and beliefs and stretch into limitlessness, flow, and mystery—a journey that many of us are afraid to take. Royce guides you in ways you may have never encountered before, sharing waking and sleeping dreams, and ultimately, if you are willing, helping you find your authentic truth."

Dr. Patti Ashley,
psychotherapist, TEDx speaker,
author of *Shame-Informed Therapy: Treatment Strategies to Overcome Shame and Reconstruct the Authentic Self*

"Run! Don't walk to get your copy!! In this compelling memoir, Dr. Royce Fitts has crafted a literary masterpiece that will resonate with readers across the globe. The book's ability to simultaneously touch our hearts, stimulate our minds, and nourish our souls is a testament to the author's endearing spirit and profound understanding of the human condition. It is a transformative journey of healing, revelation, and self-discovery that will remain etched in my heart for a lifetime. I cannot recommend this book enough; it is truly a gift to the literary world and anyone seeking inspiration and enlightenment.

Infused with a rare blend of poetic elegance and raw authenticity, readers are invited on an intimate voyage along the ancient Ridgeway National Trail. With every page, the author skillfully paints landscapes that come alive with vibrant hues, evoking a sense of wanderlust that leaves the heart yearning for adventure.

Dr. Fitts masterfully takes readers on a transformative expedition that transcends the boundaries of ordinary memoirs, offering a profound exploration of the human spirit, dreams, and the landscapes that shape our existence.

Viviana Guzmán
GRAMMY Nominated album artist,
TEDx speaker, internationally performing flutist,
faculty member, University of California, Santa Cruz

"...*The Geography of the Soul* is a lyrical, heartfelt exploration of what it means to be human. You see yourself from a new perspective."

Laura K. Deal
Storyteller, Poet, Dream Worker

The Geography of the Soul

Dreams, Reality, and the Journey of a Lifetime

Dr. Royce Fitts

Flint Hills Publishing

The Geography of the Soul
Dreams, Reality, and the Journey of a Lifetime
© Royce Fitts 2023
All rights reserved.

Original cover oil painting by Bonnie J. Gibson

Bonniejgibson.com

Cover Design by Amy Albright

stonypointgraphics.weebly.com

Flint Hills Publishing

Topeka, Kansas
www.flinthillspublishing.com

Printed in the U.S.A.

This book reflects the author's present recollections of
experiences over time and from his perspective.
Some events and dialogue have been recreated.

Paperback Book: ISBN: 978-1-953583-54-3
Hardback Book ISBN 978-1-953583-55-0
Electronic Book ISBN 978-1-953583-56-7

Library of Congress Control Number: 2023913983

Dedication

For Mom and Dad, for your wounded wisdom, and your love for us as children. Your lives were born of pain, nightmares, joys, faith, and prairie dreams. All this grows in me each day.

For Ellie and Shane, flying. Soaring with heart, soul, creation, and love. Don't ever stop. Be safe and be adventurous, and, if you must make a choice, be adventurous.

O ye worn soul,
come, walk,
stravage with me,
stray defiantly!
through the shadows of wounds and time,
through dreams unbidden,
hidden,
shocking our souls into deep awakenings,
exploring our geography,
our landscapes,
and healing our souls.

Royce Fitts

Contents

Foreword

A s soon as I met Royce, I understood him to be a man full of wonder and trust, hope and doubt, vulnerability and wisdom. He had such an eye for the beauty of the natural world, the tenderness of the human heart, and the modern mess of it all.

We met on a summer afternoon at a retreat center deep in the Catskill Mountains of New York. The previous autumn, Royce had taken the hike of a lifetime you're about to read about, and this book was tugging at his sleeve. In the years since I've had the honor to know Royce and his stories, I've come to realize that my first impression was right on.

On first glance, Royce and I wouldn't seem like creative partners. Three decades separate us (Royce and my dad were born the same year). He was raised on a farm in the Midwest and grew up in a fundamentalist Christian faith before enrolling in seminary. I come from a seaside town in New England and decided I was a witch while attending a Jesuit university. But we share so much that feels *universal*: a passion for the wisdom of the landscape and the ancestors; a curiosity about the unseen realms of the mind and the spirit; grief over "the way things are" in our disconnected culture; and a yearning to be part of the change we wish to see in the future.

Shortly before publication, Royce sent me a note regarding the subtitle for *The Geography of the Soul*. He was certain he wanted to highlight dreams and his life transforming journey, but did "reality" really work? Was that word accidentally perpetuating the misconception that dreams and the so-called real world are truly separate entities? Were dreams being relegated to make-believe?

Once you get to know Royce over the course of these pages, you'll understand that nighttime dreams—and the ways they shape waking life—are very real, for him and for all of us who dare to pay heed to the movies projected in the sleeping mind. The inner dreamscape is as vital as a 1500-year-old church in the British wildwood, an alley in Peckham district of London, a dining hall at a U.S. army post, or a beloved cottonwood tree on the Nebraska prairie.

As you see on the cover of this book you hold in your hand, Royce decided to stick with that word, and I'm glad he did. Though you're invited to wonder about the mysteries of creation and ponder images that have emerged in dreams (both Royce's and those of his psychotherapy and Dream Work clients), "reality" remains close to both author and reader on every step of the journey. You're invited to enter into conversation with the fullness of the beautiful, battered Earth and its striving, stumbling society. You're guided by a writer who is a wounded healer, an eyes-wide-open wise man, and a gentle soul who nonetheless rages at the inequity, greed, and cruelty that mark much of human history.

I think we all could use a bit of practice reckoning with both dreams and reality. From Royce, I've gotten to know this precious piece of the planet, England's Ridgeway Trail. And, I have learned so much about the power of the interior realms, all crafted from experience, projection, yearning, and more than a little inexplicable magic.

Marisa Goudy
Writing Coach, Story Healer, Author,
& Host of KnotWork Storytelling

Introduction
Place Forms Us

In modern life, we are inundated with some version of "the pursuit of happiness." Many people believe that our ultimate goal in life is a kind of relaxed, emotional, and material prosperity shrouded in perpetual bliss. Maybe, at some level, all we really want is to be rich and smiling! In my explorations of the *Geography of the Soul*, I'm not particularly interested in happiness. Although being happy is an honorable and pleasurable experience that sometimes flows like a rushing mountain stream, refreshing our souls and lives with new energy, laughter, and even euphoria, those feelings are temporary and cannot sustain us through the long-haul of life. Mere happiness won't hold up to the awful tragedies, joys, and crazy complexities of our human existence. Instead, I am interested in living out life's true callings. My quest, and the quest I hope you'll take with me, relies on living out your heart's deepest values and life's deepest meanings. It's a journey marked by the struggles, doubts, pains, and joys that invariably color a life that is dedicated to integrity, vulnerability, and authenticity.

This book explores the deepest longings of the human heart. It's an invitation to roam beyond conventional thinking. Throughout our journey together, I'll be asking you to do what I am asking myself to do: stray from the usual, acceptable, pre-programed paths of our existence.

We seem to have inherited unconscious habits of being

that prevent our spirits from taking the greatest risk: bursting open with courageous openheartedness. These habits, like habits do, become natural, "safe," unexamined reactions to life. These ruts become the trail and we get entrapped in "the ways things are."

I was entrapped by the habits of a lifetime. Circumstances—many of them chosen and self-made—forced me to live a kind of conventional, boxed-in existence. For years, my soul cried for change, as I longed to burst out of the constraints and live with more openheartedness, adventure, and courage. Fearing disruption, shame, rejection, emotional and financial poverty, I avoided that call. Deep down, however, I still needed to break free, to stray off the trail—way off— and wander without a set direction in order to discover a whole new way of being.

So, I took a hike.

I took the hike of a lifetime along an ancient trail that had seen uncountable wanderers over, at least, its 5,000 years of existence. I became one of them as I wandered along the Ridgeway National Trail and as I wandered into myself. The walk across the English countryside became a metaphor, a living symbol that enabled me to explore my past and create a new future.

Our Stravage is Calling

What might happen if you strayed from the old habits and paths of your lifetime that entrap you and keep you from embracing a more authentic, courageous life? I invite you to be curious, *radically* curious, and to wonder about your inner and outer geography as you explore your own undiscovered country.

I heard the word *stravage* for the first time while in a counseling session with an especially challenging psychotherapy client. Some months before this conversation, he had confessed to me that he often lied during our times together. He lied about his war experiences, travels, and friendships. This revelation was disconcerting, but, in the end, I didn't really care. I didn't take it personally, because, therapeutically, he needed to lie. His fabrication was *his* story, his edgy waking-life dream. He *needed* to lie to me, to stray from the facts, to capture me with his stories, to defy convention in order to feel more connected to me. We both recovered from that therapeutic glitch and kept working together.

This man was well-read, better read than me. A few months before I began what I called a self-made sabbatical, I sought to prepare my clients for my departure. As I informed him about my upcoming journey, he pulled himself up out of his chair, used his cane to balance himself, stood tall, shook my hand, and said, "You are going on a *stravage*." Puzzled, I asked what he meant, and he explained the word's rebellious Scottish origins. He described that *stravaging* was to engage in a defiant walk, a decision to *stray* without limits, to freely, aimlessly, roam. He later wrote an essay for me describing the meaning of the word and why he used it to describe my call to wander. *Stravage* came from an even older word, *extravagate*, and this old Scottish idea of audacious roaming was a tremendous gift. It would become the theme of my hiking journey and this book. *Stravage* describes a way to *be*, a necessary, edgy act of defiance. The word gave me permission to go on a mission that would take me beyond the rigid boxes of conventional life, and create radical new meanings in a beautiful, wounded world.

We are Stardust that Talks

The ancient biblical stories of creation on which I was raised refer to a most intimate relationship between Earth and us: *out of the dust of the Earth, we are formed, and we return.* In an intuitive, poetic moment, the Hebrew writer described what science thousands of years later would discover: the universe and all it contains, the planets and stars, is simply made of settled stardust. You and I are made of molecules and particles of the stars too. The mysterious clouds of universal dust have drifted here, adhered with unknown forces and, of all things, *we* emerged. Perhaps this drifting and settling of dust comes from the touch of cosmic artists who used their evolutionary brushes to paint landscapes or trace the shapes of new life forms. Some people, of course, call this grand creative act the work of god. Sometimes, I do too. (My decision throughout this book to not capitalize "god" is not meant to be disrespectful, but rather reflects my opinion that using a lower-case "g" equalizes all belief systems.)

We are stardust that talks. We are in an eternal conversation, in a constant creative exchange of forming and reforming with the earth and sky. We are also stardust that walks and shapes the earth with each footfall. In the Lakota stories from the American prairie, we are a part of *the all that is,* forever. Earth is engaged in an eternal process of formation and reformation. We mirror the Earth. Earth forms us. And, in turn, we form the Earth.

We are always in an intimate relationship with the physical world. Sometimes our relationship is beautiful and nourishing. Other times, painful and destructive. Sometimes we are destructive, and sometimes it's the physical world that seems intent on destroying life as we know it. Storms. Droughts. Erosion. Eruptions. Explosions. These words describe the landscape as well as the actions of the humans that dwell upon it.

The soul, that which is mysteriously *us,* reflects and mirrors the Earth. The soul has a geography of its own. The soul, also, has weather systems and is constantly engaged in formation and reformation. We are indeed made from the dust of the Earth. We survey the place and space in which we live—an apartment, a hut, a farm, a forest, an island, a desert, a mountain, a city. Consciously or not, we are conversing with *the all that is* around us. Geography forms us. Place forms us.

The winds of the Earth can be experienced as living beings, capable of carrying messages from the spirits. Indeed, sometimes the wind itself is called god, carving and re-forming all it touches. The ancient Hebrews had a word, *ruach.* It refers to the breath of life, the fierce and gentle wind of god, Yahweh. Jesus described the spirit as something like the wind, "You know not where it comes from or where it goes, but you know it is there, you feel it…"

The *ruach* blows across the Earth, blows the chaotic unformed dust, and then, the dust settles. High prairies form, steppes across the vast openness of sky and land, intimidating and wondrous, eventually giving way to mountains that pierce the heavens. Yet, the wind ceases not. With the patience of eons, the wind continues to blow the dust fiercely and gently across the Earth's surface. The Earth is a living cathedral—dynamic, evolving, and forming all life it holds. The spirit of the winds and the dust of the earth conspire together to nudge, carve, and sculpt the hardest stones into mysterious, mystical shapes that beckon us to stare, to gather, to worship.

Place may be the vast, arid prairie of the American West, diminished by nineteenth century Anglo-European ignorance as the "Great American Desert." Place may be the majestic urban landscape of London. Place may be a medicine wheel on a high plateau in the Wyoming Bighorns that is thousands of years old. Place may be a tiny island off the coast of Scotland that holds some of the oldest rocks on Earth and carries memories of some of the most ancient spiritualities in the world. Place may be a U.S. military installation in the forests of northern New York that supports democratic ideals and yet serves the needs of selfish politicians and greedy industrialists. Place may be a tiny village in southern England surrounded by massive standing stones that marks the beginning of the most ancient trail in England and Europe. All of these places, and more, have formed me and form this narrative.

You and I cannot tell the stories of our lives without, in some way, sharing our stories of the places from which we have come. Our places, whether or not we love them, have life-long influences upon who and how we are. We are forever connected to place. This unavoidable and eternal link is part of our living geography. It shapes our past, our present, and where we seek to go.

Let's Allow Our Separate Paths to Diverge
for a Little While

I am a child, as are you, of place. In my case, I am a child from that arid vastness of Nebraska, a land of purported nothingness that had actually nourished millions of bison and thousands of people for tens of thousands of years. My Scandinavian and English ancestors arrived on those western prairies in the most recent whispers of time. However, this journey that I invite you to take with me covers a vastly different terrain. I would like you to come with me along a trek—a *stravage*—along Britain's 5,000-year-old Ridgeway National Trail, known as "the oldest road in England and Europe."

Put simply, I needed this journey. Over the years in my professional life as a spiritual counselor, psychotherapist, dream worker, and now—in a most unusual calling—serving as a consultant and counselor with U.S. military members and families, I challenged numerous clients, many of them professionals and caregivers, to consider the necessity of balance and self-care. Generally, I have practiced what I preached. But in 2014, I suddenly discovered myself immobilized. After much soul-searching, I made the soul-wrenching choice to end my forty-year marriage. I was shocked, guilty, ashamed, that I had made this decision that caused enduring harm to my former partner, to our adult children,

and my extended family. Yet, even in this awful, self-pun-
ishing anguish, I knew I had to make this decision. Though
I had often walked beside clients and friends through the dis-
solution of family and relationships, now it was my turn. I
was disoriented, depleted, and unable to get my bearings. In
the months following the divorce, I would sit at my dining
room table, weeping, unable to move, staring off into the
wilderness of pine trees and canyons that surrounded my
home on the prairie.

Spent in body and soul from a lifetime of over-giving, I
needed to push out of my old life and release myself from
the constrictions and habits that I had unconsciously used to
entrap myself. I studied and delved deeply into my nighttime
dreams for wisdom and healing with my spiritual counselor
and dream mentor. I consulted with trusted friends, read vo-
raciously, hiked endlessly, cursed, cried, and fell apart. I
prayed to the god I didn't necessarily believe in. I prayed to
everything and nothing, to the prairie spirits, to *the all that
is,* and finally I collapsed. My old story melted and dissolved
during purifying ceremonies in a sacred sweat lodge of the
Lakota people. Slowly, I began to understand the nudges and
callings that told me I *must* expand and change. Among the
many decisions that needed to be made, one became clear:
even though I loved my work and my clients, I had to stop. I
was burned out.

In the midst of all that numbing, blurring, out-of-body
dissociation, and wretched anguish, I recalled a yearning to
explore a land I had never seen: England. In a move of surprising boldness, I put my private practice—in fact, my entire life—on hold. I sold my home in the mystical prairie
canyonlands and created what I needed most: a sabbatical

for personal healing, traveling, hiking, and writing. It would begin with a nearly one-hundred-mile hike along Britain's Ridgeway National Trail.

And I am *still* hiking and writing. This is my calling. I am traveling the world, at once next door and thousands of miles from everywhere. When I began in 2016, I called it "The Sabbatical of the Soul." Self-created, self-funded, often unplanned, this journey was sourced by inspiration from the heart, the tug of the inexplicable, conversations along the way, synchronistic intuitions, and dreams of the night.

You are invited to join this trek. Perhaps your inner siren, "that still small voice" within, has already invited you to heed your heart's deepest values and seek out life's meanings. As you read, you may be prompted to take your own wandering stravage into unexpected territories. Together, we will roam across a physical and spiritual geography, saunter through the stories and memories of lifetimes. We will explore nighttime dreams as never before, receiving wisdom, healing, and experiencing eternal growth and change. Joyfully, we will explore the beauty, history, and wonders of the English landscape—and so far beyond—into other lands and geographies. The trek will also take us into the deep, often dark, spiritual caves that yearn to be transformed into passages of light and knowledge. Together, we'll traverse landscapes obscured by swirling clouds of our unknowing, until the mists of confusion part, and we discover insight and transformation for ourselves and one another. Let's do this, together.

As you become more whole, as you create more meaning, you influence the beauty and meaning of our world. The world, because of your risks, your edgy compassionate *straying*, becomes more whole because of you.

May these journeys inspire, provoke, and support you. Your life's meaning is at stake, as is mine. Listen to the wind, the spirit wind. Your stravage is calling.

Royce Fitts
Autumn 2021

Chapter One
Subversive Compassion

"You're in the Army now!
You're in the Army now! You'll never get rich, You son
of a bitch! You're in the Army now!"
(1917, by Isham Jones, Tell Taylor, Ole Olsen)

I was not drafted. I applied.

In the spring and summer of 2017, I served the U.S. Army as a civilian Military Family Life Counselor. If you know me at all, you would likely say that was out of the box for Royce. If you know me deeply, you would say I was fuckin' crazy.

I was about a year into my sabbatical of the soul. An often difficult and sometimes unanswerable question: how do you pursue wholeness and meaning while you also pay your bills and earn a necessary income? Though I couldn't have known it then, this would be the first of many postings at American military installations. For reasons that I hope will become clear to you as you journey with me, this stravage into foreign territory on domestic soil is the story I *must* tell you first. It's a necessary tale about walking into my own shadows and into our nation's collective shadows. Perhaps you'll find you encounter your own shadows too.

A few months prior to accepting this unusual assignment with the military, I had finished my dream-come-true hike through the majestic English countryside along the Ridgeway National Trail. The Ridgeway had challenged me in ways beyond imagining. It was as if that ancient road knew how to stretch and break old, limiting habits so that my mind, body, and soul could expand. Now that my feet were back on American soil, I had to ask myself: if I were serious about growth and healing and was truly ready to continue this exploration of the geography of the soul—*my soul*—how would I continue to push myself to discover the parts of myself I did not yet know? The Ridgeway Trail, with its idyllic beauty, ancient stories, and compelling energy, propelled me into an unknown physical, emotional, and spiritual wilderness. My time in the United Kingdom was an intentional vision quest. In contrast, landing on an Army post in upstate New York was the sort of transformative experience I never would have asked for. Suddenly, rather than "finding myself" as I strolled across a lovely stretch of countryside, I found myself spiraling into a human landscape littered with moral and ethical conflicts I understood in theory but had never faced directly.

A Wizard Without a Wand

It was early spring when I arrived in upstate New York, and I had a couple of days to fill before I began my assignment. I'd recently been back to my prairie homeland of Nebraska, and I was struck by its contrast with this region. There was so much water here with all those lakes, ponds, and rivers. These vast farmlands, bordered by budding deciduous forests and nearby mountains, seemed so different from my own. I parked near the main entry gate of the post and simply sat in the car for a very long time, observing this place and what it might mean to become part of it. I was also hoping I would not be spotted and ticketed for illegal parking. Every molecule of my being was shaking with nervous insecurity, telling me to not go through with this decision. At the same time, I knew I would. Conflicting voices—both equally powerful, both equally compelling—boomed and whispered in my mind. I prayed. Not with eloquence, but in crude, anxiety-filled breaths. For me. For those still nameless, faceless soldiers. For, if nothing else, an out-of-the box learning experience for all of us. A sacred adventure—maybe.

"It's not easy being green," Kermit the Frog sings. It's not easy being unique, different. It's not easy being sensitive. It is not easy being a man, a macho man or a soul man. It's not easy to be a soldier in the U.S. Army. Not easy being green, camouflaged or not.

My whole adult life had been arranged to never do what I was about to do. I was, with deep ambivalence, "anti-military." I do understand the need for a powerful military. I have lived a rich, secure life as the result of some of our military accomplishments. I will not deny that truth. And yet, I've also perceived what I believe is "fear-mongering" inflicted upon the U.S. citizenry by self-serving politicians and industrial giants who, for their own gain, bloat our military and push for economic international imperialism. This evil energy is pervasive, deceptive, idolatrous, and seductive. It is often abusive, diabolical, nasty, and just plain mean. And, as I am forced to look into my own sacred mirror, this military industrial machine looks like parts of me.

"Will they make you cut your hair?" How many friends

and family asked that? Secretly (and neurotically) I wondered if once the Army saw me, someone—some general, someone with authority in the system—would order me to the barber as soon as I set foot on post.

Eyes closed, I sat in the driver's seat of my illegally parked car, and I took a long look into that internal sacred mirror and gazed into my own past. Months earlier, when I was hiking on the Ridgeway Trail, I met a warm, gregarious family enjoying a morning walk. The small boy was bicycling up the trail with all his might. "It's his birthday present," said the daddy, as both parents watched.

We exchanged bits of biographical information. The father said he was home on leave from Kuwait where he served in the Royal Air Force as a flight instructor for helicopter pilots. Noticing my backpack and American accent, he asked where I was from and why I was doing the hike. I explained my attractions to the historical and spiritual significance of the trail and told them that I was writing about my experiences. I surprised myself by blurting out that I was a psychotherapist, theologian, and dreamworker and how fascinating it was to explore the ancient traditions and stories of England. The man, charming and quick witted, smiled mischievously, a glint in his eye, and said, referring to my hair, "Well, whatever, you look like a wizard." We all laughed together. I appreciated his spontaneity. "The Archbishop of Canterbury needs to visit with you," he said, giving a playful poke at the rigid structure of the Church of England.

With long white hair grown well past my shoulders, I guess I do look like a wizard. With a collection of fascinations and skills like I have, you might even think my work looks a bit wizardry. Well, this wizard was about to enter a

14

structure that might be even more rigid than the Anglican Communion.

Crazy. Like a dream.

A Memory of Now

This choice to work as a counselor on a U.S. Army post was like a crazy, surreal dream that was about to shock me into a whole new kind of wakefulness.

Years ago, I learned from my spiritual counselor, mentor, and deep friend, the late Jeremy Taylor, about a process of dream understanding called Projective Dream Work, which I'll explore further throughout this book. It honors many theories humans have used over the millennia to understand dreams, using ancient and modern psychological, philosophical, and spiritual belief systems. Projective Dream Work posits that each person is the best and final interpreter of his or her own dream. The "projective" aspect of this work indicates the understanding that virtually everything you say about someone else's dream—whether you're an "expert" dream interpreter or not—is really saying more about you than about the original dreamer. Once we own that we are "projecting" our own life experiences onto and into another person's dreams, we are placed together on a level, supportive, compassionate playing field. Rather than judging each other, we can explore a mutual mystery inspired by our instinctual and evolutionary process of dreaming. Indeed, dreams are a mystery that heals. They offer insight, wisdom, and constant opportunities to transform who we are.

There is no better way to discover what we do *not* know about ourselves than to stravage into the chaotic and threatening realms of our nighttime dreams. Dreams allow us to explore the deepest darkness of our inner caves without taking any of the waking-life risks that might get us into real trouble. As a way to normalize how outrageous and bizarre dreams might be, I often say to my dream work groups and clients that if you knew what I sometimes dreamed, I would be arrested! That is true, of course, for all of us. And yet, paying attention to our nighttime dreams in our present world is often labeled "crazy." We often feel silly, like one of those "woo-woo" people if we listen to our dreams rather than focusing on our logical, advanced, supposedly sophisticated world.

Considering that we don't tend to take dreams all that seriously, it's ironic that we often use the word *dream* in a positive context during waking life. We gaze on a crush from afar and say, "Wow! They're *dreamy.*" Or we declare, "I just landed my dream job," when describing an almost unimaginable success in life. We use another word for dream to describe an awful event, like a tragic automobile accident, or a war that destroyed thousands of homes and lives. We call that, of course, a *nightmare*. It seems that our dreams are always present, and yet we carry around an "anti-dream" prejudice that keeps the true benefits of our dreams at arm's length. I invite us all to change that.

Let me share with you a nighttime dream I had a couple of months after my first assignment as a Military Family Life Counselor. On the surface, it might seem quite bizarre, but I think it does a great deal to illuminate my feelings about working with military service members.

My brother and I own a camper trailer together. We are waking-life age, lingering on either side of seventy. I have an awareness that I haven't invested any money into this camper, but the sense is that we own it together. There is some guy, a younger man, maybe in his 30s, who is harassing and threatening us. He wants to have a fight, a physical fight with us. I do not know why. It is nighttime and very dark. The guy is chasing or following us on his motorcycle as we are driving a pickup truck pulling our camper. The street may be wet, or maybe there is a railroad track, but our pursuer skids out of control. I see sparks as he slides the motorbike on its side on the pavement. He is unhurt, but this accident seems to have made him more angry and more determined to fight.

Now we are out of the truck. The accident happened just outside a garage where other men are working together on their projects, like their own cars or trucks. The threatening man is trying to entice the others to fight us too. They all seem to be about the same age as the threatening young man. They all come out into the street. My brother and I are just standing, and the others are kind of milling about in a sort of semicircle. I'm afraid.

I've been trying to dial the police on my cell phone, but I cannot get the dial pad to come up. I keep trying, but to no avail. I feel anxiety, fear, and dread. I even try to get the other men to call the cops too. But some or all of the men are hesitant to call the police because this will alert the police to possibly target them because they

17

all have had run-ins with the law, and the men do not want to call attention to themselves.

Puzzled, I sought to understand this dream by working on it with my dream mentor. Using the style and approach of Projective Dream Work, Jeremy borrowed my dream as his own, and reflected upon it with "I-messages," speaking as if the dream were actually *his* dream.

This approach of borrowing someone's dream and speaking of it as if it were your own allows the dreamer to release the defensiveness that comes up when being analyzed, interpreted, and probed by another. I could simply listen to what Jeremy was saying about himself, not about me. I was given the room I needed to more objectively contemplate the meanings of my dream through *his* imagination. This way, I could more easily absorb what and how the dream was speaking to *me*. Consequently, in this gentle, relaxed, communal space, I could feel the *ahas* of insight and wisdom about my dream. *Relationships heal* is an axiom often used to describe how psychotherapy works and I believe that axiom is even more truthful and accurate in the world of dream work. Dreams shared within trusted relationships heal deeply.

As Jeremy and I worked the dream, I became aware of a theme that occurs often in my dream and waking worlds. I carry a feeling of "not-okay-ness" within me. It's a kind of "out-of-place-ness" that I have with certain groups, especially certain kinds of men. In this dream, all the men except me, are "mechanically inclined." They are comfortable with projects that require the use of their hands and brains to repair or make things. I am not that kind of man. My waking world has been built around avoiding such projects, tasks, and responsibilities. Instead, my waking life is built around the world of the soul, the interior life that seeks an existential and spiritual understanding of who we are as individuals and as a part of our universe. These dream men represented undeveloped sides of me. Jeremy reflected that these men in the dream seemed to be uncomfortable with the "interior world," the world of soul-searching and meaning-making. They certainly seemed uncomfortable with being emotionally vulnerable in relationships. Perhaps these men were afraid of me, just as I was afraid of them.

I was born a sensitive, introverted soul into a world that didn't quite know what to do with such a boy. I was raised on a farm in western Nebraska with an extended family that had a history of ranching and cowboying. I was ill a lot as a child and I'm sure that influenced what I learned and what I was taught. Never comfortable with the concrete tasks and jobs of farming, the mechanical stuff was like an incomprehensible foreign language. Instead, I loved the poetry of the land, the seasons, the colors of the prairie. The earth was sacred to me. My family was religious, and we took seriously the "Bible-teachings" of family and church. My own prayers and my beliefs about how to live were shaped out of poetic images of Jesus and a "capital G"—and male—God. On hot summer days, I would drift through the air on our tire swing that hung from a sturdy limb of a farmyard cottonwood tree. Back and forth I would drift, feeling at one with god, trance-like and absorbed in the stillness of the quaking leaves from a passing breeze. The peace of that contented moment was always juxtaposed with lots of shame-based teachings and judgmentalism. I absorbed both deeply.

As I worked through the dream, I began to understand that the feeling of "not-okay-ness" is *a memory*, a feeling of how it *was* for me in my past. Yet memory can feel so *present*. All the associated feelings in the dream that came from my memory (sadness, fear, heartache, joy, insecurity, contentment) felt present *right now*. The dream was trying to free me from my past wounds of insecurity by playing out in dramatic movie fashion how I *used to* feel and be. *But now*, the dream says, *Royce has a choice!*

A key to understanding and healing in this dream comes at the end: I'm trying to call for help and I cannot. The dial pad doesn't work on my dream cell phone! I feel desperate and afraid, helpless. *And that is the point!* This is my dream's way of saying that I don't need outside assistance. I don't need to call for help or backup to cope with this moment or any other. In the dream, I am my *present* age, and this is an important clue. I have all the skills I've gathered over nearly seven decades of learning. I can do this! The dream is saying that no matter how I feel, I can deal with this bizarre, scary moment, just as I have dealt with countless other emergencies, and I can do it with power, knowledge, and confidence.

As a child, I had learned how to connect with men who didn't get the "interior" side of life, even if it was uncomfortable, scary. When I grew up and became a professional helper, I was drawn, unconsciously, to work on the undeveloped aspects of my own personality by working with such "manly men." It was as if I hoped that by connecting with and helping these men along their interior journeys, I would somehow get the help I needed to take my own exterior journey. To go even deeper into my psyche, it's possible to say that I believed if I could make these kinds of men my friends,

I would be safer. I would be less abused as a child, and less likely to be humiliated and afraid as a man. In my twenties, I became a pastor of such "exterior men" in a religious denomination that I'd eventually understand to be a source of shame, humiliation, and spiritual abuse. With time and maturity, I saw these conflicts and awarenesses and left that religious group and went on to pursue advanced degrees in order to become a psychotherapist. Again, to serve men like these. Why did I keep walking—straying—into these situations? I wanted to break the cycle so our religion and society would stop creating cruel, abusive men. I wanted to be a part of their healing. I hoped I would be able to teach this type of man the foreign languages of the interior world. I wanted to be with them, discomfort and all, to teach them about vulnerability, feelings, and the relationship-centered realm of the soul. Then, as now, my life—and I believe, theirs, too—is at stake.

In the waking world as a psychotherapist and dream worker, whether in my private practice or as a counselor at a military installation, it has not been easy for such men to be with me, or for me to be with them. I have sometimes felt their sarcasm and hostility and I know some have harbored fears about my sexual orientation because I happen to be liberal, tender, kind, and very long-haired. Sometimes in public presentations, I refer to Mr. Rogers, the public television icon and my hero, as one of my spiritual models of male strength, fatherhood, and how to be a different kind of man. It's no wonder that, in my dream, the men were "hostile" and wanted to fight. After all, "those men," as they appeared in my dream, were actually an aspect of who I am. The urge to "fight" in this dream is a desire to bring together the opposing parts of me, to integrate what I perceived as my opposites. Sometimes, "dream fighting" is a way—a first step—toward reconciliation, intimacy, and healing.

A Child and A Porcupine

Despite my trepidation, I would report to duty as planned. When I began orientation, I hid my anxiety. Or thought I did. I did everything I could to look cool, confident, well-dressed. Maybe I just appeared a bit nervous, like anyone would when starting a new job. I reserved the real hammering anxiety for my insides.

In those early days, I drove around the post, wandering and wondering what the hell was I about. I discovered hiking trails and streams, and even a small lake. Surprised by the beauty of the post, I walked deep into the woods, recalling the autumn beauty of the forests of England. I immersed myself, meditating upon the aliveness of early spring on the post as flowers and trees were budding all around me.

One cold, rainy afternoon, I drove into a beautiful, wooded housing development located in the far back section of the post. I pulled onto the muddy shoulder of the quiet residential road, worried if I was risking a parking ticket. I strolled across the soggy grass, but I certainly wasn't dressed for it. My sports jacket, shirt, and tie were supposed to make up for that long, grey ponytail. *Oh, the lengths I go*, I thought, *to build bridges of connection.*

Still finding it hard to believe that nature could thrive in the heart of the military industrial complex, I noticed something high in one of the trees. An owl? Hawk? No. It was a mammal about the size of a small dog. The animal's dark coat stood in contrast to the fresh, small green leaves, but I still couldn't figure out what sort of creature I was looking at.

Imagine me there on that stretch of wet, upstate New York grass squinting into the woods, and reflect with me about these ideas of "fresh" and "green" for a moment. In new situations, or in situations in which I feel neither secure nor competent, I often feel like a young child. It's a bit like the feelings from the dream I described earlier, a sense of being out of place and threatened. These are "memory feelings" that loom large in the present but are not based on the *facts* of the present. My adult self "knew" how to handle my new assignments, but my child self, the memory self, felt insecure. I felt like these tree leaves: fresh and very, very green. Vulnerable. I'm only able to write about this, to share it, because I have a feeling that you too know what it's like to carry this small, insecure child inside.

Here I was, the man with the doctorate, charged with the mental wellbeing of servicewomen, servicemen, and their families. And, in the same moment, I was the young boy who wanted to be at home in nature, who felt a little abashed that he couldn't identify the animal that was just a hundred feet away. Despite the rain that seeped down my collar, I pulled out my phone to snap a photo. Just then, a van pulled out of a nearby street and headed toward me. The driver stopped, rolled down her window, greeted me with a warm smile. "Are you okay?" she asked.

"Oh, yes," I answered. "Just trying to figure out what

that animal is up in the trees." Without so much as turning to look at the tree she said, "Oh, that's a porcupine! We have all kinds of wildlife back here in the woods. It's amazing." With another broad smile, she waved, "All right then. I was just checking to make sure you were okay. Didn't want you to be stuck."

I felt embarrassed. A porcupine, of course! But it was so high up. I didn't know they would climb trees, never mind climb so high. My child self—the insecure self—who was in a new job, a new environment, and was thoroughly green, was coming through now. We didn't have many porcupines on our prairie farm. So, in this moment wandering around the forests of the U.S. Army post, I was, indeed, a child again, a child who felt foolish because he'd never had the chance to learn about the living habits of porcupines.

I stumbled to introduce myself, said this was my third day on the job as a Military Family Life Counselor and I was trying to get to know the post. She immediately recognized my job title, "Oh, welcome!" she exclaimed. "That's a great idea! Drive around back here. It's beautiful."

We said goodbye and she drove off. I would see her a few times that spring and summer. Wife to one of the primary commanding officers, she led volunteer efforts to build a community for the soldiers and families on the post. Alone again—cold, wet, young, green, and on my own—I walked back to my car, reflecting on this touch of warm, welcoming humanity.

If wildlife was unexpected in this military bastion, then so was kindness. But then, here was this wild porcupine and this open-hearted woman. Here was I. While I might see aspects of myself reflected in the evil energy that propelled the

U.S. military, I could also see the good in each of us. Mirrors. Mirrors indeed.

Shabbath, To Rest

Less than a year before I found myself on the post, I had declared myself to be "on sabbatical." There was just one drawback in this perfect plan: I did not work in academia where sabbaticals were a blessed part of the norm. Oh, the privileged existence of the professor who is given a regular chance to do research, write, or engage in specialized studies for a year or more— and be *paid* by that college or university to do so. That was not my life. Instead, I had spent years in private practice as a psychotherapist, most often fully self-employed and vulnerable to the ebb and flow of client numbers and health insurance fees and reimbursements. For me, this sabbatical was an audacious declaration of independence. And it had its risks, enormous risks.

I loved my work and the clients with whom I worked, but I was worn out. Exhausted spiritually, financially, emotionally, I had been divorced for about two years. The huge, necessary change of divorce was painful, shattering, disorienting, renewing, and transformative. Even in the expansive and tumultuous result of a marriage ending, I saw that the divorce represented only one of the many changes I needed to make.

Who am I, if not married? Who am I, if not living in the sacred prairie space where I had spent much of my life? Who am I, if not a psychotherapist and spiritual counselor in a traditional setting? Who am I, really?

I had discussed the idea of a sabbatical with the clients who saw me in my Nebraska and Wyoming offices. Informing them of my need to write, travel, and heal, I was surprised by their support and acceptance of my journey. I was relieved. Though I had no idea if or when I would return to my traditional practice, most clients accepted this news with grace. I felt in awe of their wisdom and encouragement.

My humanity, in all of my vulnerabilities and rawness, was supported by my clients' understanding. I often recommended deep, good self-care for my clients, and did my best for myself as well. But never like this. I needed new adventures, adventures in healing. I needed to expand my universe into uncharted waters. I needed to face my own shadows, my nation's shadows too. I needed to walk where I have never walked before, not seeking traditional comfort, but expansive, uncomfortable growth.

"A Crazy-Assed Job"

Hello, U.S. Department of Defense. Hello, U.S. Military. Hello, collective shadows. We need to talk...

I've long held deep ethical and moral positions surrounding anything military. My raging skepticism concerning anything political was always close to the surface too. To think that those god-awful politicians and corporate behemoths would seek to make war, cheat, lie, and steal to feed their wounded egos while they made themselves wealthy and powerful by using humans—citizens of our nation, our soldiers—as holy pawns in their poison Ponzi scheme... It sets my teeth on edge and makes me feel dizzy, angry, and lost all at once. It's all in the name of national defense, of course, but what's real? What's the genuine con job and what's legitimate national defense? Given the outrageous hyperbole from those sources, we can hardly know, really.

And yet, I had applied for this job. While preparing for my self-made sabbatical, I had read about an interesting counseling model used to serve the U.S. military community. It could be an opportunity to earn some money, serve people in ways I had never served before in locations I had never lived. Adventure. Travel. Meet new people. Challenge like I never knew.

Crazy, like a dream.

It took me three weeks to figure out the layout of this particular Army post. Actually, I never did figure it out. Google Maps worked in certain areas, but not others. We never knew the full story, but the conspiracy theories as to why were delightful. My colleagues were a gift. I knew that I would get along with my fellow counselors, because that's what I'm good at. It's what I do. It's what we all do on our best days. I never expected that some would become dear friends. One colleague was particularly helpful, coaching me through the ins and outs and encouraging me to remain playful in the face of this strange job. On her last day—these positions are always temporary—she laughed and said, "Royce, this is a crazy-assed job!" I laughed too. *So* on target! Such a confirmation. That little moment was a gift. She told me to do this job like I wanted, to follow my instincts and still "stay in my lane!"

Our understanding of our "scope of service" came

through official training and volumes of information from both the Department of Defense and the mental health contracting companies who hired us. As a private practice psychotherapist, there were always ethical boundaries that ruled the profession and the therapist-client relationship. There was a lane to stick to, but it was wide, and the road was generally long and mostly predictable. However, this assignment was called "casual counseling." It is modeled after "walking social workers," the professionals who walk the sidewalks of cities and drive the rural roads to connect and build helping relationships with residents. This concept in the military is to, in my words, prevent soldiers and families from falling between the cracks and getting lost in military life. This particular and unique service is classified as "non-medical counseling," meaning that counselors do not provide any mental health diagnoses for the people they meet. We would refer anyone who needs more formal psychotherapy to the available mental health resources on the post or in a nearby city. It was not within our lane, or scope of service, to serve anyone who was a potential harm to themselves, or to others. We had a clear protocol if we met anyone with immediate, emergency needs and knew how to guide them toward appropriate intervention.

Casual counseling reminded me of being a priest in a parish, as I once was. A priest who drops in for coffee at a parishioner's home, sharing spiritual communion with a family. A priest who walks her beat in her small town and neighborhood. A priest who visits a farm or ranch or city business and hangs out with the owners and workers, even offering to help with the tasks. A priest who has deep counseling sessions in a local pub with one of his flock. A priest who holds a newborn and gives them a gentle kiss of welcome. A priest who prays goodbye as a life fades away. I doubted that the folks who created the "casual counseling" model even knew or thought about the long history, since time immemorial, of priests and shamans. These "social workers" of their day lived in the midst of their community, serving the needs of their people. Priests and shamans were as natural to the landscape as the sacred breeze blowing through the tribal camp.

As everyone who held this kind of position before me did, I had to invent this job over and over. It reminded me (and I could not say this when I was there because turf issues in the military are rigid) of my experiences not only as a pastor in a parish, but also as a chaplain in a medical center. Military chaplaincy is an esteemed service and accidentally describing my work on post as similar to that of a chaplain could cause conflicts. Beyond the scope, out of my lane.

In this specific assignment in New York, we casual counselors had no formal office in which to regularly consult with soldiers and families, and so we hoofed it, traveling all around the post. My job was to invent ways to meet soldiers and families, to engage them in some form of connection and conversation, to begin the process of establishing trust so if needed, they would ask for an appointment to consult with me or another of my colleagues. I am an introvert, so walking up to people, whether in the food courts, coffee shops, or on the playgrounds, and casually introducing myself as a counselor was never comfortable. In the beginning, I secretly and playfully teased myself and compared myself to young Mormons, the first-year elders who are assigned to a city and go door-to-door, politely knocking, smiling, and introducing themselves to residents and hoping to share the goods of their life and faith.

The most powerful service we provided was to simply consult with any soldier or family member about whatever they needed to talk about. Never taking notes about what was shared, "off the record and undocumented" was our number-one rule. The only exception, as described earlier, was if there was some indication of possible harm to someone, past, present, or future. We then were quick to do a "warm handoff," as it is described, so other professionals could intervene.

It was refreshing, comforting even, to know soldiers and families could talk about anyone and anything, even about their commanding officers. In fact, many commanding officers would refer their soldiers to us directly, even ordering some to come to us. Again, off the record, this work was grounded in safety and privacy. No one knew. And it wasn't just the enlisted folks. In fact, many commanding officers would seek us out for their own needs, as well.

Interesting that the military, so rigid, and so often controlled by corrupt industrial groups and self-serving politicians, would even conceive of such a service. I shake my head in wonder and appreciation. Not all is lost.

Crazy, like a dream.

To make the most of this choose-your-own-adventure job, I decided I needed to create some kind of routine that was natural. I needed to give myself structure to do my work, receive referrals, and consult with people in private. What to do? How to do it?

I went back to my old family systems training, an approach to psychotherapy that I often used in my private practice with clients, both in the business world and in therapy with individuals and families. Family systems teaches us to observe how we are functioning and living within the larger system, be it our professional or family worlds. This approach teaches us that we can and must own that the only thing we can be in control of is how we are managing ourselves. *The only one I can truly change is myself. Am I functioning in a way that is strong, thoughtful, and calm? Am I catering to others and losing a sense of who I am? Or am I keeping a solid sense of myself? Am I seeking connection with others and, at the same time, am I being solid in my principles and clear in my goals?* I decided that the best way to serve in this new environment was to first take care of myself in a non-selfish, proactive way.

How would I meet soldiers? I decided to join one of the fitness centers on post. Imagine, 6' 3" me, slim, 67 years old, long grey hair working out every morning with America's finest. "Be All You Can Be!"

Crazy, like a dream.

I did it. Proud. Scared inside. Showing up to work out. Watching, being watched. Who were we, them and me? I built friendships. Heard stories. Told stories. Shared communal bathrooms. My favorite part of the day was eating breakfast in the dining facility with scores of soldiers. Communion with these men and women, breaking bread, mediocre coffee, great eggs, and all the best trimmings. Sometimes I would see clients there, nod in a kind of secret way, never wishing to expose anyone. Some soldiers would sit at my table and simply talk about life. *How do I get out of the service? What will my next assignment be?* Sometimes they needed to talk about the suicide of a friend, a fellow soldier. One soldier could not make sense of his friend's killing himself. Staring off over my shoulder, this young man, trailing his words as he spoke softly said, "He was weak..." I felt sorrow for them both, the living and the dead. I sigh. How do we do this to ourselves and each other? What politician or industrialist gained something due to the death of that man?

I never talked to any soldier or family member about my deep anti-military ambivalence. What I did offer was myself: a concerned, caring, curious, insecure, anxiety-ridden, highly-trained, seasoned, compassionate professional. I am intuitive. I know the deep anxiety I often felt was not mine alone. The signals and energies of anxiety were being emitted from the psyches of nearly every soldier and family member on that post. I felt their anxiety, along with my own. They were trained to ignore it, repress it, to try to eradicate it. Me, on the other hand, well, I was trained to be subversive, to not ignore the moral conflicts of taking orders, of collateral damage, or of saying "yes" to any commander in chief who is ruthless to democracy and to humanity. And I was trained to pay attention to the dreams of the night and how not to ignore the nightmares that come to challenge, confront, and heal us.

Sometimes, I would be with a married couple and realize that their youth, their lack of life experience, their new babies, their being so far from home, meant that I was the only adult in the room. When the fighting and emotional conflicts would break out between them, it was up to me to be the anchor, to be the grown-up who could create a sense of calmness in what might be very chaotic lives. I would often say, "Calmness is not a feeling, it is a choice and a thoughtful way to act." Sometimes that worked, for a moment. I became their calm touchpoint. I was honored to hold that space for them.

How does it feel to be a soldier who has walked the landmined roads and hills of Afghanistan and then returned home with permanently damaged eardrums and a constant loud ringing in his head? How does that soul come back after his tour, make love to his partner, have children, and find ways to talk about intimacy and vulnerability? How does his wife relax and give him space, all the while hoping that since he came back alive, he can become fully part of their family life? These are age-old questions carried back from every battlefield and every nation, past and present.

Crazy, like a dream.

A Labyrinth of the Heart

I carried these questions in my soul every day as I went through my routines. I would walk the forest trails of the post and pray, surrounded by trees, communing with the natural world that surrounds this military machine and all this human pain.

One day, I found a labyrinth near a forest trail. Here was an ancient symbol of soul searching, a sacred technology devoted to meditation, prayer, and peace hidden amid an institution that is designed to use violence to resolve conflicts. A labyrinth represents the power of wandering and finding oneself and, mysteriously, is used all over the Earth. In the Hopi world of the American Southwest, the Mother of All is symbolized by the labyrinth, a path one can walk to the source of all life. Perhaps the labyrinth on the post symbolized the mystical feminine energy of nourishment and healing that insists on bubbling up as a warm spring of healing wisdom in the heart of this warlike masculine construct. Unconsciously, of course. I had no choice but to walk the labyrinth, the path to the Mother of All.

Just the evening before, I had learned of the death of a good friend from Wyoming. I walked the path, holding his memory, his long struggle for health and peace, as well as our imperfect, sometimes conflict-marked relationship. A labyrinth for peace and prayer on a U.S. Army post, of all places. How could I hold space for these strange realities? Somehow, the strangeness of opposites naturally became friends.

Crazy, like a dream.

Every soldier was polite and addressed me as "sir." No matter what. No matter how weird I may have looked to them, so out of place beside all that military dress and protocol. I have rarely received such displays of respect in any place, required or not. I would sit with officers as they reflected with me about their years in service and explored deep questions about the nature of the soldierly lives they'd lived. I did my best to hold non-judgmental space for their questions. Sometimes, the way of my being, the way I looked so different from them, the way my presence *felt* so different from those they commanded and obeyed, invited them to talk deeply and openly about their journeys in ways that they could not discuss with anyone else.

People who knew me in my "real world" would ask what I was doing on a military installation. I would say, "I am offering subversive compassion and subversive curiosity." It became my answer to myself, to my soul, even though I was still uncomfortable—and always will be—with the outrageous and unjust way that people in our government and industry exploit our soldiers and use them to exploit our world. I sought to hold that subversive space, a secret closet, for those I was there to help. They needed the space to wonder, to be curious about their own journey. They needed space for compassion, for self and others.

It might seem strange to spend all this time on an American army post when you're settling in to read a book about a man making a solo pilgrimage across a stretch of English soil. These stories are woven together, not just because I walked them, but also because they're part of our great human *stravage* and Earthly soul. They are a part of our saunter into the geography of our souls. Before we set out on the Ridgeway, I'll share one more story from what would be my first of several stints as a casual counselor with the U.S. military during my ongoing personal sabbatical.

It was late Friday afternoon, and my day was supposed to be winding down, when I received a call from a colleague asking for assistance. A colleague was fielding the telephone calls for counseling requests and walk-ins that always seemed to multiply before the start of the weekend. All at once, she was trying to visit with two separate soldiers, catch phone calls, and deal with a third walk-in.

I rushed to the office. The building was closing for the weekend, so I met the soldier, an officer, outside. We walked to a picnic shelter nearby to visit. She was hurting. She and her wife were having a painful crisis. What a normal crisis to have: two people misunderstanding each other, deeply in love, and yet accidentally hurting each other. The soldier was wise to want space to reflect with a neutral person, a counselor, before their weekend road trip.

I am proud of this development in our military. So much has had to change to reduce racism and sexual exploitation and to increase status for minority groups, women, and the LGBTQ community. Any such change in our military is cumbersome, painful, slow, and always against the grain of wounded tradition. But now, a same sex couple—in love, married, and serving each other and our nation—reminds me how grace and progress sometimes surfaces in the most delightful, unexpected places.

The officer and I had a deep, reflective conversation. On the other side of this intimate chat, she felt clearer, hopeful, and ready to enjoy the time away with her spouse. As we were saying goodbye, the clock struck 5 p.m. and, as tradition required, taps was broadcast throughout the post. We were in the now-empty parking lot. No one around. A hush fell. Even the rush of traffic on the nearby road ceased. The music of the trumpet softly echoed through the nearby forest, through the breeze on this warm summer's eve. The officer became silent, excused herself, stood at attention, and saluted.

A tear gently rolled down her cheek. I stood silent; head

bowed. When taps was over, she quietly explained she had friends—sisters, and brothers—who had died while serving in the army, "I always tear up and think of them, no matter how often I hear the taps."

Crazy, like a dream.

Chapter Two
Solo to London

Through the glaring morning sun, I looked out my tiny window in the crowded airliner. I was filled with awe and giddy enthusiasm. I was a child again.

Whoa! That's England down there! I thought. *Golly, they have trees and fields too! Looks like Ohio or Indiana!* I exclaimed to myself in my little-boy Ameri-centrism. The famed lush and green English countryside was real. Moments later, I watched the concrete earth rush up to meet the wheels of the plane.

Landed. In London. Solo. Speechless. Wordless. Excited. Ready. I felt naive, vulnerable, and wonderful. I was a wide-eyed little Nebraska farm boy, gushing, eager, scared. Alone. I knew no one in England.

It was the fall of 2016, and I was about to go on a hike. *The* hike.

This all unfolded a year before I would find myself joining the Army as a civilian counselor as described in the previous chapter. It was the beginning of my great adventure, my open-ended sabbatical. But it started long before I would gaze through that airplane window, overflowing with anticipation, worry, and wonder. Way back in November 2009, probably on a Sunday afternoon, I was reading the online edition of the *New York Times* travel section. I was captivated by a story entitled Hiking History: England's Ancient Ridgeway Trail:

> *THE Ridgeway is the oldest continuously used road in Europe, dating back to the Stone Age. Situated in southern England, built by our Neolithic ancestors, it's at least 5,000 years old, and may even have existed when England was still connected to continental Europe, and the Thames was a tributary of the Rhine. (Henry Shukman, "Hiking History: England's Ancient Ridgeway Trail," New York Times, 2009)*

I was instantly in awe of the description of the Ridgeway National Trail. History beyond history. A journey beyond a journey. The article described standing stones *older* than Stonehenge, placed by ancient humans in what was now a tiny village at the start of the Ridgeway Trail. These stones stood as gigantic, intimidating markers along what was once part of a vast highway used for commerce, migration, and ritual. There I was, at home in Nebraska, imagining what it would mean to hike the oldest road in Europe as it stretched along a natural ridge above the English plain, often following the path of the River Thames. Just by reading a few thousand words of this travel feature, I knew the Ridgeway served as a portal for all sorts of mystical communion: worship, burial, the ancient business practices of the day. The Ridgeway spanned the metaphorical ridges between worlds. Then, at that moment, at my dining table in Nebraska, I promised myself I would hike that trail.

I archived the article and occasionally took it out to savor the possibilities. The hike was so very *doable*. Though thousands of miles from my prairie life, the trail was less than a hundred miles long. It was all that had been preserved after a millennia of service to the multitudes that used the trail. I imagined the history. First, animals walking the natural ridge as the Ice Age retreated, then humans so similar and yet so different from us. I envisioned them all following the melting glacial streams of an emerging land. And I imagined myself there, long before the safe, secure American life I had so carefully constructed, a life that like the ancient glaciers, would someday melt away.

Wander Defiantly

I have a passion for hiking. Walking. Sauntering. Wandering.

I've shared with you the story of my client who, upon hearing of my dream to hike this tiny corner of England, spontaneously described my mission: *stravaging* across the wilds of the Earth. I had never heard of the word, so he explained that "stravage" refers to a kind of defiant wandering. I did more research and found that, in addition to its origins in the rebellion of the fallen Scottish clans, stravage had its roots in the archaic word extravagate, which means "to go beyond proper limits." Somehow, the Scots, still reeling and healing from the devastation of both land and community, invented a word that inspired life and determination. The Scots—at least some—began to wander defiantly and roam "aimlessly," to stray across their land, daring their English oppressors. Well said. Well done. Stravage. Stray. Roam defiantly.

It is one thing to explore the vastness of miles and miles of land by car, but it is another to come to intimately know a small path of earth by walking. Whether it be the rugged canyons, bluffs, prairies, sandhills of Nebraska, the mountains of northern Wyoming, or the stunning and unexpected beauty of the Adirondacks in New York, you learn the land when you tread gently upon it. The land talks with you. Walking the earth is healing. And though I had dedicated my life to healing and to walking, I now needed to stravage. I needed to heal in a defiant, even aimless, way.

And here I was. Sleepy. Hyper. Spacey. I tried not to show it. I deplaned. It was important to look "normal." I wandered through the airport corridors, following the signs and arrows, but mostly just drifting with the crowd of passengers. Surely, they knew where they were going. I did not. I finally found the huge cavern dedicated to passport inspection. Long line. I struck up a conversation with a woman near me. American. New York City. "I've been to London a lot. My boyfriend lives here. A clothes designer. He always says, 'You must see the Tower of London!' I have seen it so many times. He loves it."

The Tower of London? Inwardly, I asked *why*? That tourist destination was not on my list of priorities. I felt confused. I started worrying about whether I had made the "right" decisions. Had I missed something? This was *London*. History! Elegance! Royalty! Then I caught myself. Wait a minute. I remembered *why* I was here. I didn't want to be, wouldn't be, couldn't be a conventional tourist. I had a calling. A hike. I'd been dreaming about this defiant wandering for years. Should I explain this to her?

"Ah-umm—I'm going to be in London for a few days, then I'm going hiking. Up on the Ridgeway National Trail. Heard of it?"

"Noo—but I love shopping here." We neared the passport officers' cubicles and drifted apart.

"Hello," I said, as I handed my passport to the officer. Without being conscious of it, I was my child self again: insecure, vulnerable, as I tried to look big and confident. It wasn't like I had never traveled overseas. I had visited family in Switzerland and Singapore. Why was this utter naïveté emerging now? Why did I feel so vulnerable? Why did I feel so young? Because this time was different. I was different. I had a mission: to meet myself. Alone. There was no one to greet me. There was no companion to pick up along the way. Just me. I was to navigate this geography, this physical and spiritual place and space, alone.

"Morning," the official nodded as he received my passport. "How long will you be in the UK?" How strange. I hadn't anticipated that question. "Ah-umm..." What to say? In my thoughts, I was to be out of the States for, like, seven weeks. But I had no idea if I was going to stay in the UK. I had thought of going to Europe, yet I had no definite plans. I suddenly became aware, again, how unstructured and unplanned my trip was, and how strange it may have appeared to others.

"Well, several weeks, I believe....". The officer needed specifics. "Several weeks?" He looked firm, eyes furrowed. "How long? What are you doing in the UK?" "Ah-umm...I am a—writer, and I am hiking the Ridgeway National Trail.

I am going to write about the hike and explore the English countryside. It'll take me a while to hike." I paused for a second, then added, "I'm on sabbatical..." He lit up. Bingo! "Sabbatical." He liked that word. "Okay. Have a good trip," he answered curtly. He stamped my passport and waved me on.

Cool. I wasn't arrested for being a man without a plan. I imagined that if I had said I was going shopping and wanted to see the typical tourist sites, like the Tower of London as my new friend had suggested, I would have been waved through rapidly. I looked up to see where the woman had gone, but she was long out of sight.

Finally, I was in the open, spacious airport! Sunshine filtered through the windows. London sunshine. I walked and gawked my way through Heathrow International. I shyly visited with vendors about the monetary exchange rate and got good advice as to where to go to get the fairest fees. I bought good coffee and visited more shops and bought a map of London.

Have you ever felt the joy and excitement of discovering something new? Have you looked onto a new flowing trail that has artistic twists and turns as it winds up and down a hill or a mountainside? You may see it from afar, and then it tugs at your curiosity. Before you know it, you are on that path wondering and wandering. A bustling airport may seem like a wilderness, as you look for signposts to guide your way through the confusing maze of hallways, vendors, and rushing crowds. You stare out the windows at the parking lots and impatient traffic, wondering which exit to take to find your taxi. You wonder about the wiles and wilds of the city beyond, about safety, adventure, and discovery, and you worry about doing this all alone. And then, the worries are shelved, the wondering takes a new, empowered form. Fresh determination to live out a dream swells in your chest.

The Rattlesnake Within

Still, I felt like a little boy wandering in the airport. We all tend to unconsciously slip into a version of our younger self in unfamiliar situations, and, in my case, I become a paranoid child. I touched my backpack all the time because I had been coached to never, ever set my pack down and step away. Not in the toilet, not anywhere. I had my passport, billfold, and valuables stored in such a way that it would take a direct assault to take them. *Pickpockets,* my paranoia said, *were lurking everywhere.* Underneath anxiety and neurosis is the ancient will and wisdom to survive.

When not wandering airports like a lost kid, I help people explore the visions of the dreamworld and the realities of waking life. As I work to illuminate "the people dynamics" in my clients' relationships, families, companies, and organizations, I train them to become aware of and use their "new" brain to think logically, choose to act with calmness, and use facts and deep values to function and make decisions. My goal is to help clients monitor and reduce their reliance on the "old brain," including the brainstem and the amygdala, which are reservoirs of powerful emergency instincts like anxiety, reactivity, and impulsiveness. Drawing on my prairie world where fearsome reptiles often lurk, I like to call this the "rattlesnake brain," and I describe how it is always ready to strike or flee. The old brain is survival-based and, when we use it in moments of crisis without the proper degree of awareness, curiosity, and thought, it often leads to destructive decision making and rash action. "Brain-stemming" and "rattlesnake reactivity" strike when we give in to that ancient, raw, survival-based energy. Sometimes, the results are dangerous.

We have politicians, religious leaders, greedy corporations, news organizations, social media, and special interest groups—whole power bases—that are rich, dangerous, and hellbent on tapping into our ancient fear of survival. Across the globe, they are feeding paranoia and terror. This sort of thought control is called religious fundamentalism (It doesn't matter which religion). It's called right-wing and left-wing hyper partisanship. It's called North Korea. It's called Syria. It's called racism. It's called white supremacy. It's called sexism and homophobia. It's like a rattlesnake striking, and it's toxic. It calls itself faith, worshipping ideology and power while ignoring ethics, compassion, and integrity. It calls itself religion and purports that god, or The Great Whoever, has a plan and everything is as it should be—generally meaning that white, rich, male, and greedy should get ahead and stay ahead. It's called Brexit and America First. The powerful few are getting richer and ratings are soaring, as we give up our legal freedoms through "fear legislation." We, the general populace, are duped. And it's all because we, naturally, want to be safe.

The problem is, of course, there *is* danger out there. The world *is* dangerous. I took this journey in 2016, in a world now known as *pre-pandemic*. No one had heard of COVID-19 then, but now, millions have died. For well over a year, non-essential travel virtually stopped. The global economy was halted practically overnight, and at least for a time, daily life was rendered unrecognizable for just about every person on the planet. There is no place on Earth—no place!—that has not been touched and transformed by this universal horror.

We have lived through a time when a trip to the grocery store or visits to a loved one became potentially life-threatening encounters. These experiences could have unified us as we faced a profound common problem. Sadly, rather than engaging in conversations about how to heal, and agreements about how to recover, we've come together to point fingers, spread anger, and feed fear. Science is often reviled and dismissed, even though it was science that developed, in record time, vaccines to curb the virus.

I wrote most of this book from inside Trump's America, not knowing if the 2020 election would bring any sort of hope or change and unsure of how long the pandemic might last. Conspiracy theories have abounded throughout this time, from the belief in malicious, martial origins of the virus to suspicion that the vaccines contained microimplants to track, sterilize, or somehow control anyone who received it. Paranoia, promoted by some radical conservatives and even those on the far left who preached radical individualism, became the new pastime and led to dire real-life consequences. As the pandemic became a religious, racist, and political tool, the presence or absence of a face mask indicated your party affiliation. Rather than being seen as a wise act of patriotic compassion that offered protective care for vulnerable neighbors, the "anti-maskers" used these strips of cloth to aggressively announce "You're not the boss of me!" In the face of crisis, our rattlesnake origins—those primitive, un-thinking, reactive brainstems—often took control.

Real danger is often blended within false danger. You can't easily tell the difference from one or the other, espe-cially in the midst of a global crisis. It takes work—hard, soul-searching, fact-based work—to separate our primitive reactions to the false dangers lurking in our lives from the *actual* life-threatening perils existing in our wounded world.

What if I were to have walked through Heathrow Inter-national Airport during the pandemic? How much more out-rageously anxious would I have been? Fearing not only that my backpack might be stolen, but I might have been exposed to a deadly virus. Or worse, the fear I might have been a car-rier of that virus and caused the illnesses—or even deaths—of others? We all have a child, a vulnerable, anxious child, inside of us who is susceptible to fear and exploitation at the hands of those more powerful. How do we deal with those moments of fear and learn to separate the facts from the ter-ror? Whether it is traveling alone in a strange land, watching a politician make excuses for racist speech or actions, allow-ing our young child to walk across the school yard while hoping she is not shot, or choosing to get vaccinated when so many declare it's all fake—a big government-big pharma conspiracy—how do we *truly* know when it's the right in-stinct and when it's mere paranoia?

It's hard to be smart. Hard to gather facts and follow logic. Hard to *not* use histrionic social media as our primary news source. It's hard to be thoughtful and not just go with the instinctive coiling rattlesnake within that is getting ready to irrationally strike or flee. So, what to do? How do we deal with all the conflicting energies and screams of danger and confusion swirling around and within us? Here is our tough choice, in fact, the only true and mature choice we have: We must manage ourselves.

I must think, observe, seek hard facts. Willing to be curious and insightful about my personal history and my internal anxieties and do my best to know where those anxieties come from, I must listen to my deepest heartfelt values. I must come to know the instinctual rattlesnake within and manage that energy. It's not possible to eradicate it, unfortunately. The only mature choice is to recognize that the reptile always lurks within and continue to take responsibility for myself. I *cannot* change others. I can only change myself. *Correction:* I can only *manage* my brilliant, curious, frightened, wounded self. And then, act accordingly.

We cannot control the outside, but we can manage ourselves. Simple to say, and oh, so very hard. My adventure of life is on me. Yours is on you. Whatever happens on the *inside* is up to me. That is my freedom. One of my existentialist heroes, Viktor Frankl, psychoanalyst and survivor of the Holocaust, wisely insists that our greatest and final freedom is the freedom to respond to whatever happens to us. So, whether it is hiking in England for the first time, or contemplating the meanings of life, or both, the existentialist reminds us that, ultimately, we *are* alone. We do our best, and maybe we get lost. Hopefully, we give and receive grace and compassion generously wherever we are on the journey, losing ourselves or helping someone else find themselves.

For me that day, as I sat in the airport trying to settle my traveler's nerves while sipping deeply the darkest roast coffee available, I felt my aloneness. It was good—both the coffee and being alone. I was not responsible for anyone else on this hike. There was no one to disappoint. Just me. All the mistakes and successes were mine. All was an adventure.

Again, I checked my backpack, my burnt-orange backpack that would be my one, true steady companion for weeks to come. Nothing lost or stolen. Everything to gain. I saddled up. It was morning in London.

Chapter Three
Days & Dazed in Peckham

Sir, a-hh, why are you going to, a-hh, Peckham? Why not, well, somewhere else?" The Uber driver kept glancing toward me in his rearview mirror. "Most people," he continued, "who come to London stay, well, near the sights of downtown, at a hotel." He was puzzled. So was I.

"I want a neighborhood," I replied, "I don't want to stay in a tourist area. I looked for a bed and breakfast online while I was planning my trip. I had no idea where to look." His eyes were concerned while he nodded his head, politely and skeptically. After a few minutes of this questioning, I began to doubt my decision. I struggled to push those feelings away.

Back in Nebraska, I had done my research about where to stay in London. Knowing I'd need to recover from jetlag and would want to explore for a few days, I wanted to do things my way—whatever that meant! Hoping to experience life from a Londoner's perspective, I wanted to spend time where real people lived. Thanks to Google, I found a bed and breakfast with excellent reviews on the south side of London, in a town called Peckham. I wondered, admittedly with some trepidation, what adventures awaited me.

I fell into silence and gazed out the windows. The sun was bright and cheery. I watched the famous red double-decker buses pass and noticed the late morning traffic and the crowded sidewalks. The driver, though polite, spoke broken English, and it was hard for me to gather information about the city. It was hard to settle into the back seat as I worried about where we were going and where I'd be staying. We followed the River Thames on some main thoroughfare. I watched buildings, old and elegant, turn gradually into homes and apartments. I saw people jogging along the river, amongst the trees, and felt a kinship with those running a trail. I watched the sun sparkle off the water and tried to breathe in the city.

The driver's curiosity lit the fuse on my growing anxiety. It was true. I did not know what I was doing. Except, I reminded myself again, I was learning. I was alone. I was on an adventure. No predictions, few plans.

Out of my backpack, I grabbed the map I had purchased at the airport and tried to make sense of the drive. I asked the driver for confirmation, using landmarks noted on the map. "No," he said, and he tried to explain, but I couldn't understand him, his version of English. I felt embarrassed. I saw a bridge as we passed. I mentioned the name. He didn't know the name. Did he know where we were going?

This, I suspect, is a modern-day dilemma, a problem created by our relatively recent dependence upon high-tech information, like the map apps on our phones. It's a blessing and a curse. We do not need to pay attention to landmarks. We listen to the disembodied voice, watch the red arrows on the display, and notice only the streets we need to track the route. The existential metaphor of being guided, actually being told what to do and where to go, is representative of our reactive time and age. It's easier to be told what to do, what to think, to follow a god, or follow a representative of that god, than to take the risks of thinking for ourselves, to get lost. The longer arc of human history would tell us that sometimes getting lost is the only way to be found.

We missed a turn to take a bridge to cross the Thames because traffic was heavy, and the streets were blocked. We drove on. Where was I staying, anyway? Finally, we took a turn and crossed the river. Again, I asked for the bridge's name and the driver identified it, but I couldn't understand him. I faked it and smiled.

We arrived in a residential area, a neighborhood. We passed an old, historic pub. The driver's reactions to my choice of location away from the city center made me concerned that I had somehow booked a place in some impoverished, dangerous section of town. This location seemed, in my American judgmentalness, deeply blue collar. It was old, grimy, post-industrial, and probably concealed some areas that were downright destitute. I moved out of anticipation and into the reality of my choices; I was just as nervous as before.

He drove onto a dead-end street. I saw a small cottage, a rowhouse, connected to others. The driver pointed to the address on the low brick wall. I double-checked the address and location. Yep, that was it. I took a breath. I began my new adventure.

I rang the bell on the cottage door and was welcomed. The host and her adult daughter were Portuguese, having come to England many years before. London is, of course, a fully international city, and I found it fascinating to experience the flow and rich mix of cultures. I observed this especially in Peckham. Having settled into my small, cozy room, I sat on the edge of my bed and took stock of where I was, what I had, and what I was doing. This burnt-orange back-pack—my only trail buddy and as important to a hiker as a saddle is to a western cowboy—was stuffed with the as-sorted necessities of my stravaging life: clothes, running shoes, sandals, water bottles, medications, vitamins, a treas-ured old leather notebook, passport, mobile phone, laptop, and hope.

I sighed deeply. Dazed. Fumbling with disbelief. Yet fi-nally, I was here.

Raw and Unpretending

It was early afternoon. Even though I was exhausted from a long overnight flight, I wanted to explore. The host explained the general layout of Peckham. She pointed to the walkway on the side of the cottage that was a shortcut to the business district. I felt uneasy. It looked like an old grimy alley. My American fears kicked in. Big city alleys could be *dicey* and *dangerous*.

I walked outside in the opposite direction of the alley, toward a supermarket a few blocks away. I soaked in the au-tumn afternoon sun. I made mental notes of my location and easy-to-remember landmarks. I expected to get lost. My anx-iety was still flickering in my heart like a steady flame. The streets and buildings suddenly all looked alike. If I were in arid western Nebraska where the sandhills only turn lush and green for a few short months a year, where every sky-reach-ing dune of sand looks like every other grass-covered dune, and where foreign wanderers have indeed been lost and not always found, I knew I would be at home and able to find my way. But not here in Peckham. Not me. Not this prairie foreigner in this old city of the world.

When I was a child, my brother, sisters, and I would listen to stories of my mother, grandparents, and other relatives who lived on cattle ranches in the sandhills of western and central Nebraska. It is an invisible sort of land. The land hid itself for many years from opportunistic land-claim hunters and other Anglo-European settlers by disguising itself as a nearly treeless desert. Roughly, the sandhills comprise the land between the Platte River on the south and the Niobrara River on the north. Underground, sometimes just a few inches below the sand, exists a portion of the largest aquifer of pure, naturally soft water in the world.

The sandhills, discarded as worthless desert and essentially invisible to most Anglo-Europeans, were the sacred center of life for the native people for thousands of years, and home to the holy bison, elk, deer, prairie wolves, pronghorn, beasts of prey, and birds beyond imagining. If I thought the buildings of Peckham suddenly all looked alike to my rural eyes and made me feel disoriented, vulnerable, and lost, the sandhills could do their own magic. One story from the late 1800s describes how the Cheyenne people disappeared from the pursuing U.S. Calvary by shapeshifting into the sandhills and grass. They were cloaked by the sacred land for days as the soldiers searched for them, riding in endless, fruitless circles. Relying on their own raw, beautiful patch of earth, the tribe, though starving and wounded, endured to resist U.S imperialism for another day.

This bit of urban landscape was not my native land, but as I got more comfortable wandering Peckham, I could see the unpretty beauty of the buildings, the broken sidewalks, the giant mounds of trash that were heroically picked up by the rubbish crews every other day or so. I was also able to calm some of that anxiety that made everything feel so urgent, so very life-or-death. As some of the tension melted away, I began to hold my story, my sabbatical, and my present experience in a new way.

I found a delightful coffee house on a side street. One day, I was visiting with the barista as she was fixing my delicious brew, and I mentioned how I enjoyed this part of London, how Peckham was intriguing, full of every color of the human rainbow, and so busy with energy and life. She smiled and said, "I know. That is why I live here," pointing across the street to a small building. "I moved here several years ago. I love it." Peckham was raw and unpretending. I imagined its secrets and stories, tucked behind the doors and within the hearts of pedestrians as they rushed in and out of the shops and restaurants. Peckham was home for these folks. *Home.*

I had promised myself and others that I would blog my sabbatical throughout my English adventure and wherever else I journeyed. I envisioned writing the details of every moment, recording the stories both good and bad, sharing some of the secrets of my inner child and adult self, learning, teaching, and experiencing. But here I was on my first night in Peckham realizing that I already had to break that promise. Back in my hotel in Denver, Colorado, before I even boarded the plane that would take me to London the next day, I suddenly realized I had lost the power cord to my laptop. It was late and not possible to take a quick taxi to find a store in that part of Denver. I tried to calm myself thinking that it would be relatively simple to get a new cord at a computer store somewhere shortly after my arrival in London. This was a Google product after all and, well, Google-god is *everywhere*, omnipresent. I was wrong. It turns out that my particular Chromebook, an older model, was never sold in England or Europe. I could order a new cord from California or Asia, but it would take weeks to deliver.

It was time to go shopping. Now that I had found my bearings in this friendly little neighborhood, I was on a new kind of mission with a fresh source of worry. With my limited budget, I dreaded the expense of a new computer. I fought panic. I fought discouragement and failure. I feared that every electronic store in Peckham would take advantage of me. I was ten years old inside, trying to solve an adult problem with logic and smarts I just didn't have yet. Impossible.

Finally, I was referred to a small computer store down the block from one of my favorite international food cafes. I explained my predicament to the manager. His assessment: I could buy a new Chromebook or a used laptop. Either way, I was going to end up with two computers, my old one, unusable and untradable in England and Europe, and whatever I purchased. The added weight in my backpack and the expense were daunting and painful. My amygdala, shooting anxiety into my brain, sarcastically reminded me, *Everything is an adventure*. Shit.

I blubbered about how awful my life was, seeking some sort of sympathy from the man behind the counter. He looked at me directly, dead-eyed. This man was an immigrant to England and replied in a musical sort of accent, "This is not awful. This is an inconvenience. Problems like this happen every day." I stuttered and mumbled something about the expense. Again, he shook his head. I asked what he meant. He replied, "Where I come from, we have lots of death. Friends and family have died. A thousand people have died in one day."

I fell silent and then asked the necessary question, "Where are you from?"

"Afghanistan," he answered.

The hills of Afghanistan, the sands of Nebraska, the streets of Peckham. They all hold stories of joy and heartbreak. And there was egocentric me, the center of the known world. Yes, I was a stranger in a strange land, but how strange was this place, really? Yes, I had a heightened sense of lostness and puzzlement as I tried to navigate this new place, but how difficult was it to manage this small corner of the city? I had no excuses for why my little crisis felt so large and consuming. I had nothing to compare with the life experiences of that frank, straightforward manager of a neighborhood computer store in Peckham. He didn't just manage a store, he managed a life. The used two-hundred-dollar laptop I purchased that day suddenly felt cheap and weightless. I was embarrassed. Rightly humbled.

The Handwriting on the Wall

For almost four days, Peckham and I conversed. One cold and rainy day as I explored and walked her streets, I was feeling the emotional rain in my soul. Wrapped in melancholic meditation, I stopped in the middle of a long block, sensing the energy of the city, feeling the shamanic connections of spirit and urban place. Moving out of the way of pedestrians, I backed close to the wall of an abandoned steel building along the sidewalk. Feeling as if I were invisible to the crowd as they rushed through the wet weather, I felt the chill of the rain even through my new English-made waterproof jacket, purposefully oversized so it would cover me and my backpack on my upcoming hike. In the sacredness of that moment, I wondered, yet again, of my callings. Wondered about this city, wondered about being alone here, far from the center of my prairie, and wondered about the daunting journey that was still yet to be.

Standing silently, the rain dripping off my wide-brimmed hiking hat, I glanced at the old, corrugated steel wall that lined the sidewalk. The anonymous building's barn-red paint was scratched, dented, and fading. Suddenly, I saw the handwriting on the wall, as clear as the words must have appeared to the ancient biblical prophet Daniel. A scrawled message on a small piece of cardboard, attached with some kind of industrial-strength duct tape, ink smearing in the rain. It read:

I dreamed of this moment and finally it came.
Thank you for changing my world.

I quickly turned and glanced around, seeking the author but knowing it was futile. How long was this note here? Who placed it? I had walked by this spot numerous times and had never noticed the note before. Was some poetic lover celebrating a mystical connection with another? Or did someone, an angelic spirit in human form, follow me to Peckham, knowing I needed encouragement for this journey of my life, leave it for *me?* I was dazed, joyous. This felt so personal. My rational logical mind tried to minimize this message, but deeper down I knew it was a spiritual affirmation of my path. This waking dream, this handwriting on that old wall, out of the blue and in the rain, bidding me... *Welcome, Royce, this is the place where you are called, where you belong—your stravage. You dreamed of this moment, and finally, finally, it's here. You're here.*

A Home on the Range

Place is vital to our survival. Place forms us. Place calls us. In a spontaneous meditative moment, my mind and heart drifted to the meanings of *callings.*

I drift far away from Peckham, across the oceans of grass and sand, and reflect upon the discovery of how deep the sense of place and geography pulsated within my mother's veins, her place where she belonged...

For years, I had wanted to visit the specific ranchland home where my mother was born. We would occasionally visit cousins who lived near the original ranch-stead. We children were thrilled with the experiences of visiting our ranch-cousins, riding horses across the sandhills, digging massive tunnels and hideouts, oblivious to the dangers of collapsing sand caves. One hot June day long ago, we even helped with a genuine western cattle drive, moving the cattle from one section of the ranch to a far pasture. My brother and female cousin rode their horses across the prairie dunes, becoming silhouetted against the blue sky as they gazed down upon us. Their shapes across the distant horizon looked straight out of a western painting, capturing the images of long ago. Later, during the cattle drive, a wild afternoon thunderstorm suddenly exploded across the prairie. Lightning striking. Rain pouring. We reached the swollen Niobrara River, pushing the cattle across. I didn't know what to do. "Just let the horse swim!" my adult cousin yelled above the deluge, "Relax the reins! He'll take over!" I did. He did. I couldn't help but giggle as my cowboy boots filled with river water, as my horse simply swam the deep water with me on his back. Effortless. Memories so golden.

We were so close, but we had never visited the actual site of my mother's home. I often wondered why. Later, I would learn that my mother and her siblings were not only raised there, but also abused there. Abused, not by the land, but by an erratic, impulsive cowboy father. The land offered a healing salve for these children and their own mother. The land, so stark and beautiful, was their refuge. Gently, fiercely, it still holds untold secrets.

One spring, on an Easter weekend when I was fifty, I insisted on being let into that secret realm and she reluctantly agreed to be our guide. Looking back, I understand the painful ambivalence my mother carried with her on that visit to the land of her birth. She had spent her whole life carrying poetic and beautiful memories of life on the ranch and trying to deal with the horror of the rest.

My mother was thirteen when she and her family moved out of the hills. Sixty years later, we brought her back. Leaving the paved highways behind and driving onward, it was another waking dream. The ocean of sand parted and welcomed us. I felt joyous disbelief as my mother, now nearly blind, remembered the twists and turns of the old sand trails, navigating by memory, intuition, and love. We drove through ranchers' yards, passing shallow lakes and ponds. Wild swans swimming, their white feathers glistening in the spring sun. Newborn calves romping across the grasslands. I felt her longing when she said, "I always miss the songs of frogs after a spring rain."

She directed us to follow a faint course of a nearly invisible path, an older, now unused trail. We followed the rise of the land and then she spotted it. Home. A lone, ragged tree standing next to a windmill and a small water tank for cattle. That was all that was left of the place that had raised her.

We parked our four-wheel drive vehicle. The prairie spring day was bright, glorious, and gentle. We got out and I watched her walk in the beauty of the land, touched by the sun and quiet breeze. The fresh tall grasses were waving and welcoming. She was four again, or eight, or ten, sharing stories of "riding fence." She'd pack her lunch and ride out on horseback to repair the barbed wire fences, alone. She was in her own dream. She wandered by herself, up the hill behind the site of her house. She turned around and around, gazing, gazing in all directions.

From a distance, my father watched his wife. Softly, he reflected, "I have never seen her like this before." No one had. My mom was home. Home, where she belonged.

In Peckham, thousands of miles and many lifetimes away from the American prairie, I also felt strangely at home. I continued to stare at this sign of synchronicity, the handwriting on that old metal wall, all of us dripping in the London rain. I took a quick photograph to forever preserve this message of longing and belonging.

How could I, a prairie farm boy, be at home in a grimy district of London? It's because I felt community. I felt the connection of people to each other, and to place. Peckham, a place called home. Isn't that what we all seek, a place to love, and a place to lovingly make love?

Of Carnivals and Kings

This small post-industrial town deep within London, far from the River Thames, was full of surprises. Peckham, it turned out, was not dicey and impoverished, but a safe and welcoming friend. It's still a mystery what drew me to *this* town. It was something more than search engine algorithms. Some unconscious process beckoned and seemed to know I needed to see all the colors of her humanity and all the costumes of her people. I needed to stand in the midst of sidewalk preachers and their flock of believers, singing and shouting on a Sunday afternoon. I needed to breathe deep the aromas of the International Spice Cafe as they mixed with the familiar odor of the McDonald's a few doors down.

I felt I needed to visit the sights of London, to do my tourist duty and to say I was there. Still an amateur traveler, I had to ask the double-decker bus drivers how to find central London, but they were gracious and took their time with me. I overwhelmed myself touring the banks of the Thames, drifting amongst the heavy crowds. Big Ben tolled and I marveled. Cotton candy, ice cream, Disneyland style rides, and hyped-up tours of The Tower of London violated my historical sensibilities as I imagined V-2 rockets bombarding London during World War II. I looked in judgment upon the clowns and acrobats and cheering tourists. The grey ghost of smoke rose still from the bombed buildings, and the distant echoes of screaming children and blaring sirens seemed more real than this contemporary commercial circus.

Disoriented, I walked across the bridge that spanned the massive river. I wondered about my own family's heritage in this land called England. My land and this land, intertwined with exploitation, greed, and military and economic dominion of peoples across the Earth. I walked through Trafalgar Square and felt lost amongst the towering statues. Mostly white, mostly male, mostly about military power. They were specters of violence rather than benevolent guides.

Grief and loneliness took over. Turning in circles, I watched the flow of traffic, human and machine, and felt myself judging the wandering tourists who seemed unaware, oblivious, to the stolen souls we have extracted from each other and the rest of humanity. Of course, these were my projections and did not ring true for many of the residents and tourists who came from the far edges of the empire and who might know the weight of British colonization firsthand. I reflected how imperialism, whether it be English or American, exploited millions across the Earth. I grieved humanity's injustices—mine and those that belong to all of us. A prayer bubbled up through my grief.

The depth of human history enveloped me as I paced the tiles of stone. I felt outside of my body, dissociative, as I observed myself walking, moving around the square. A tourist I was, like the hundreds of others, chaotically milling and drifting toward ancient buildings. Other groups, herded by guides, snapped pictures compulsively. But I left my phone in my pocket. It wasn't what I needed in this moment of disorientation. I knew where I was and yet I did not. I was lost. Off to my right, the crowd swelled and started flowing together in a specific direction. I realized they were headed toward Westminster Cathedral. It was time to celebrate Evensong. Unexpectedly, in a rush of holy need, I knew I *had* to attend. For a thousand years, humans have sinned, repented, plotted, avoided, and sinned again in this castle built for god. And now, this lost wounded soul that was me, yearned to go to church, to briefly be part of a church with its own wounded soul that represented both greed and grace. Seen that way, you could say that a church is a place for us all, for all souls. Flowing with *the all that is*, and merging with the crowd, I stravaged toward the cathedral.

The ghosts of kings, queens, priests, holy commoners, and sacred sinners communed together in this place. The hymns of Evensong and words of the ages washed over us. The stones cried out, sang with us, our voices echoing through the massive cavern. The priest (a woman!) smiled as we filed past and I thought how even this ancient, rigid hierarchy has changed, ever so slightly. Had the stones, less rigid than the archaic church itself, noticed that molecular shift of the graceful smile of the goddess? I felt centered again, anchored by the singing stones of the year 1090. As beautiful, wounded, and holy as all this was, I simply wanted to leave central London, and go *home* for one last day in Peckham.

Chapter Four
The Dreams of Averbury

The next morning, bright with the warm autumn sun, I saddled up my pack and sauntered through the now familiar streets of Peckham. The early morning traffic was light, this being a weekend. Store clerks were busy hosing off the sidewalks of residue from the last evening's crowds. I wandered and gazed and wondered again about the mysterious callings that brought me here to this urban enclave. I felt grateful. I had honored my desire to experience a London neighborhood. I had been welcomed beyond imagining. I felt meditative as I silently conversed with the inner-city landscape. We were friends, Peckham and me. We bowed and bid each other farewell.

Wandering through the now friendly alleys and shortcuts, I made my way to the train station, a worn-out building at the end of a worn-out lane. I purchased my ticket and joined the passengers waiting for their scheduled trains. It was time to head to Swindon, the rail stop nearest to the Ridgeway National Trail. Settled into a comfy seat, I hooked up to the free Wi-Fi and watched as the city gradually changed to country. Again, I felt young. I noticed the trees, pastures, and farms and how similar all this looked to mid-America. I was full of joy, but also felt traces of embarrassment. *How else would England look?* my critical-adult-self asked. The little one inside me bravely refused to give in to such logic and insisted on being surprised. His wide-open eyes took in the sights with awe and a playful *gee whiz*. Silencing my internal critic, I simply soaked in the wisdom of my internal child's spontaneous delight.

Before I left western Nebraska in 1968 to go to college in Indiana, I had seldom seen a forest of deciduous trees. That fifteen-hundred-mile car trip was revelatory. At eighteen years old, I was like the hatchling who bonds with the first images of life outside the shell. The forests to the east of the Mississippi River captivated me. I've always loved trees, but trees on the western prairie were few. The grasslands would roll, mile after mile and, maybe, near an oasis of water, a small grove of cottonwoods would appear. Oh, the sacred cottonwood.

Our family's farm was located on a gentle hillside. We could stand on the rails of our corral fence and look west and south and see the North Platte River valley. We would watch storms build in the west, scores of miles away, and track their advance with awe and sometimes terror. The wind would blow giant clouds of dust and sand, mixing high in the sky with the storm clouds. Sometimes, gentle life-giving rain would fall. Sometimes, winds of dry sand would rip buildings apart, forming massive tornadoes that swept across the land, ripping through towns with unbelievable destruction. Or it might be hail that would destroy crops, roofs, windows, and farmers' livelihoods in an instant.

The western slope of our farm gave way to a large borrow that collected the wastewater from rain and irrigation runoff. In the summer, the borrow became a swamp of deep mud and shallow pools, the perfect place for farm children to hunt for frogs. Sometimes an old cottonwood log would become a raft and we would float the swamp like Huckleberry Finn. This borrow marked the farm's boundary line. There were numerous cottonwood trees clustered there, but one in particular became our family's sacred tree.

The Grandfather Tree

If trees could talk—and *this* tree, at the bottom of our fields, at the end of our farm, wanted to tell its story—it would tell you a tale and speak of the land and the sky, and the beings that lived above and below. It would tell sacred stories, stories that mattered to all, especially to the first peoples of this prairie land. The cottonwood tree, as a species, was and is sacred to the indigenous ones who came before all the rest. The prairie cottonwood was a tree of life, a prayer tree that offered healing wisdom and served as a spiritual conduit for the tribes.

The mighty cottonwood, the tree of trees, has served a sacred duty for the people of the plains, from the far north to the far south, for thousands of years. The old dead roots, gnarled, seasoned, and twisted by time and weather, would be carved into kachina dolls and ceremonial masks by the people of the Southwest. The great boughs would be used for funeral shade. Elders and other honored ones would choose a tree to represent the Tree of Life, cut it down, being careful to not let the tree touch the earth, then re-erect it in the center of the ceremonial Sun Dance. Prayer flags were hung from the branches. Dancers, the skin of their chests or backs pierced as part of the ritual, would move for days, fasting and seeking wisdom. The dancers, taking on the sufferings of the people, served as a loving, willing sacrifice for the healing of the tribe.

As a child, I did not know the native stories of the great cottonwood trees. I only knew that the tree at the bottom of our farm, at the end of our fields, was special. My earliest memories are anchored there: being held by my father, standing in the shadow of the tree's massive limbs, watching people picking potatoes, stuffing huge burlap sacks with produce. It was autumn. I wasn't even two years old.

The cottonwood tree was always there, through wind, lightning, blizzards, droughts, and floods. The tree was naturally sacred to us. Its energy beckoned us without our conscious knowing. We climbed the great arms and perched ourselves in the folds of the thick bark. One day, playing with a cousin high in the tree, I grabbed a young, green branch. It snapped. I fell to the ground. The wind knocked out of me, I writhed on the ground, sure I was dying. Later, we laughed and told stories of that moment. I grew to call this the Grandfather Tree. One time, home from graduate school and getting ready to attend my high school reunion, feeling nervous about seeing people with whom I had never really belonged, I climbed into the tree as high as I could and prayed. I walked on the giant branches, talked with the tree, deeply and privately about my life. Grandfather Tree listened and spoke to the wisdom deep within me. The gentle movements of the heart-shaped leaves of the cottonwood tree whispered compassion and acceptance. The words of healing from Grandfather Tree were as real and audible as any conversation I have ever experienced.

Dr. Royce Fitts

Droplets of Mystery

I am an atheist, an agnostic, a believer, and a dreamer. Sometimes I am all of these at one time. Other times, my soul picks only one or two. Sacred is about being in touch with the energies of life, the mystical mystery. I do not believe in the supernatural. I believe in the *unknown* natural that is sometimes described as *super*-natural. Supernatural implies that there is a kind of intervention from something outside, an arbitrary force for good or ill that strikes like lightning upon the earth, and upon us. I believe in flow, the natural evolutionary river of life that, essentially, has always existed. This river has many tributaries that branch in and out, experimenting with new directions, sometimes succeeding with new, creative results, other times reaching only evolutionary dead-ends.

I believe in synchronistic energies, or, for lack of a better term, *coincidences* that fall like droplets of rain. Sometimes we notice them and call them miraculous, unusual, but most of the time we never see them at all. We treat these droplets like we treat nighttime dreams. Though we experience thousands of both each year, we mostly ignore them, letting them wash down stream and down our memory drain. We dismiss our dreams, and we dismiss moments of synchronicity as mere coincidences, often saying, "It's just chance." We brush away the goosebumps that appear which, oftentimes, confirm the beautiful strangeness of the mystical mystery.

I felt the droplets, these remarkable blessings, as I rode the rails to Swindon. It felt miraculous, and yet, at the same time, it was as natural as a nourishing springtime shower.

My dreams were coming true. I knew I was following my calling. Arriving at my destination, I was less than fifteen miles from the ancient village of Avebury, the beginning of the Ridgeway Trail.

The taxi driver who picked me up from the station said he had not been to Avebury in years, and though I gave him the address of my bed and breakfast, he delivered me into the village proper. My host actually lived in one of the outlying housing developments a mile outside the village, but I didn't care. I thanked the driver and said goodbye. I would walk the remaining mile on a tree-covered path, over a stream beside a sheep pasture. I gawked at the old cottages, with their cracked white stucco walls that revealed brick just beneath. I gasped in astonishment. Unable to help myself, I reached to stroke the dried straw of a thatched roof, hoping the homeowner would not notice this tall, strange child from the prairie touching their private property. The late afternoon sun was shining golden. *I was in an English country village.* I was walking through history. I was in an enchanted dream.

And then, there they were. The massive standing stones. I stared in disbelief. They were almost within touching distance, so close to the walkways, hedgerows, and tiny streets. I could not reach out and touch them. Not yet. I would not let myself give in to the energetic rush of being a "groupie," a gushing fan, a goofy tourist taking in these ancient monuments. I gazed, steadying myself as my emotions wavered in this new, unreal reality. For thousands of years, they have stood there. Bounding up to touch them seemed sacrilegious. I savored the moment and breathed in the knowledge that they would be there at dawn, as they had been for uncountable dawns before.

Over and over, I whispered to myself, "I am here. I am actually *here*." My memories of first reading about these stones and this trail in 2009 resurfaced in my heart and soul. These sentries served this lovely green land, moved here from afar by a mysterious, brilliant people thousands of years before this village even existed. Sentries for centuries. This was my moment at last. I had promised myself to come here so long ago. Against great odds and a very complicated soulful geography, *we* had arrived, *both* my inner child and my adult self, now at one. Courageously, smiling in awe and wonder, we walked the mile to the bed and breakfast.

The next day I would introduce myself to the Standing Ones, the Stones of the Ridgeway.

The Whispers of Stones and Hills

The sun was hanging low in the western sky when I found the bed and breakfast. After offering a warm welcome, my host Sara intuited my persistent sense of, *Am I really here?* disorientation. She invited me for an early evening stroll upon Ridgeway soil because she seemed to know such a walk would help ground me, help connect me to the reality of this place. She suggested we explore nearby Windmill Hill, a mystifying human-made mound constructed over five thousand years ago. In the warm early evening, we walked along a tree-shrouded farm road and felt the cool, gentle westerly breeze. Everything had the mystical flow of a dream.

We passed through a farm fence gate and took the small path the last few yards to the hill. Sheep were grazing and then gazing at us. They were used to human visitors yet still possessed a sense of curiosity about those who would stroll through their pasture. Sara respectfully hung back as I walked up the mound alone. This moment, a walking meditation, unlocked a spontaneous flow of gratitude for this dream come true. I turned toward this English sun in the western sky and watched the cotton-white clouds drift across the blue. I was so very present, but I could also see myself. It felt as if I was watching from far away on a bluff high above western Nebraska. It was as if I were in two places at once and it made both places all the more palpable and potent. Bearing the weight of all the dreams and all the years that took me to this day, I held out my arms to the sky and the sun, reaching to the faraway western prairie from which I had come. I thanked all that brought me here. I thanked all the beings who were a part of my journey. Faces of family, friends, clients floated by me like the soft clouds above. I thanked each one for who I am, for all that brought me to this moment.

Months before, I had done some research about the Ridgeway National Trail and Avebury, the village that the National Trust of the UK designates as the trail's beginning. Due to the winds, most hikers begin in the village and walk the easterly direction to the end. It's basically an eighty-seven-mile trek (assuming the hiker does not get lost, as I did several times). All advice I read coached hikers to plan at least three months in advance to secure lodging and know where the drinking water locations were along the trail. With a few exceptions, camping (called "wild camping" in England) is not allowed along the trail. Try as I might, I could not force myself to plan. I knew I would be in England for seven weeks at most, but I couldn't bring myself to commit to specific times and dates for the hike until I actually arrived in Avebury. I needed to *feel* the land, *feel* Avebury, *feel* the stones. I needed to hike this hike in a moment-by-moment, day-by-day way. It was to be a meditative soul walk. A saunter. A defining and defying stravage.

It was good that I was alone. Very good. I can only imagine the anxieties and conflicts that would have emerged if others' legitimate needs, expectations, and justifiable demands were clashing with mine. Up until I left the States, I'd had a desire to share this trip and hike with someone, but my unconscious—my soul—knew better. *I must be alone.* Only in retrospect do I understand how very necessary it was that this would be a solitary pilgrimage. I needed to discover what it's really like to inhabit time without the restriction and demands of some external schedule. Time must be allowed to unfold naturally, intuitively.

Yearnings of Earth and Sky

I was fascinated to learn that no one knows where the original trail began or ended. Thousands of years before the first humans walked upon it, this ridge was carved by the movement of glaciers. Once, the Ridgeway would have extended across the land-bridge that connected England and Europe. What's left of this trail cuts across what we now know as central southern England, occasionally following the flow of the River Thames. The ancient connections between earth, rivers, seas, and the beings that walked, swam, and sailed across it all intrigued me at the intellectual and spiritual level. They represent a kind of eternal conversation that exists between all elements of our universe. This earth and sky are alive with the yawnings and yearnings of every birth, death, change, expansion, and holy mundane urge to build and experiment.

After a glorious sunset, the stars came out. I could see the shadows of other standing stones in the near darkness of a distant alfalfa field. Not far to the south, beyond the neighborhood homes, other human-made mounds invited exploration. These high mounds and massive boulders, somehow moved from a quarry perhaps fifty miles away, were placed here by an unknown people. It's a wonderful mystery for us humans living five to eight thousand years *into their future* to ponder. What meaningful purpose did these landmarks serve? What duty was being honored? What holy fear, intimidation, or welcoming invitation was being offered then and—so mystifyingly—is still offered to us today?

I slept with a peaceful, contented, *I am finally here*-awareness. Early the next morning, I awoke eager to meet the stones face to face. Low-lying clouds and fog drifted across the grounds of Avebury that first chilly morning. The sun rising and the fog drifting, moving in and out of the stones, conspired to weave the mystery of time. Thousands of years ago and *right now* are simply one and the same.

A few days before, I had visited London's Westminster Abbey. Its construction had begun in 1090. I considered those building stones of the Abbey as I now stood in the midst of these great monoliths placed in these pastures over five thousand years ago. These guardians soared in their own cathedral of green fields and milky blue skies. Humans have a need to delve into the deep stories of the soul and universe.

We seem to long for a sense of protection, to yearn to feel that we've been chosen by the powers beyond our human powers. We need to feel special and in communion with all that is beyond and uncontrollable in our mysterious existence, whether we walk in Westminster Abbey, sit in the shadows of great uncarved stones, or stroll upon the sacred sands of the Nebraska prairie.

During one of my many saunterings into the Wildcat Hills back home, a family member and I delved deeply into one of the hidden canyons located there. I had never seen this particular canyon before, not in the nearly twenty years I had lived in and explored thoroughly those hills, even though it was less than a mile from my home.

Twenty-three million years ago, those canyons on the prairie did not exist. Nor did humans. All the land was level then. The bluffs that are visible now and rising hundreds of feet above the present prairie, did not exist either. The land had been submerged and existed for eons as the bottom of a shallow sea teaming with aquatic life. Then the seas disappeared, and mountainous volcanoes rose and exploded in the west. New rivers in the new western mountains formed and plunged toward the east, eroding the high plateaus and former seas of this region. One of those ancient rivers, according to the findings of an archeological dig, flowed nearly right outside the door of my former Wildcat Hills home. Ancientness is everywhere on our Earth. As is sacredness.

Twenty-three million years later, we wandered through one of those erosion-sculpted canyons. Tall ponderosa pines, some hundreds of years old, reached elegantly to the sky. High sandstone cliffs formed this rugged horseshoe-shaped canyon. We stared up, shielding our eyes in the shade of the pines, up at the cliffs and at the carved troughs where water-falls would tumble during massive rains or snow melts. We were in awe, viewing this semi-circular sanctuary, gazing upon the altar of Mother Earth, and the insects and birds offering a chorus of sensual music. The holy beings of the Earth danced in the breezes and welcomed us. This cathedral of the most holy order was as sacred and holy as any human-made cathedral in all the world. This sandstone canyon of soaring pines, dry waterfalls, sage brush, yucca, and prickly pear cactus rivaled the holiness of any sacred place, whether it be the Standing Stones of Avebury or Westminster Abbey. In the mysterious ways of the earth, the canyon, less than a mile from my home, became hidden, invisible. I was never able to find it again.

From the Stars

I intuitively understand the ancient humans of south-central England who needed to invent ways to search outward and bring stones, gigantic boulders, to their homes and to their places of awe. I understand without words. Words can't do justice to these urgings of the soul. I walked among the stones of Avebury, touched them, marveled, read the various plaques, and watched the other tourists do the same.

These Standing Stones of Avebury, older than Stone-henge by a thousand years and separated by only twenty miles, are not nearly as well-visited as their famous cousins. I wondered if the builders of the Avebury site inspired Stone-henge. Or maybe there was an ancient threat by rival tribes and a "stone-erecting race" erupted, like our crazy modern military arms race. Whatever the case, my inner child's contrariness, defiance, and a need to simply stravage, caused me to ignore Stonehenge, that heavily-touristed place. I may visit Stonehenge someday, but this journey to the Standing Stones of Avebury and the Ridgeway Trail was a single-focused mission.

The Avenue of Stones, the remnant of a wide thoroughfare that probably went on for miles once upon a time, invited me to wander. I walked across pastures and hayfields with the stones at their borders. I projected my own dreams upon these treeless grasslands and the placements of the boulders. There was an elementary school group dutifully following their teachers up and down the paths of the historical land. They had their own professional guide from the local National Trust Museum. I fell in with their little troupe, tuned into their curiosities, and to the explanations offered by their Ridgeway guide. It brought back memories of my childhood field trips that were offered in our rural schools. How exciting it was for us as children to take a bus ride during school hours to visit some local historical site. As I joined these children, some turned and smiled, as did their teacher. I felt welcomed. We followed a long moat and together we guessed about why it existed.

Later, as I was taking pictures of the stones, I met a man standing near one of the massive boulders. He glowed with a sort of passionate intensity as he handed out flyers and booklets about the origins of these circles. He believed that extraterrestrials had assisted the humans in the creation of this place. His materials had fun, crude drawings of flying saucers and powerful anti-gravity light-beams. He went from person to person handing out his information with an odd,

in-your-face energy that reminded me of Christian fundamentalist evangelists pushing their desperate truths. I faded
away, heading for the pub and an early supper with a draught
of warm English beer.

The evening would take me to St. James Church, a thou-
sand-year-old parish. The building was constructed, in part,
with pieces of the original standing stones. No matter what
time or space we inhabit in this world, there has always been
a tense mixture of cultures and belief systems trying to occupy the same piece of physical or philosophical ground. At
least five thousand years ago one tribe of people built their
own open-air cathedral. And then, a few millennia later, an
entirely new tribe judged that pastime as godless and used
the sacred stones to build their own new artifact, their
church.

Now, a large covered trellis welcomes all who enter.
The pathway wound through the church's graveyard and to
the massive wooden doors of the sanctuary. A welcoming
note was attached to the doors, inviting you to offer silence
and respect as you step inside. The coolness of the stones
also made the air cool. The dim light of the waning day
drifted through the windows, musty aromas of dust, rock,
and wooden pews wafted in the air. I felt a kind of holy confusion. Though I appreciated this building built a thousand
years before, it felt odd and sad that some of the Standing
Stones had been stolen and chiseled to build a belief system
that condemned those ancient ways. This is not rare, of
course. In the names of whatever gods and goddesses of any
time, self-righteousness and judgment are often cloaked as
eternal goodness and truth.

I left this holy building and its centuries of irony and

walked back through the churchyard and amongst the stones of grave markers. There I met a woman sitting on a bench under a massive oak tree whose story paralleled my own in many ways. An American, she was from Ohio and was fulfilling her many years' dream to visit Avebury, but at this moment she was lost. She had gotten confused by the twists and turns of the walking trails around the village and got a bit disoriented. She couldn't find her bed and breakfast. She said she had been a drama student in London some thirty years before, fell in love with England, and vowed to return someday. Just retired from a mental health job, she was burned out and recently divorced from an abusive and alcoholic spouse. In Avebury, she was following her own ancient, healing dream. She felt called to this place. As I showed her the proper path to take her to her accommodations, she tearfully shared that she felt strangely at home in this village of stones and hills. Along the way, we met some warm-hearted locals who had moved to Avebury years before and loved it. My new companion shared her callings with these new friends. They encouraged her to move here and explained how to rent a small, affordable home. After we said our farewells, I imagined what it would be like to live here amongst the ancient ones, the stones, the hills, the early morning mists, all juxtaposed with the present. There is a part of me that could do that. Still, I think about whether that woman from Ohio ever followed her dream, ever moved to this, her Avebury home.

Back at my own bed and breakfast, I struck up a conversation with my host, Sara, who described her own journey to her Avebury home. She too felt called to this land of hills and stones and described her own way of communicating with the spirits of this land. Sara believes that Star Men, from long ago and even now, made of energy and light, come and go from this place. They stravaged across the galaxies and stopped here for a while to help build the hills and stand the stones. This land, she says, offers a series of portals, both for them and humanity. Sara sees and senses them and is here to learn. Her work in this world is dedicated to offering restoration and healing retreats for her guests. I suspended my skepticism and simply held space for Sara and her Star Men. I have myths, beliefs, and knowings of my own. How could I judge another's story, another's calling, another's dream?

Chapter Five
The Chamber of Dreams

The next morning, skies clear, sun bright, and an autumn briskness in the air, I set out for a run, heading south along a muddy, spring-fed ditch that led toward Silbury Hill. The land around the hill is flat, covered in grass and alfalfa. The hill, though less than one-hundred thirty feet tall, looms high in sharp contrast to the surrounding land. It has a broad symmetrical base covering about five acres. I was glad I wore my long running pants because stinging nettles were thick on the narrow, unmaintained path that took me up the steep climb. More nettles, some reaching as high as my chest, grew on its small flat top. The views, however, were magnificent in all directions and made the risk more than worth it.

Alone on this human-made hill, I meditated upon this land called England. I could see vehicles rushing along highways and roads. I noticed sheep and cattle wandering and grazing in pastures. I felt the rising warmth of the air, heated by the rising sun. I could see walkers on the Ridgeway Trail, far to the east. Soon, I would be on that trail, stravaging my soul's unknown geography with each new mile. I prayed to the Four Directions, to *the all that is*, in all our worlds, above, around, and below. I prayed for all I know of who I am, my lonely, wounded, healing self. I prayed for my dream self, my past, present, and future self. I felt my boldness. This journey to England, symbolized by my climb to the top of this lonely hill, was a metaphor for my dedication to being fully alive, open-hearted, ready to feel fear as well as courage and grace.

The run inspired and enthused me. I had traveled thousands of miles for this moment, standing like this in the midst of the English morning. The moment was dream-like, ethereal. Energy needs to move within us, or it gets blocked. Energy, be it in the form of dreams, insights, intuitions, anxieties, angers, or pains, is often without words or beyond words. It's like the old English saying that existed before the word *unconscious* was invented, a phrase that my friend Jeremy Taylor was fond of quoting: *That which is not yet speech ripe.* Who knows if I were praying the prayers of a people five thousand years ago, or the prayers of unseen beings surrounding me, or the prayers of people faraway in my mid-western worlds of Wyoming and Nebraska, or simply praying as myself. It may have been all of the above, all at once, and more. Energy needs to move, and moving the body and the soul unlocks the spiritual and emotional logjams. When confusion reigns and mental stuckness immobilizes us, we can find some measure of freedom when we move, stretch, walk, or run. Moving through our immobilization is often painful because the emotional joints hurt. Yet, as we move—pain and all—we move toward clarity. We move, breathe deeply, and become unblocked and clear.

Silbury Hill was built over hundreds of years. Sticks, antlers, and sharp flintstones served as shovels as basket upon basket of earth was carried up the mound. These baskets were emptied time and again across the five-acre perimeter, probably packed by human feet as the hill grew over time. Its original purpose is unknown. It was likely tied to the other human-manufactured hills nearby, aligning with the patterns of the sun, stars, and seasons. Or maybe it was simply a way to see the land stretching out below, forever and forever, on a clear day. It has been explored and excavated only to find local soil. It has little in it that can be said to be unusual, except itself, one of the highest human-made hills in the world. And, it has its own unique power. We are drawn to the hill because of this power and this power grows because we are still drawn to it. Our wonder is a fuel for the ancient past.

In northern Wyoming, nearly ten thousand feet above sea level in the Bighorn Mountains, is a circle of stones that has no known origin. Now, it is called the Medicine Wheel, or Spirit Circle. In recorded times, it has been used as a place of vision quest, a place where people can connect with the powers of the Earth, the soul, and the unseen. It is as if the Wheel has always been there. It is a place that is hard to reach along an ancient, rarely traveled footpath that cuts across the Rocky Mountains. The location became holy, or it simply was recognized as holy, because it drew people to it. What is it about this place—this small plateau—often desolate with winds, snow, and isolation that was inherently holy or invited holiness to it? It was and is a portal to unseen powers. Across time and up to this day, it continues to be an opening to the inner soul of the universe, the Earth, and to those called to explore the sacredness within.

The Medicine Wheel in the mountains of northern Wyoming, and Silbury Hill in southern England, are cousins of the spirit. They are of unknown, unconnected origin, and are thousands of miles apart, and yet both have drawn thousands of people with a similar sort of magnetism, calling us to wonder and pray across the eons.

Free-Range Hiking

Once again, I braved the stinging nettles and made my way down Silbury Hill. Needing to keep my energy moving, I ran across the pastures. I had to explore the stones and the corners of the land more before I began the hike. I went to the National Trust Museum in the village but felt strangely resistant to their displays and explanations of Avebury and the Ridgeway National Trail. The guides were helpful and knowledgeable, but a "not yet speech ripe" sort of defiance bubbled within me. I was here for existential and spiritual purposes, and they wanted to ensnare me in modern-day speculation as they invited me to view the land, stones, and hills from a logical, human-made, linear perspective. Such facts had their place, but I was tied to the moon, the sun, the stars, the inner worlds of dreams that touch earth, sky, and the soul.

Though intuitively I knew I needed both the logical and the mystical, I was not here to simply study this land, the stones, and the myths in just a practical, scientific way. Humans, if we are honest, are both logical and mystical, always. I need both. We moderns tend to compartmentalize and misjudge facts as truth, as the only literal truth. We are often terrified of the unclear, the truth beyond the facts, the truth of the soul.

Jeremy Taylor often challenged those who held tight to rigid positions, whether they be theologians who welded themselves to literalistic interpretations of scripture, or scientists who consider their linear data as the only truth. He called this "mistaken literalism." In other words, fundamentalism comes in all stripes, including the religious and the scientific. It's not the view or the person with the view who is wrong, but the *rigidity* that is the real villain in such cases. It's one more way the ego tries to control that which is confusing, threatening, out of the box, mysterious, unexplainable. The ego tends to dismiss and diminish dreams for the same reason.

In family systems theory (one approach to therapy that serves as my foundation as a professional and as a dreamer), we see rigidness as a reaction that arises from the natural survival instinct of anxiety. We tend to react to conscious or unconscious threats to the familiar, even if the familiar is unhealthy. As they say, the old misery is better than the new uncertainty. When presented with the unknown, the "rattlesnake brain" floods us with anxiety because it senses a threat (correctly or incorrectly) to our survival. This is understandable. The unknown is scary. If we are confronted with the possibility of new facts that do not fit into our accepted understanding of life, we resist, even fight. Ask the Catholic Church, ask Copernicus and Galileo. The new facts of science disputed the old facts of the Church, so the new information was dismissed as "fake news," even to the point of excommunication and death.

Cultural and personal narcissism emerge when we believe that, indeed, the sun—the entire universe—*must* revolve around us. Fake news—in religion, politics and in personal stories—is a bitter solace because it reinforces the yearning for "the way it used to be." This was true for the ancients, and it is certainly true for us today. We want to maintain our private little solar systems in order to create a "safe" world built from our conscious prejudices and unconscious biases, our narrow view of the way things ought to be.

This habit of seeking solace in rigidity is why the U.S.

regressed (again) into more overt forms of racism when Obama was elected President. The threat was not about "socialism" and "Obama Care" (these were merely code words). Instead, we saw what happened when a Black person disrupted the "family system" established by racist white America. Trump-ism revealed something that has always been there: the chronic national disease of white anxiety. Racism, so emboldened in the age of Trump, became the false and terrible "cure" for a deeply wounded, deeply fearful, deeply reprehensible American family system, a system that was founded on, and is still deeply guilty of, white supremacy.

In family systems counseling, when an immature, undeveloped self begins to awaken, to heal and move toward a new, more authentic, healthier, even, powerful, and independent self, we call this process "differentiation." This new growth becomes a threat to the old system. Acts of conscious and unconscious sabotage seek to destroy the progress and reinstitute "the way things were." Differentiation, whether for an individual in a difficult family system, or in a nation that is struggling to heal and come to terms with its inherent racism, is scary because deep systemic change is threatening. In our America, when the old order, the old ego, personified by white supremacy and economic greed, felt threatened, we fell into "Make America Great Again." Fake news never felt so good or hurt so bad.

But I wasn't standing in the Ridgeway visitors' center to debate U.S. politics or toss around psychological theories. You could say I was there at the start of the Trail because I was on a quest to differentiate from the toxicity of my own nation and from the conditioning of a lifetime that urged me to play it safe and stay within the proscribed boundaries. I was about to set out on a hike with a "no-plan plan," to saunter eighty-seven miles, at my own pace, armed with my trusty pack, my dreams, and a few guidebooks. When I described my plans to one of the museum employees, I felt nervous and vulnerable. She responded to my request for advice about where to stay along the way with logical, linear professionalism (and, likely, hidden eye rolls). I faked appreciation for her insights when she reminded me that the hike is long, and everyone plans their accommodations months in advance. Leaving the museum, I did my best to calm myself: this is England, a country that is full of villages! This was nothing like being set loose into the isolated wilds of the Australian Outback.

As I wandered the grounds, I met another guide outside the museum. He was a volunteer and a recent retiree from a large corporation. As I explained my desire to wander in my own way, he offered encouragement, suggested I research some maps online, and was even gracious enough to give me his home phone number. Relieved and full of appreciation, I knew I probably wouldn't die.

Tombs of Life

On my last day in Avebury, I planned on a quiet evening, devoted to packing my backpack and getting to bed early, but I kept hearing about a site a couple of miles to the south called West Kennet Long Barrow. It is a high, natural hill that easily fits into the aura and mystery of the standing stones and the human-made hills nearby. Large boulders and sod were placed on the site beginning around 3600 BCE and it seemed to be the home of tombs used by various peoples for at least a thousand years. My bed and breakfast host believed that the site featured more than burial chambers. In fact, Sara said they were not burial chambers at all, but mystical portals used by the Star Men to go to and from other worlds.

The sun was going down. Darkness was barely an hour away. I knew I would not be back in Avebury for a long time, maybe never. The "never" hooked me. I made a last-minute decision to do the two-mile run to the Long Barrow. As I arrived and hurried up the long slope, the formation of the Barrow took intriguing turns. The sky was clear, and the sunset reminded me of the glorious orange and red hues that soared above my beloved prairie. The massive boulders and the sod and stone chambers were silhouetted against the western sky. A man and two women who had parked on the side of the main road were making their way up the hill toward me.

Still not ready to engage with these new people, I was absorbed in the process of taking pictures, framing the massive boulders against the beauty of the heavens. I was also meditating, listening to the whispers of the cool evening breeze brushing over the stones and the entryway into the chamber. I stepped into the darkness within. The scent of earth and stone reminded me of moist, freshly tilled soil. I wondered about my host's beliefs about the chamber's true purpose as a mystical portal to other worlds. I felt like I was in a waking dream again. The logical, familiar, touchable Earth blended with the mystical possibility of portals and dreams. Can the scientist and the mystic hold a gentle conversation about perceptions and perspectives, about seeing and experiencing different realities, perhaps all at the same time? Can we allow ourselves to be open to multiple realities, entering in one door and emerging through another? Can we use dreams to take us from one understanding of the universe and "the way things are" into a whole new way of seeing everything?

I decided to enter the tomb before the newcomers arrived and stumbled in the darkness, eyes not yet adjusted to the lack of light. At first, I chose to walk only a few feet into the tunnel. How could I say it was anything but spooky to enter these burial chambers? What lurked in the darkness? Was I desecrating a holy space? I imagined crazy things, like getting mugged or stumbling and crashing my head into a stone wall. What if this place *was* a space-time portal and I tripped into another universe? My primitive brain was flooding my logical brain with fears and illusions of danger.

Walking into the tomb was to walk into a dream, and dreams have no rules. Dreams insist on being outrageous, allowing us to do outrageous things, like fly or die. Dreams exceed known limits for the sake of our expansion, growth, and healing. One minute you may be losing your teeth or unable to speak because there's gooey gum stuck in your mouth, and in the next minute's dream you are making love with your grandmother. Dreams, even the dreams that shock and shatter the rules, never lie. You may dream your beloved partner has left you for another and is having a wild, raucous affair. You wake up, sickened and sulking, so you cook up a fight in the waking world, doubting them and seeking to confirm your worst waking nightmares. You may not have had these dreams specifically, but they are real dreams of mine or of people with whom I have worked. Almost inevitably a person who shares a dream will preface it by saying something like, "This dream is weird, but…" and then proceed to describe the dream story. Often, I gently reflect and remind them that dreams, by nature, *are* weird because, without rules, they will use anything to get our attention for the sake of our health, healing, and wholeness. So then, the question begs to be asked, "What *are* your weirdest dreams?" In them, you will find the golden nuggets of grace and wisdom you need.

I believe dreams are our most ancient, enduring human resource. They help us continually change, to evolve our thinking and living toward the direction of health, wholeness, wisdom, and healing. Dreams aren't logical. They will break any waking-life rules to get us to listen, pay attention, and change for our health's sake, either individually or as a collective. Dreams speak truth to power, to you, to me, to our world, in order to offer visions of personal and universal healing, wholeness. and justice. Dreams are unvarnished, elegant, raw, crude, rude, insightful, healing, and truthful.

I moved through these chambers of dream life, knowing the dream worlds and the waking worlds are as close to each other as breath is to non-breath, as death is to life. Using my phone as a torch, I gave myself to the portal tomb of West Kennet Long Barrow. I could see the small rooms and cubicles that might have held the remains of humans long ago. I stopped before I reached the stone wall far to the end of the room, sensing that I needed to cease my exploration. It was impossible to know why the ancients had constructed these passageways, but my curiosity had begun to feel nosey rather than sacred. I placed my hand over my heart and bowed, holding respect for the belief that these mysterious chambers are, indeed, portals of some kind into the worlds beyond, into death and life, and perhaps even more. I turned and quietly took my leave.

When I emerged from the chamber and stepped into the early dusk, I saw the two women wandering nearby. They smiled and whispered a soft greeting, taking care not to interrupt my quietness. The man who accompanied them was standing nearby, smoking a cigarette. I sensed he was waiting for me. From a distance, I smiled at him. I offered a slight bow and quietly thanked him for waiting for me to finish exploring. He smiled warmly and walked over to me, "I knew this was your first time here," he said. "We did not want to disturb you."

His name was Chris. He said he had been here many times, sometimes twice a year. He and his wife were bringing his wife's best friend this evening because she was soul searching, seeking new direction in her life. Chris had taken the day off work, and they'd spent the day traveling to several sacred ancient sites in the region to support their friend's meditations.

It was almost dark now. We walked down the long slope together, the four of us. Chris and I discovered a spontaneous bond with each other. It was as if the chambers on the hill created a portal that brought Chris and I together. We were connected by a mutual sense of wonder. He wanted to know about my journey and asked about what drew me here to take this hike on the Ridgeway. He was a scientist from Birmingham and worked for an industrial company. He shared about his childhood, how he was an altar boy in his church and how meaningful it was to him then, but it became stale as he grew and matured. He now read books of psychology, theology, and mythology, and made frequent pilgrimages to sites across south-central England, as he did today. He's on a perpetual sort of quest to touch the past and to contemplate the spiritual meanings of these sites for himself and others. He then looked at his wife and her friend and, after a moment of silent communication, invited me to get into their car and take a short drive to another nearby site. I must have looked startled, because Chris quickly laughed and reassured me they would not kidnap me. I laughed too, brushing away my worries about being mugged and allowing myself the luxury of feeling welcomed.

We crowded into the small car. Chris drove about a mile and turned into a grassy fenced off area. He explained that this place had recently been discovered but may actually be older than the standing stones themselves. There were a few markers and signs outlining a small structure that had existed there thousands of years ago. The only remnants were crumbling pieces of wood that seemed to serve as the foundation of a building. The beams, mostly just slivers now, were buried deep in the earth and somehow survived the centuries. The site was being slowly excavated and they were discovering the full outline of the structure. Scientists and seekers were now left to ponder its purpose and meaning. We walked around the site and speculated. I was moved to be a part of this little journey, marveling at this gracious spontaneous moment.

It was now completely dark. Chris offered to take me back to Avebury and I gratefully accepted as I was exhausted and needed to pack for the next day's hike. After a short drive, we bid farewell. I gave them my business card and we all said we hoped to stay in touch. We didn't. But then, we didn't have to. The gift of spontaneous connection between strangers can be a droplet of life-giving water that sustains us for the next leg of the journey.

Chapter Six
Our Dreams Shall Set Us Free

The next day, with anticipation, joy, anxiety, fear, and the trusty burnt-orange backpack that carried all of my Earthly belongings (including two laptops), I took the first steps of my hike on the Ridgeway National Trail. A day into the hike, I recorded the following dream:

> *I'm living in England long ago. I feel at home. I notice that much of the forested land is gone. I'm saddened. I feel the loss of the forests. The images of the Green Man and other spirits of this lush land come to my awareness. I understand, I feel, how natural it is to imagine spirits in these forests.*

Depending on our perspectives and orientations, understanding this or any nighttime dream is a challenge. To encounter a dream is to encounter countless conscious and unconscious projections. That dream, depending on whoever happens to explore it or ignore it, can be viewed in limitless ways. Perhaps a linear-thinking sleep scientist may say the dream is self-explanatory. They might say it's just a way for the body and brain to process information from the day before and assimilate this new experience with the long-held goal to hike the path. Some would say I was remembering another lifetime, a past life when I lived in England long ago, and being on the Ridgeway prompted a literal past-life memory. Others might believe that we absorb the energies of life around us, including those of the deep past, and this dream gave me a glimpse into the flow of life back then. Still other approaches invite us to imagine that I, the dreamer, am trying to integrate aspects of myself that are, in a sense, split off from my conscious, waking self. The forests that are gone in the dream represent a part of me that is seeking to adjust to grief, loss, and change in my waking world. This approach reflects, also, the environmental catastrophes that humans have wrought upon the Earth. A Jungian analyst might explore the meanings of the archetypes of trees, land, and time, exploring the collective unconsciousness of a kind of universal memory embedded within our psyche. A Freudian interpretation might reflect that I am yearning to merge again into the womb of my mother, symbolized by Mother Earth and Mother England. And the rest of us may simply run to pick up our dream dictionary, or search online the various parts of the dream and find out what the internet dream "experts" would say.

What do you say? Whatever you say, you are right! All these interpretations of dreams, and more, are correct. Welcome to the world of projections. I offered a dream, and you offered your projections. You couldn't possibly do otherwise, even if you dismissed the dream as stupid or meaningless, because that dismissal in itself is a projection. Welcome to being human.

The problem is not that you are right. The problem is that you, I, we accidentally assume that what we project is the *one and only* truth.

Projections are the movies, both simple and complicated, that constantly run through our heads. Their subject matter is infinite. We make these internal movies about everything that is happening, past, present, and future, in our waking and sleeping worlds. You may discover a lovable puppy that you know for a fact was abandoned and abused by past owners. You notice the puppy is skittish, afraid of you, and yet, you are kind and loving. The puppy is projecting her past movie of abuse-experiences onto you. You are assisting the puppy to change her movie from one of terror to one of love and healing. The fact that you feel drawn to rescue and love the puppy into healing is, in itself, a projection from your conscious and unconscious worlds. Why are you so drawn to this wounded puppy? Explore your inner movies and projections.

We cannot *not* project. We can, however, learn that we are projecting, become aware of our projections, and reduce the thoughtless reactions that emerge when we assume that our projections—our inner movies—are the literal truth of life. Our inner movies are one truth among many truths. As my dream mentor Jeremy Taylor used to say, "Just because it is true does not mean it is not a projection, and just because it is a projection does not mean it is not true."

If we were to sit down and talk about this dream, I'd grow wiser, healthier, and more whole as I take a deep spiritual breath to calm myself and listen to your projections about my dream. As I listen patiently, and as you, patiently, accept that your projections are yours, you are offering your movie to me as a gift, not as an objective fact. This allows me to take in your truth and see how it speaks to me, alongside my own truth.

The Poetry of Dreams

I interpret the above dream through the lens of my personal, built-in limitations, some of which I know, and many

I do not. I find that exploring the meanings of dreams works best in the company of trusted companions. I put my raw dream out there, and my listeners borrow the dream and consciously project their own movie upon my dream. In a poetic and gracious way, my dream becomes the dream of my trusted circle. This approach, known as Projective Dream Work, was most fully introduced to me by a great pioneer in the field, my friend Jeremy Taylor, who died in 2018.

In my dream, I am most drawn to my *comfort level* of living in England long ago. I am drawn to the forests and the spirits. There is a part of me, in the dream, that imagines life forms that thrive within the rocks, land, and trees. This is my projection, not a literal fact. It is my truth, however. There is a part of me that believes this dream is a memory of my long-ago life. I believe I am transported to another time and space. Time in dreams is like water, fluid. There is no past, present, or future as there is in the waking world. Time flows in and out through dreams.

In my dream, I am alone, except for the spirits who draw me close. What does this mean? The spirits, in part, represent my inner self or spirit. I go deep into my own reflections of what I know as my soul. I have wisdom deep within. I have intuitions beyond my conscious knowing. My waking self has many insecurities and anxieties and I often forget my wisdom. My dream of the forest spirits anchors me. It is important that I am without human companionship and am anchored by my inner self. I must walk this path alone. The dream reminds me of my own core of wisdom and strength and how deep my roots go in this life. I have good instincts and must follow them.

This dream sustained me, gave me confidence in my

waking world, and helped me follow my own path; my own ancient past, present, and future trail. Before this trip, I had taken huge risks: selling my home, leaving all that I knew that was predictable and secure, and setting out to travel the world. I put my private practice on hold, setting aside the financial and emotional security, comfort, stability, and meaning it offered in exchange for new risks, aloneness, loneliness, unconventional living, unknown adventures, money worries, and *lots* of deep breathing. I feared I was crazy. So did others. Anxious projections from many, including me, cut deep into my soul.

But here was this dream, coming to hold me, support me. The timing of the dream, on the first days of the hike, was just right. *I had come home.* Home to Self.

Silence and the Wind

The Ridgeway National Trail is quiet, almost empty of humans, just as it was in my dream. I'd venture to say that nearly anytime of the day or year, there is a gentle hush along the Ridgeway. This oldest road is a quiet road. Stonehenge, a few miles to the south, more famous and younger, is overwhelmed with sightseers who are bussed in for a minute, or an hour, to glance at the works of humans thousands of years ago. The Ridgeway, on the other hand, asks you to make a gentle, quiet saunter in a gentle, quiet land.

To leave the village of Avebury and join the trail, I had to walk through somebody's muddy, sloppy corn field. Already my running shoes were soaked with English mud. Suddenly, I met a couple of teen farmhands barreling past me on the farm road in their beat-up pickup truck. (So much for my quiet saunter!) I smiled and asked if I was headed in the proper direction, and they pointed me toward a signpost that I had yet to see.

Even in these first strides of my trek, my backpack felt unwieldy. It wobbled and shifted on my back and waist as I walked. It pulled on my shoulders, and I imagined the next eighty-seven miles would seem like eight hundred. I resolved, again, to figure out a way to mail back some of my excess stuff. The unusable laptop that added so much unnecessary weight had already been rejected by the Royal Post in Peckham, so I was stuck with it for the time being. I kept adjusting the straps, shifting the load. However uncomfortable this was, I would not allow it to cloud my bright sunny day, or to stop my happy dance along the Ridgeway.

This dream was alive! I was *walking my dream.* I talked to myself with joyous breaths. I prayed to the spirits of the land and felt the inner doors of my soul begin to open. I speculated that distant cousins of mine might have lived somewhere near, long ago. What would these ancestors have thought of me trekking across their land, sauntering under the English sunshine with barely a cloud in the deep blue sky? What would it be like to walk with them in my world, as my guests, showing them the vastness of the rolling landscape, arid and treeless, strolling under the brilliant prairie sunshine? These comforting thoughts filled my mind and body and I felt as if the trail was welcoming me home.

Clusters of ash, beech, and oak sprung up around me. These groves were filled with small boulders, and I realized they were preserved Bronze Age burial sites. Soon, I met a bicyclist who asked me for directions—as if I knew! I met a woman pushing a child in a stroller on an early morning walk. I passed secret lovers in a hedgerow, kissing. In a pasture nearby, equestrians were preparing their horses to jump hurdles. The Ridgeway: so quiet, and yet so full of life.

From its beginning point near Avebury, the trail winds along the higher ridges, looking down on farms and villages below. I had a nearly ten-mile hike ahead of me before I reached my next bed and breakfast. This was doable and would allow me to stravage, wandering with an amiable aimlessness and maintaining my gentle defiance of convention. In time, silence and the wind became my only companions. The warm autumn sun, sometimes hot, washed the hillsides in white. I had worried about the English rains, but, as it turned out, it would barely rain at all while I was hiking. Whatever the weather, my first day's giddiness would propel me along my way.

The corn, grains, alfalfa, and beans were mature as the fall season grew closer to its conclusion. Soon it would be harvest time. Cattle, sheep, and horses grazed in the distant valleys. I could smell the heavy scents of autumn in the grasses and fields. The neat shapes of fields, square or odd rectangles of crops, added design and color to the land. I imagined life in the tiny villages below, so close together, yet obviously separate. I imagined what it was like in those hamlets five hundred or a thousand years ago. Why did they emerge in that spot rather than another? What stories drifted through the wind, from ancient times through today?

The prairie town I came from was founded in 1900, a mere one-hundred twenty years ago. It emerged beside the new railroad that connected Omaha, which lay five hundred miles to the east, to points west and north. This railroad was built to capitalize upon the exploding farm, ranch, and mining developments that had begun to crop up across this vast region of the country.

My father's mother was born in 1903. Her family rode the train from the Ohio River Valley to join this new white settlement when she was about three years old. For a while, they lived with other immigrants from the east in makeshift canvas tents just north of the emerging town. She remembered crawling out of the tent in the morning and walking barefoot through freshly fallen snow to go shopping for supplies with her parents. Life was hard and crude for these pioneers who dreamed a new life into being on this vast, flat land. They'd certainly come a long way from the ancient villages of their English forebears. As I considered the people who dwelt in the picturesque hamlets beside the Ridgeway, I thought of how I can barely know the stories of my own parents and grandparents, never mind the lived histories of the little villages I passed. At once so close and so far, I, their long-lost American son, will always be a stranger to the people who call this English land home.

Farewell to Old Dreams

In the broad valley below, I could see church steeples rising toward the sky. I pondered what it would be like to be the priest of a church in a tiny village in England, imagining walking the narrow lanes and paths to visit parishioners, stopping by shops, enjoying tea, sitting in an old study and gazing out the windows overlooking the churchyard and gravestones. Romantic notions drifted with the wind and wafted toward melancholy. I missed pastoring sometimes. I missed the intimate connection between priest and people, death and life, and the way we created meaning and community, even in the most adverse conditions. In this moment, I felt the profound loss of my early pastoral years. I'd followed a calling to serve churches and religious institutions until I could no longer abide with what felt, for me, like a set of too-rigid beliefs, expectations, and practices. Even now, I could recall that visceral feeling, the ferment of my own spiritual development with its smoldering theological conflicts and heated internal debates. My identity as an atheist, agnostic, believer, and dreamer had begun to emerge long before I had a conscious awareness of those concepts. I embodied these ideas long before the courage to use those words to embrace such a fluid, hybrid relationship with god. Back then, I just knew there was a vague, and often painful, genesis unfolding within my own firmament. Eventually, I would say farewell to that faith and that job, and, with fear and trembling, be glad for the growth and even the wounding I experienced. Mostly, I was grateful I had found the ability to expand beyond it. I would leave that particular house of god behind so I could worship in my own way and speak my questions to the eternal blue sky. And yet, an old, not quite forgotten grief drifted with the English winds.

I was raised in a small Christian group that, even now, resists calling itself a religious denomination. In the late 1800s when the group first emerged, it named itself simply: *the church of God*. In the late nineteenth and early twentieth century America, the group's tradition was to never capitalize the letter *c* at the beginning of the word *church*. The belief referred to New Testament writings that the *church* was a gathering of believers and had no name other than *the church of God*. Any other name was divisive and encouraged competitive denominationalism which was rampant at that time in America's religious history. The rule was conveniently discarded, however, when it was discovered that official ministers of the *church of God* could not receive discounts for train tickets unless they were tied to an organized church with an official name—and a capital *c*. Practicalities (and saving a buck) sometimes gets in the way of idealism.

The group saw itself as a spiritual movement of god's purifying fire. Thus, it became known as the Church of God Reformation Movement (with capital letters!). The church identified itself as being in the spirit of the first reformation originally led by Martin Luther, the German monk who instigated the rebellion against the Roman Catholic Church in 1517. The Church of God, for the most part, interpreted the Old and New Testaments as the literal word of god, except for the last book of the Bible, Revelation, which, remarkably, was treated as a symbolic, subversive story of spiritual survival within the evil Roman Empire. It was unique for a conservative Christian church to interpret some scripture as a non-literal metaphorical story. It was unique, even progressive, for the church to call all Christians everywhere to drop the competitive denominational structures and move toward the unity of all Christians. This "non-denominational denomination" required followers to militantly reject formal membership in *any* church denomination. However, patterns of shame-based control, strict dress codes, hellfire and brimstone preaching that compelled everyone to rigidly believe in a particular path to salvation, made the church into yet another agent in the divisive galaxy of American Christendom.

The Church of God Reformation Movement also followed the early holiness theology of John Wesley of England, who was the founder of what became the United Methodist Church. Wesleyan theology was crucial to the Church of God. Beyond simply converting to become a follower of Jesus, a person had to be infused with what Wesley described as *a second work of grace*. When a new Christian was "saved," they needed to specifically request a "second step" from god: sanctification or the infilling of the holy spirit. This phenomenon made it possible for one "to be perfect, even as your Father in heaven is perfect." In some other denominations that were also influenced by John Wesley, the sanctification step involved intense emotional expressions, such as speaking in tongues, which are a kind of spiritual orgasmic utterance of angelic languages. My church, however, *strictly* opposed those emotional expressions as unruly, ungodly, and *not* scriptural. The Church of God always had its way of tilting the lens and doing Christianity in its own alternative, insular way.

As I look back now, I can't help but think how it would have been if this belief in sanctification conveyed a genuine sense of grace that blessed all human vulnerabilities and forgave all faults. Instead, it transmitted a compulsive, even obsessive, fear of inherent human frailty. Being imperfect meant that if and when you sinned, you betrayed Jesus. Unless you quickly repented, you would die for eternity. The harshness, even cruelty, of this belief system cuts deep into the hearts of children and adults. Unhealed scars develop. Grief lingers. These wounds become nightmares of the soul.

I was trained and educated in the church and attended services three or more times a week as a child. Eventually, I'd go to college and the church's seminary in Indiana and answer the call to parish work upon graduation. This was the expansive and rule-shattering period of the late 1960s and early 70s. The college and seminary I attended, though steeped in Church of God teachings, history, and conservative beliefs, also included a community of students, staff, and professors who were willing to ask subversive questions about our cultural and religious inheritance. We had our version of turmoil and campus unrest that included both opposition to and support for the Vietnam war, as well as protests against racism in the church and society. In addition to casting off bras and burning draft cards, just like secular college students across the country, at our institution this was also a time to question literal interpretations of the Bible. This new radicalism was juxtaposed with attendance (or not) of thrice-weekly chapel services and participating in conservative religious revival services designed to get folks saved and sanctified.

Where was I in this moment of change and contradiction? Confused, of course. I was trying to be attentive to these conflicting energies as I tried to be myself: a conservative, liberal, kind, thoughtful, bridge-building student. Generally speaking, I was a lonely, guilt-ridden, curious, inquisitive soul.

While in seminary, I eventually made a more deliberate commitment to become a liberal Church of God minister. Friends, professors, and pastoral colleagues who were on the cutting edges of these progressive efforts supported my growth as I became an advocate for social justice issues.

Along with a small band of progressive fellow ministers, I sought to challenge our organization to support economic equality and engage in anti-racism work and peace movements. The religious power structures were, for the most part, deaf to our efforts. "Not biblical. Too liberal," they'd say and shut down the conversation immediately. Now, in these awful years of more blatant right-wing, racist, anti-feminist, homophobic ideologies they'd probably include, "Not Republican enough," equating Republican ideology with the spirit and work of Jesus.

Breaking Free, Breathing Free

As I continued to pastor and stay involved in the activities of the denomination, I became increasingly disheartened and depressed. I kept trying to maintain a connection with the church, but my views of theology, spirituality, and world culture were expanding and deepening well beyond the bounds of the institution. Eventually, I went back to graduate school to work on my doctorate in counseling. This time, however, I attended a theological school outside the Church of God, which did not adhere to my church's strict Wesleyan roots. This new school invited me to explore process philosophy and theology, a liberal approach to thought and the creation that seeks to apply its perspectives into the worlds of social justice, politics, counseling, and parish ministries. I discovered open, spiritual kinship with like-minded people in that program. Perhaps for the first time in my life, I felt the beginnings of spiritual safety, a new way to emotionally relax and breathe the *ruach* of god. I felt freer.

Throughout college and my graduate programs, I was deeply curious about how personal growth groups could help people along their inner spiritual and psychological journeys. I knew that small gatherings could help people to experience connection, intimacy, and contemplation and find creative ways to live out their faith in the secular world. In retrospect, I realize I was on a quest to heal myself and others who had experienced the wounds of a rigid religious upbringing. These gatherings were an attempt to "level the religious playing field," and to take faith "out of the pulpit" and put it into the hands of simple, common believers. I wanted to bring others with me on the journey to embrace liberal views of the incarnation, to embrace the deep "earthiness" of Jesus, and what it meant for god to become human. I wanted to celebrate the earthy, imperfect humanness of us all.

I came to realize there was no distinction between mental, emotional, and physical health. It was all one, it was all spiritual, all of it. It was circular. We didn't need spiritual and religious language, "god talk," to describe this stuff. Instead, it was about naming the beauty and agony of our existence. It was about recognizing that the quest for meaning and purpose in life takes us down a lonely, joyful, painful, enriching road. We can choose to explore this soulful, uncharted geography—our risky stravage!—or we can stick to the safe track laid out by familial and religious expectations. It is as one of the writers of a New Testament letter incisively asks, "How, then, shall we live?"

As I progressed in my doctoral program in counseling, I knew, at some level, that the stravage into my soul was going to be arduous, expansive, and life changing. During this time, it felt like a natural, necessary decision for my wife and I to delve into marital therapy with a counselor associated with my program. During this experience I had a dream which took me back to my *first* theological school:

> *I am in a large, crowded church auditorium, far up in the bleachers. I'm surrounded by many people, some of whom are waking-life mentors and former theology professors. I stand up and start to speak. I am trying to make jokes and humorous comments. But instead, I blurt out profane words, cuss words. These are funny, but I'm embarrassed and apologize. I try to correct myself, but instead, I can't stop. I keep speaking with embarrassing, funny profanities.*

Perhaps, after nearly thirty years of contemplating this dream, I should have a clear understanding of its meanings. As is our way with Projective Dream Work, don't just take my interpretation at face value. I invite you, dear reader, to enjoy your own projections. *If this were your dream, what would you say?* For me, the dream became a playful expression of my growing differentiation from the church and my family of origin. I was expressing my "earthiness," my connection to the raw, honest, joyously unpredictable energies of life. The dream helped me take myself and rigid heritage less seriously. It helped me build the waking life courage "to take a stand," speak my raw truth, and to eventually leave the church. And yet, I was not leaving spirituality. In fact, this dream affirms my heart-centered dedication to grow and process my vulnerable feelings in the presence of others because sharing with others in a safe atmosphere heals the soul.

The fact that I remember this dream after so many years says I am still working on these issues. (And I'm celebrating my decisions too!)

Therapy became a space where I could discuss my theological transformation. I needed to explore my differences, growing openness, and liberal inclinations while, *at the same time*, I worked hard to stay connected to my denomination. I hoped I could do both. The goal was to stay in the Church of God and be a change agent who could help lead the church into more tolerance, healing, and progressive positions.

During one session when I shared the anguish I experienced in the face of such a dilemma, my therapist gently interrupted, "Royce, you sound just like an abused spouse who keeps trying and trying to get it right, to say the right words, to try to figure out how to fix the broken marriage. You speak like it is all your fault and it is up to you...." I fell silent. Stunned. I hadn't put it together that I was "trying and trying" like a victimized partner trying to make a bad match work. The truth of my therapist's words sunk in. I had been married to the church and it was a bad marriage. Until that moment, I did not realize that I was acting like a spiritual martyr. Suddenly, I began to feel relieved, healed, and I knew I could let go of that spiritual tug-o-war. *I don't have to carry that responsibility anymore,* I thought. Freedom. I began to breathe...the *ruach* of god.

Spiritually, I left the church that day, though, for pragmatic reasons, I took a couple of years to do so formally. I became more honest and integrated. I was relieved. Eventually, I sent a resignation letter to the denominational executive describing what I believed were my fruitless efforts to play a positive part in an institution that was designed to control, oppress, and abuse. I said I could not and would not continue to be a part of such an organization. I could not bring change, so I let go. I gave up.

It is vital and important for me to say this: I did *not* give up my calling and deep sense of being priest, counselor, and follower of dreams. Instead, I unshackled myself in order to do this work in a way that was infinitely more effective and profound. One of my favorite moments in the Jesus story is when his followers complained that no matter how hard they worked to spread the good news, many people did not care to even listen. Jesus's response was direct, simple, and perhaps shows us he was a bit pissed off. "Shake the dust off your sandals", he said, "and go on to the next town." Don't waste your time. Let go. Give up that silly, simplistic compulsion to change those who don't want to change.

When I was pastoring in a city in the American south many years ago (all the while questioning my call and place in ministry), I pursued clinical chaplaincy training in a large medical center. Clinical chaplaincy is an intense, introspective program that assists the trainee in "knowing thyself" and learning to "be with" patients and staff with a non-judgmental, free-of-religious-agenda, gentle, reflective presence. A trained chaplain will provide a solid self to anchor others going through stress, crisis, and death. One of the chaplain educators, a brash, aggressive Southern man, said that no matter what happened to his job or his relationship to his denomination, "I will always be a preacher. I may work at a fast-food joint stamping out hamburgers, but no matter what, I will always be a preacher. I just would be a hamburger-stamping preacher. No one could ever take that away." Then and now, my heart shouted: "Amen, Brother! Amen!" It is now and shall always be.

Still, all these years later, I think of my therapist's insights about how I was unwittingly locked inside an abusive relationship with the church that declared it was there to love and shelter me. As a licensed psychotherapist and spiritual counselor, I have often worked with individuals who have suffered abuse in couple's relationships. Though some men in intimate relationships found themselves in this situation, most have been women. As a male therapist, I can never know the extent of the abuse that a woman in our culture experiences. Abuse is systemic, meaning the abuse is normalized *within the system* and is often invisible, even to the victim. Abuse is physical, spiritual, emotional, financial, sexual, cultural, and on and on. Abuse is approved, consciously and unconsciously, within the psyche of the system, permeating our culture within the concepts of family, schools, government, spirituality, and, indeed, all institutions.

Sometimes, I therapeutically reflect with an abused spouse that "some of the hardest work you will ever do is to *stop* trying. Drop the tug-o-war. Let go. Walk away." Hike a different path. Stravage a new trail. Stray defiantly, walking, breathing free.

Giving up is sobering and scary. And yet, it is also freeing. It is always freeing. *The truth will set us free...*

Chapter Seven
Wars, Wars, & Rumors of Wars

The wind picked up, blowing hard, as I walked those first miles of the Ridgeway. I hiked the steep slopes of Barbury Castle, the first major landmark going east. Not a castle at all (at least, not anymore), this ancient ring fort was made of mounds of dirt, not stone. Once, its perimeter was held by spears and shafts of wood thrust into this great natural hill. The remains are gone, decayed, except for the earth ramparts and deep moats. The castle area was massive and offered a phenomenal view of the lowlands. Two and a half millennia ago, this was the site of a small village. *What would I have done for a living back then?* I wondered. How would I have survived an environment of marauding forces, constantly threatening and attacking? Would I have been a warrior? A farmer? A priest of the goddesses and gods?

As I descended from the heights of Barbury and left behind thoughts of my career prospects in the ancient agrarian workforce, I met Eric, a man in his early eighties. He and his wife were out for a sunny, windy walk, up and down the rigorous castle paths. His wife was shy and did not join our conversation, but Eric paused and leaned on his well-worn hiking staff when he heard my American voice bid him hello. Instantly, he was telling me about the American military forces that had been stationed down in the valley during World War II. He pointed down the long hillside to the west, to sprawling brick buildings that now served as the head-quarters for a massive solar farm. The solar energy collectors spread across acres and acres of open land and gleamed from miles away. Eric told me how he and his childhood friends used to walk to the base to visit with the soldiers, and some-times they'd even get a few squares of military-issued Her-shey's chocolate bars. It was clear he had a longing to share this story of his boyhood. This elder needed me to under-stand the sense of admiration and appreciation that this com-munity had for the Americans stationed amongst them. Those soldiers stood between them and the terrifying possi-bility of a full-fledged German ground invasion of the Brit-ish Isles.

Oh, the irony of exploring the remains of a 2,500-year-old fort designed to protect the inhabitants from some long-forgotten invasion while speaking to a man who had grown up under the threat of the Nazis. To think of where things stand today, all the history we seem to be forgetting or re-writing, and to gaze at the remnants of that American mili-tary base, juxtaposed with this ancient fort just a short dis-tance away. The enemies and the regimes may shift, but war remains a constant force in our world.

A Country Boy Without a Country

Except for the swimming trunks and a cheap towel from my hotel, I was naked. On my sockless feet I wore my shiny slip-on Sunday shoes. I was sixteen years old, and I was rid-ing a city bus in San Diego, California in August of 1966. My buddy and I were skipping the afternoon services of our church's international youth convention and heading to the beach. I had never seen a beach. Or the ocean that goes with it.

There were few other passengers on the bus. I felt self-conscious, suddenly realizing that I should have worn some clothes and just changed at the beach. Neither my friend nor I had thought of that. Such country boys, such prairie boys we were.

A soldier in uniform sat across the aisle. I don't remember his service branch, but, being in San Diego, I imagine he was Navy. He was quiet. Then he suddenly looked at the old man beside him and simply said, "I just got back from Vietnam." In my sixteen-year-old brain, I imagined this soldier needed something. A welcome, a thank you, a handshake. Instead, he got nothing. The other man barely nodded in acknowledgement. We all just rode in silence. This moment was soon lost on the beach, dissolved in the sun and the crashing ocean waves.

The unjust U.S. Selective Service System, commonly called the draft, worked well for me. I still have the original draft card I received at eighteen. Unlike some, I didn't burn it. As a white guy who had educational opportunities, some emotional support, and financial loans to put me in school and keep me in school, I could apply for a deferment called college. Somehow, college education qualified someone to sit out a war. I was able to use the system to my advantage. Not all white males avoided the draft, of course, but it was men of color who had even less of a chance to avoid the war in Vietnam.

At some point during my college years, those deferments were nullified, and the military draft lottery began. I have no idea, and have never cared to know, how the strange lottery worked. It was, as they say, *complicated*. It was sort of based on the year and month of birth. I remember my draft number was in the mid-range, like 150. That meant I wouldn't be drafted unless there was some kind of a huge national emergency. The draft ended with the Nixon administration when the country reverted to an all-volunteer military.

During the brief time when I was faced with the possibility of being drafted, I visited with a minister I admired and talked about evading the draft and going to Canada. The minister became a role model for me because he was able to live out a calling to social justice, deep spirituality, and compassion. He reflected that many young men my age were in an awful dilemma. My parents happened to be visiting me from Nebraska at the time, having taken the long, rare drive to Indiana. I asked my dad to go out for coffee with me between my classes. I told him I did not want to be drafted, serve the military, or go to Vietnam. I told him I might evade the draft and go to Canada. I asked for his support. Naturally a shy man who was never good with words, he stuttered, "I would have to disown you...."

I sighed, smiled defensively, and dropped it. My induction into the military was not imminent, nor even likely, so I avoided any further confrontation. I did not know how serious he was about disowning me if I fled the country. I knew it would be a crisis for him, for me, our immediate and extended families, and friends. I knew it would challenge my religious heritage, which was founded on serving God and Country. Our "Christian" nation exists in a state of symbiotic sin that melds faith, patriotism, and imperialism. To refuse to serve in the military would expose that sin, and I'd be the one who looked like he was violating a sacred covenant. My father and I have never brought it up again. This little incident, now almost forgotten, still gnaws at me, a strange, unresolved moment from a strange, unresolved time.

Waking from a National Nightmare

We need the draft back. Don't worry, I am fully aware of the irony of this statement. I opposed the war in Vietnam and feared the draft as a young man because I believed, that if I were called up, I would die. As a child, I was physically weak and often ill, and I had very low self-esteem as a result. Imagining myself in training for violent military activities filled me with the dread of a boy who couldn't keep up with the other kids on the playground. If I survived boot camp, I assumed I would perish on some battlefield. I even had dreams, still do, of battles. Shot. Stabbed. A deep, brutal pain tearing into my stomach.

This dream of mine about dying on a battlefield is the nightmare of an entire nation. Dreams come with universal symbolic meanings, not just for the individual dreamer, but for the collective—or the family, the tribe, the community, the country, for all the Earth. We need to redefine, revise, reform what "service" means in the U.S. of A.

I also understand this dream to mean that something in me, in us, in the universe, needs to die to be reborn. "Death dreams" always, on some level, reveal a need for new life. The old life no longer serves the dreamer. The dreamer is being called to move into health, healing, and wholeness.

Something, a *radical something*, needs to change within—
for the individual and for all people. Dreams about mortality
emphasize that the choices we're facing in waking life are
"life or death" choices. We must change, or we die. The good
thing is that it is safest to die in a dream. The dream is an
experiment in which we can explore major life transitions. It
is a wakeup call to change—and live!

And so, I declare that we need a new draft. With a perspective rooted in maturity and the seasoning that comes
with a long life, I feel called to say, for the sake of our nation,
we need it. The draft needs to be *radically broadened*, indeed, the old draft model—a nightmare!—needs to die. It is
a nightmare that resembles a death cult because it imagines
that the *primary* way to serve our nation is to learn how to
kill. The draft needs to be reborn to require that *all* women
and men of draft age have national compulsory service *without deferments,* no matter one's wealth, political power, or
privilege. The service to country may be to the armed services, of course (I am not a pacifist), but could also include
service in the national parks and forests, the Peace Corps,
AmeriCorps, or other emerging organizations that contribute
to our nation's safety and deeper, soulful, empathic strength.

Think of what the social and environmental landscape
would look like if millions of young people applied themselves to teaching in underfunded rural and urban schools,
providing healthcare in impoverished neighborhoods and
mountain valleys, or caring for the rivers that flow through
our cities and fields. This idea of national compulsory service is not new and has been proposed by others. Service to
and with our fellow citizens and the world would infuse us
with a deeper capacity for empathy and creativity. It would

also take some of the arbitrary military power away from politicians and the industrial machines to which politicians bow and put it into the hands of those who serve—*all of us.*

The Dreams of the Father

Years after our conversation about the Vietnam draft, I grew to understand some of the harshness and rigidity my father carried about military service. He felt deep guilt for not serving in the military in World War II. He and his older brother had each been called up when they came of age. They followed orders to leave their Nebraska farm where they'd grown up with their father, mother, and baby sister, and reported to the U.S. Army Depot in Denver, Colorado. After having a routine physical, his brother, who had a slow-healing broken leg from a previous horseback riding accident, was rejected. My father, when his turn came later, passed the physical but was suddenly rejected. The powers that be simply said, "We need you to farm for the war." He was immediately sent home.

The grief and guilt seemed to permeate my dad, especially in later years when he would visit with family and friends about their military service. He became obsessed with watching the History Channel and old newsreels of WW II. This seemed to be compounded by his deep psychic wounding that, in my belief, stemmed from spiritual abuse. The fundamentalist teachings of the church and family shame dynamics ripped at his self-confidence, esteem, and self-image. He never recovered. He has never, as I have known him, experienced the kind of spiritual, contented joy that springs from being a husband, father, farmer, or from simply being a human alive on this wondrous planet. I can track the wounds of self-absorption that are etched into his psyche. My father is in his nineties now, and outwardly, he seems to have little or no conscious capacity for insight and change. In the seven decades I've known him, he never has. And yet, the inner self—*the not yet speech-ripe, dream-making, unconscious self*—often has a remarkable ability to offer deep healing to the soul. This is the kind of healing that happens in the realms that exist beyond a person's conscious knowledge.

Not long ago, I witnessed my father's unconscious healing when he described a dream he had recently experienced. My father is known for having scary, disturbing, anxiety-producing dreams, but this dream was different. He'd shared it with another family member who later described it to me. One day as we walked together in the warm prairie sun, my own long strides abbreviated to match the gait of a man trying to negotiate a rough sidewalk with a walker, I gathered the courage and asked him to tell me his dream. I also asked for permission to reflect with him what I thought the dream might mean. Shyly, he shared with me:

> *I was walking, herding cattle up a long narrow canyon. There was no water for the cattle in the canyon. It was hot and they were very thirsty, but they were calm. I felt sorry for them, but I was calm too. I could see a rock wall up ahead, where the canyon ends. In the wall I could see a cave. We were going there. I could see sunlight through the cave on the other side. I knew the cattle could smell water and grass. I was herding them to get*

*there. I knew they would be okay then. I knew they would
have what they needed. I was relieved.*

It is crucial—life or death—for ranchers and farmers to
provide water for livestock in the near-desert climate of the
prairie. As a child, I remember a cow that got trapped within
some old, unused farm machinery stored in a pasture. The
cow was unable to maneuver out of the trap and she died. No
one could hear the cow calling, mooing desperately for water
and help. I knew my father's guilt and sorrow over the suffering of the cow, not just because he lost an expensive asset,
but because we'd lost a life. I knew he imagined the cow's
pain and suffering. I knew he felt responsible.

I was careful as I worked on this dream with my father.
He is in fragile health and has nearly died several times in
the last two decades, and yet he has a tenacity to live. I set
aside the obvious projections that this dream is a literal message of "I will die soon." A dream doesn't come to simply
tell us what we already consciously know. My father is, due
to his age and frail health, always close to death. He knows
he will die. Using this dream to imagine that the dreamer will
literally die soon, which is shocking enough, "accidently"
takes the dreamer away from the invitation to go into the
deeper, yet undiscovered healing wisdom. Dreams guide us
toward our healing wisdom into the places we need to go and
into *that which we do not yet know.*

With my father's permission, I "borrowed" his dream. I
imagined the dream as a walk into the biblical Old Testament
23rd Psalm, a poem from our heritage that we both knew and
loved. I reworded, reordered, and paraphrased the beautiful
poem as we walked together, and reflected to him, "Dad, this

reminds me of the 23rd Psalm: 'Yea, though I walk through the valley of the shadow, I'm not afraid. I fear nothing. I see light through the cave. I know on the other side of the cave is water and food. The cattle will be fed and watered.'" I hesitated, both of us in silence for a moment, then said, "God loves you, Dad, and spreads out a feast for you. God leads you beside the still waters. Your soul is restored. You are okay now and will be okay, forever."

"I never thought of it that way," he said. "I just thought it was a stupid dream."

"Dad," I replied, "it is a good dream. It is a gift from God. Remember how you were taught to fear sin and God? How you never felt okay? How you told us often of the awful sermons and preachers that told you if you die in a car wreck on the way home from church, you could never be sure you were saved and that you may go to a burning hell forever?" We were rolling his walker up the sidewalk to the little home he shared with my mother. My questioning backfired because he immediately began to remember the painful, cruel words of one of his childhood preachers who screamed shame and fear into him and the church. Instantly, my dad lost the beauty of grace and love he had started to feel because of the dream. I knew his old habits of shame and guilt were surfacing. I stopped him, touched his arm, and said, "Dad, remember the dream says you are okay now. *Now.* The dream is from God. Can you remember that? The dream is telling you that God is with you and is leading you to the feast. The old sermons are not the truth."

Self-consciously, he smiled and said, "Yeah, I guess..." Yet, knowing him, I knew he wouldn't believe that.

I yearn for my father to consciously, *eternally*, remember that he is held by loving grace, but he can't. His old habits, formed from nearly ten decades of shame and guilt, would not let him remember this good news. The wound he carries, the wounds that penetrate to the core of his sense of self, overwhelm his conscious thinking and his own self-worth.

The waking self, the conscious part of us that is conditioned to cope and survive in the world, is often wounded deeply. It might even be wounded beyond repair. The conscious self may never fully grasp the healing wisdom that dreams offer. I do not think my father will ever consciously believe he is healed of the wounds of shame and guilt. Perhaps he will come to understand this when he dies. There is a reason to hold onto a gentle hope that he is, deep down, healed, because *he* dreamed the dream. In other words, his dream-self, his soul, *already* knows he will lie down in green pastures, beside the still waters...his soul is restored. This is his truth because *he dreamed it.*

Chapter Eight
The Freedom to Roam

The walkers I passed along the Ridgeway had buzzed with rumors about a food and espresso truck that was sometimes stationed in the visitors parking lot of Barbury Castle. I imagined the delight of rich, dark brew while hiking the glorious English countryside. Alas, no such luck. I continued on, moving away from the small crowd of day-trippers, and followed the path through thick, lonely hedgerows. Eventually everything opened up, and I began to follow the lines of pasture fencing. It was as if I were on the prairie. I even encountered a small herd of cattle. The humans milling in their midst seemed to be inspecting the health of the cows in preparation for sale. The men and women were quite intense in their task, and I barely squeezed a word or a nod of acknowledgement from them as I passed.

Soon, the trail became a narrow, barely visible thread through the high grass, but everything was well marked in this part of the open country. I passed through a large, beautiful farmyard marked by freshly painted red barns. They raised quarter horses, an expensive and popular endeavor in England. I marveled at the ease with which I was able to simply walk through people's farms, gardens, and backyards. The time-honored tradition of hiking in the UK, and in many nations of Europe, is rooted in a basic respect for the land, the gates, the fences, and the livestock. The gates are clear, easy to open and, most importantly, easy to close. Their freedom to roam law sets some limits on what hikers can do, but essentially, you're given the simple right to pass through the land, to appreciate the majesty and beauty of the Earth. Few landowners look at walkers with suspicion. Sometimes I received a friendly hello, but often no one seemed to notice me at all.

In this book, I often speak my favorite word associated with hiking and walking: *stravaging*. John Muir, a hero for our Earth and a powerful voice as we face universal ecological crisis, had his own favorite word for experiencing the spirituality of walking in nature. Muir, in fact, had strong views on the term *hiking*. He implied that the word was superficial and was not engaging the whole being of earth and person. Muir preferred another holy word when he said:

> *I don't like either the word [hike] or the thing. People ought to saunter in the mountains—not 'hike!' Do you know the origin of that word saunter? It's a beautiful word. Back in the Middle Ages, people used to go on pilgrimages to the Holy Land, and when people in the villages through which they passed asked where they were going, they would reply, 'A la sainte terre,'—To the Holy Land. And so, they became known as sainte-terre-ers or saunterers. Now these mountains are our Holy Land, and we ought to saunter through them reverently, not 'hike' through them.*

A word sometimes expresses a deep inner calling and dares to reach further than the dictionary definition would ever allow. John Muir's *saunter* compels us to go deep and reclaim our awareness that we exist *within* nature, not simply traversing across it. My own word, *stravage,* was gifted to me by a wounded, sometimes deceiving, yet wise and endearing individual. Then, as now, this new word invited me out of my rigid box of convention and revealed that I truly needed more defiant adventure in my life. The man who gave it to me intuitively knew something that I did not yet know about myself: I must *stray* beyond old habits and *stravage* into territories that I was trained to see as too disruptive, too irresponsible, too risky. Perhaps it's like a relationship that strays beyond the normal limits for the sake of adventure, health, and love. Or maybe it's like straying into the heretical. Sometimes, the greatest philosophical and spiritual insights come from such forays into the forbidden.

The word *stravage,* no longer laden with the rage of an oppressed and defiant Scottish people, still represents a powerful compulsion to follow one's own path with a sense of passion, risk, and love. I shall always, as the old German song echoes across the vales of time and hills, "love to go a-wandering, knapsack on my back," or not. Freedom to roam may be part of the fabric of life in western Europe and Scandinavia, but that's not so in America where you could easily get shot for innocently "taking a hike."

A Human Stray

Several years ago, I was preparing for my first-ever official competitive run. It would be a "ten-miler," and was taking place in the autumn colors and mountains of eastern Pennsylvania. It was a long way from the prairie where I lived, but I was called to race there because my daughter, son-in-law, and tiny grandsons lived in that area. Easy to say yes to, of course. While I often ran the canyons and trails of the prairies of Nebraska, I had never committed myself to a race of any distance. Consequently, I decided I needed to take some long runs to make sure I was in shape.

One bright September morning, I started running cross country, wearing my clunky hiking boots to protect my feet and ankles from cactus and yucca blades, sometimes following old cattle or deer trails. I lived on the boundaries of thousands of acres of wildlife preserve and had explored many of those acres over the years. This time, however, I just headed south to explore the canyons, bluffs, springs, and sandstone cliffs that I had only seen from afar. I was curious. I wanted to saunter, to joyfully explore. Even though the land was similar in terrain to where I lived, new bluffs and rocks awaited. A strange twist of a small rivulet might take me into an unknown sanctuary. I might discover an ancient artifact, a flint piece, an arrowhead, a knife point, or a grinding stone. That day, I veered onto private ranchland, not public preserve. I strayed.

Ignoring the rules and the regularly spaced "No Trespassing" signs, I folded down the sharp barbed wires on the sturdy fences, careful to not snag my running pants or stab my hands or legs with the rusty points. I made sure the fences were left intact so they could do their job of keeping cattle in the pasture. I was miles from the nearest human, hidden in a beautiful ponderosa forest. I started to run again, trotting down the slopes under the great branches of pine. I descended into the first canyon and gazed at the peaceful meadow beyond. Running on, I followed the dry streambed through the trees and grasses. In another clearing, I joined a large herd of black angus cattle. Cautiously, I jogged through the herd, speaking softly so I wouldn't startle them into a stampede. They were scattered throughout the small valley, dozing and grazing in the warm autumn sun. Some were drinking at a nearby water tank beneath a windmill. I was making new friends.

The small valley was surrounded on three sides by huge sandstone bluffs, cliffs soaring scores of feet above the canyon floor. I was running in the direction of the open range, where the mouth of the canyon began. Suddenly, I noticed movement high up the canyon wall near the top of a saddleback ridge. It was a coyote family. They spotted me at the same time, and we stared at each other from afar. One decided to simply sit on the hillside and gaze at me. I honored these coyote spirits and briefly bowed in respect and prayer. I know we humans consider them to be harmful. Coyotes do what they do to small livestock in order to survive in a land that is no longer so wild. Many farmers and ranchers gleefully hunt them as a crude sport and kill them, seeking to commit genocide to protect their land, cattle, and farmyard animals. A legendary black and white photograph of my mother's father shows him standing outside his barn next to his horse. My grandfather, shouldering his rifle, stood proud, a wide-brimmed cowboy hat shielding his face from the prairie sun. Behind him, hanging on long poles, are numerous coyotes he killed on a hunt. He expected to cash in on those pelts.

I stared up at the coyote family. There were no small calves in the cattle herd in danger of this wild pack. I knew, however, that the ranchers who owned the property would likely shoot these animals as soon as they noticed them. I whispered prayers of caution to these wild beasts: *Be wise and alert, my friends, beware of us humans so you can continue this journey of survival for another day.*

I continued to run toward the canyon mouth, gaining elevation as I climbed the lower section of the bluff. The views were stunning. I could see for miles and miles across the open plains that stretched to the south. My intention was to reach the top of the bluff and continue west aways to the old, abandoned highway, making a giant loop as I headed toward home. I reached the crest of the bluff and was startled to see the ranch-stead about a mile below. I had overshot the distance and miscalculated my location. Suddenly, I was exposed to any ranch hand or resident who happened to glance in my direction. I was dressed in my bright neon yellow running shirt and property owners in this part of the world seemed to have a sixth sense when it comes to intruders. Assuming I had been seen, there was no turning back to run the way I had come. I decided to run on and hope. Hope rarely gets you very far on private ranchland.

I headed toward the old highway, unable to use any semblance of trail at this point. Dodging prickly pear cactus and yucca spears, leaping over small washouts and bare sandstone *arroyos*, I hoped I could make it to the road. Suddenly, I heard the distant rumble of a vehicle behind me. Then, just as suddenly, I saw another 4x4 truck blazing toward me from the direction of the old highway. The prairie dust clouds were flying high behind both trucks. I was being cut off at the pass, so to speak. Suddenly surrounded, I slowed my pace and stopped. A woman jumped out of the truck that came from the road and started yelling at me, asking what I was doing. In another thirty seconds, a man leaped out of the truck that came from the ranch and yelled, "What the hell are you doing on my property?"

Hoping to sound innocent, I said I was out for a run when I crossed a fence in hopes of making a loop over to the old highway. I tried to explain that I was getting in shape for an upcoming race. "Why the hell don't you just run out in the wildlife preserve? I'm so damned sick and tired of hunters and trespassers getting on my land, starting fires and shooting game!"

I said, "Hey, wait a second. You know who I am, right? You know where I live, right?" pointing northward toward home. I felt my anger building, but I needed to stay and act calm. Years before, his family and mine had attended the same church together. "Yeah, I know who you are!" he exclaimed. I said, "You know I am not a hunter. Look at my clothes."

"Well, he's not dressed as a hunter," said the woman, sort of coming to my defense as she seemed to acknowledge our past connections. I said, "I was just heading toward the old highway. I'll be off your land in a second." I apologized as best as I could and owned my sin of trespassing. They let me go and I trotted toward the old road, carefully crossing the fence to avoid damaging the wires. Cold eyes followed me until I was out of sight. Free of their judgment and indignation, I shook my head in embarrassment, relief, frustration. That adrenaline rush that comes with feeling both guilty and defensive propelled me along. I felt bad, but I also was laughing to myself. I blew it. I knew the rules. I also knew that I was being held responsible for all high crimes and misdemeanors that strangers had committed on their property. I was the only one—not to mention the least dangerous one—who was finally caught. I get their grievances, even if the way they treated me was way over the top.

I needed to make restitution to these neighbors. I called a local grocery store and ordered a beautiful fruit basket. The clerk asked for a name and inquired what to write on the card. Ruefully, I shared my crime. She started giggling. "I know them!" she exclaimed. She wasn't surprised by their reaction. "I'll call and tell them they have a nice gift waiting." Her levity was refreshing and healing. I hope they liked the apples and pears. I never heard from them again.

"The Cattle are Lowing…"

England's rolling farm country, lush and green even in autumn, was meditative. The fences, whether made of wire, wild hedgerows, or carefully stacked stones, offered the eyes and feet a gentle line to follow. In that unusually warm and bright English sunshine beneath azure skies, my sauntering invited lostness of the most holy kind. This was walking meditation.

Arriving at a small pasture with a wooden gate for hikers to use, I entered. Immediately on the other side of the fence was a herd of serene dairy cows. They straddled the Ridgeway National Trail as if they rightly owned it. Smiling, I cooed in low tones as I approached the black and white-spotted herd. Holstein dairy cattle, I knew. The cattle barely moved as I made my gentle way through them. They brushed their noses against my outstretched hands and breathed me in. They nodded their heads with a playful energy. I talked to them with the soft, deep mooing sounds I'd perfected as a boy on the farm, walking through herds of cattle in our own corrals and pastures. Completely at home in this moment, I wondered if hikers who were not accustomed to the agrarian life would see these life forms as strange or even threatening. We were less than a hundred miles from downtown London, from Piccadilly Circus and its outrageous, exploding neon lights. The contrast was indescribable, and I loved it. There is a part of me that can love both worlds. If I had to choose, however, I'd want to be with my new best friends—hooves, udders, swishing tails, and all.

This gentle conversation with these cows of the Ridgeway brought a flood of memories of my own farm life. As I walked through the herd, I remembered a dream forty years ago, one of the most significant nighttime dreams I have ever had. That dream instantly became a living metaphor for my life, a guiding story of what my professional and personal journey would look like. Then and now, it's an anchor into my calling in this life. The dream came to me when I was about twenty-four years old, attending my first year of seminary in Indiana and excited to be preparing for parish ministry:

I am at my family's farm by the corrals along the wooden feed bunk and fence. It is spring and the corrals are full of cattle. I see large mounds of manure and soil that have been scraped together by my father. (My waking mind knows that he'd do this with a tractor and power-lift in preparation for hauling and spreading the rich organic mixture over the fields prior to the planting of new crops.)

I crawl over the wooden fence and begin to move amongst the cattle. I am talking with them, and they respond back with words I understand. This is natural and we visit like this all the time. I am their pastor. I know their language. I am connecting with them in a natural, deep way. They trust me. I walk over to one of the higher mounds of manure and soil. I climb up and begin to speak. It is like a sermon. We converse back and forth, sharing a sense of commonality. I know it is my job to learn to speak in a way that they can understand, to be with them in a relationship of trust. I know I am human, yet I feel I am one with the cattle, as they are with me. This is my calling and mission.

There's a saying in Projective Dream Work that's as playful as it is true: Dreams are the gifts that keep on giving. Dreams have no time limit as they offer wisdom, healing, and insights that can resonate across a lifetime. A decades' old dream can grow with us, appearing with a sense of power and purpose the moment you awaken, and then it can continue to offer up a new sense of power and purpose years later. This approach to understanding dreams assumes we change over time as we absorb new waking life wisdom. It honors the way the tragedies of our waking worlds shape and season us. A dream always has more than one single meaning and can apply to more than one single time of life. When someone shares a dream with me, whether it's a spiritual counseling client, a dream work retreat participant, or a friend, they sometimes follow the description with, "And I know what that dream means!" "Yes," I say, "you do…and your dream does not come to just tell you what you already know." As my mentor Jeremy Taylor was fond of repeating, "Dreams have multiple levels of meanings." Meanings, like life itself, continue to change, evolve, and weave through the tapestry of time and generations.

Time is fluid in dreams. You may dream of yourself at high school age, or as a young child, or as an elder. You may dream of yourself at your present age. I am convinced that many dreams offer us some version and vision of our future change and growth, resonating with an energy that's quite different from our present waking life age. I have experienced dreams that seem to be pointing ahead, maybe far ahead of where I am in the present waking life moment. Such dreams act like cheerleaders and wayfinders, showing us that we are capable and ready for challenges, adventures, and events in our future waking life.

The dream that came to the twenty-four-year-old me is an eternal dream. When I was a young parish minister-in-training, it was, in part, a literal message that confirmed my mission. I remember the beauty and compassion of *knowing* the cattle, *knowing* their language. To step into the lexicon of the Christian tradition, the dream felt incarnational. It reflected the literal biblical story of god becoming human as when Jesus was born on Earth and experienced life as fully human, speaking the language of humanity with such infinite love. In all seriousness and humor, you may imagine me to have some version of a "Jesus complex." And you would be right. You'd be right about yourself too, because you could not imagine this about me unless, at some level, this is also true, in some way, about you. This is all part of the natural "trick" of projection.

In Projective Dream Work, when you hear another's

dream, you take it as your own. Imagine that this dream of speaking with and walking through a herd of cattle is yours. Based on your own life experiences, you'll have projections that will shape its meaning for you, as well as for me. As my reader, you are part of the dream too. Though I do not know your particular thoughts about this scene in the cattle corral, as a witness to my dream you play a vital role in the dream's becoming. You are a bridge that carries me further into the depths of my own soul, and perhaps your own. We are all bridges for one another. We all are capable of speaking the language of empathy and offering the gifts of healing and wisdom for each other that echo across time.

In the present, I still view this dream as a reflection of my mission, only now it's about being a bridge between cultures and belief systems. As I have said before, I am atheist, agnostic, believer, and dreamer. I am all of these, and maybe more if I could put words to that which is not yet speech-ripe. I do speak with animals and humans, plants and rocks, and to spirits, and they speak with me. In my imagination, these are all possibilities, poetic bridges, between literal, symbolic, and metaphorical truths. As I am often fond of saying, "It doesn't have to be literal to be true."

Now, this particular dream also speaks of the rich and varied nature of life, the way we mix the worst with the best as part of the alchemy of being alive. The stinky stuff of organic matter is transformed into food for growth, inviting us into wisdom, healing, and change. In the dream, I was standing on top of the manure pile. I imagine the metaphor for the shittiest parts of my life, then and now, and how it's all fermenting to offer food and fuel for growth in *all* seasons, for *all* time.

It's often helpful to give a dream a name so you can remember the insight, mystery, or beauty it offers. But in the decades following the dream, it never had a name. I think I needed to wait long enough to see the laughter and playfulness in the midst of all that spiritual truth. From this day forward, it is christened *The Sermon on the Mount of Shit*.

Amen. Hallelujah. So be it.

Chapter Nine
Sacred Detours

The Ridgeway National Trail took me toward the tiny, ancient village of Ogbourne St George where I would ultimately decide to stay several nights. My instinct to avoid a strict itinerary had been a good one, and I was sticking to it. It occurred to me that a tiny outpost like this, or the larger nearby town of Marlborough, might contain a Royal Post Office that was more lenient with its international shipping regulations, and so they were. With a great sense of relief, I sent that useless American laptop back home. Carrying two computers had been a source of pain ever since I left Peckham, and I felt more than five pounds lighter when I saddled up with my backpack again.

I had planned to spend two nights in "Oggie," but torrential rains came through and flooded the roads near the Ridgeway Trail. Not wanting to slosh across muddy ole England, I chose to spend another day in this lovely little spot. During my stay, I developed a wonderful rapport with my bed and breakfast hosts. We talked at length about their lives and opinions of life in England, from local village politics to the cumbersome national healthcare system. When it appeared, I couldn't get back on the trail, they invited me to drive with them to the ancient Roman-built city of Bath. They were headed there for a family birthday party. "Would you want a ride to explore the old city?" they asked. Ironically, years ago I had a client, a university professor, who was originally from Britain. When I shared my intention to hike the Ridgeway National Trail, they enthusiastically encouraged me to visit this particular city. This detour was made to order.

It felt strange to be a passenger rather than a pedestrian on those forty-plus miles to Bath. I almost felt like I was betraying my mission to saunter and stravage. Soon enough, my hosts dropped me off in city center, and I was on foot again, taking in the strange juxtaposition of imposing Roman architecture in this corner of south-central England. More than two thousand years ago, this land was occupied by one of the most exploitative imperialist regimes the world has ever seen. This place thrived long before the Romans decided to build bathing temples to their goddess Minerva, however. The hot springs of Bath were a sacred site for the Brythons, a people with their roots in the beginnings of time.

Frankly, I found this city along the beautiful River Avon disturbing. I did not like it. The opulent buildings created by an oppressive empire that spiritually and economically raped culture after culture across the world is a scar in the heart of humanity. Bath shines as an example of the illusions and delusions of supremacy that have warped human history for centuries. It's not just the Romans, of course. In recent centuries, Great Britain and the United States have taken their places as imperial powers, but then look further. Across Europe, Asia, Africa, Australia, and the Americas, tribes large and small from every culture and every time period have been corrupted by greed. *All of them. All of us!* I cannot name one that has *not* used oppression as a tool for political leverage. I am a product of this imperialism. We all are. Some of us are powerful within this imperialism, some are powerless. We are all scarred.

Bath was a detour. It was an unexpected and unplanned experience that opened me to terrain I wouldn't have consciously chosen to explore. I walked into part of the human history of darkness, a history commonly associated with Roman grandeur, art, and light. I detoured deeper into the shadows as I imagined the toll the native people had paid to the Roman gods of oppression. It was not just their history, or a distant collective history. It was my history too. This old city put me in touch with, again, my sorrow about our species. My stravage, whether in Bath, on the Ridgeway, or on my beloved prairie in Nebraska, always bears a mixture of feelings: of joy and sorrow, enchantment and disillusionment. It is too simplistic to say we as humans are one thing or another: good or bad, mad or sad, generous or selfish. Everything is about dual feelings. *Feelings that duel.* We risk losing that duel when we buy into the false myth of separation. When we invest ourselves in the either/or struggle, we always lose.

The drive back to the quiet quaintness of Oggie was hypnotic. I stared out the windows recognizing sights and landmarks from the Ridgeway that I had touched just days before. I felt morose, longing for the trail, longing for intimate connection of feet and hands upon earth.

Back at home with my hosts, I didn't share my disillusionments. It was my private sorrow and, being in their country, this energy felt judgmental. It was too much for me to put into words at the time. Instead, I prepared to leave early the next morning, enthused to hike again. But, before turning in for the night, I shared my desire with my hosts to explore other parts of the UK after my Ridgeway hike and take more intentional detours across this beautiful ancient land. My new friends told me that they had lived on the western coast of Scotland many years before. My eyes lit up! Imagine stravaging across the land that invented that very word! I explained that I wanted to see those vast and craggy shores and experience Scotland's wild, windy beauty. They seemed a bit puzzled by my eagerness to see the rocky face of Scotland, probably because they had little choice but to live there in times past. To me, however, the thought of wind and waves crashing into crags brought visions of mystery, awe, and wonder.

They pulled out their maps and together we poured over western Scotland. Then I spotted the Isle of Iona, a tiny island located within the Inner Hebrides. Memories came rushing back. Long ago, I'd read about Iona as a place of mystery, ancient spiritualities, and dreams. The island had captured my imagination back then and immediately I realized, after the Ridgeway, I would go. I had found my sacred detour, or, more accurately, it had found me.

I rose early the next morning to the hiker's favorite smell: a traditional English breakfast. My hosts had graciously prepared eggs, baked beans, various sausages, toasted breads and Marmite spread, cereals, yogurt, and very bold coffee. I devoured everything set before me, shouldered my backpack, bowed a blessing of gratitude, and bid farewell.

The Earth as Poetry

The land itself stravages in a free, defiant saunter. Today, when we think about it, we marvel at the four billion years of change our Earth has undergone. More than just a geological phenomenon, our Earth is geographic poetry in motion. Her changing formations reflect the same processes that happen within all life forms on our planet. We all mirror her constant state of change. Like the planet itself, we have our own tectonic plates that shift, move, and evolve. Indeed, our Earth is our mother, sister, feminine companion. The Earth and everything upon her are engaged in a forever adventure of change and creativity and she constantly invites us to engage with her evolution.

The shifting plates of the Earth have sculpted and re-sculpted this planet over these billions of years. Our Earth is a joyous and playful creature who is forever moving her furniture. The landscape that lies below the water rises above and eventually gets washed away again. One piece of the planet may start in the farthest north and then flow to her midsection, and then go further still, creating new forms, and eventually founding a new place, a new land to nourish new living things. An island here, a continent there, a new seabed over there... On and on the creation we call Earth sings new shapes and adventures into deserts, mountains, forests, lakes, and oceans. It's all happening according to the desires of her hot, passionate volcanic heart. Our Earth is forever a wild, free, and raucous lover.

I write the above sentences, and, indeed, all the sentences in this book, within the context of Process Theology. This philosophy is dear to my heart because it honors the ebb and flow of evolution, both metaphorical and literal. Process Theology is relational; it's an intimate conversation between all elements of creation. Each molecule, each particle of creation, is affected and changed according to its relationship to another.

The conventional male god that dominates our present era is described as all powerful and all knowing. Such a deity exerts absolute control over everything and causes objects and situations to emerge *ex nihilo*, out of nothingness. This god, for good or ill, makes unilateral, even arbitrary decisions, intervening in the world and, specifically, with the lives of humans. This is the god that, with variations within Jewish, Christian, and Muslim ideologies, is worshiped in much of our world today.

This conventional male god has an ultimate masterplan. He exerts his will on behalf of humanity, the Earth, and the universe. According to the major monotheisms of our day, this plan is unfolding as it "should," with him in charge of the most minute of details. This god has the power to intervene (or not) into the life of the world. He causes, allows, or stops various acts of nature (tsunamis, earthquakes, raging forest fires, pandemics, you name it). This all-powerful god could step in to start or stop wars and genocides. The reason to *not* intervene is usually explained away with theologies that contend that god expresses his love for humans by "giving" people a measure of freedom. Gift bestowed, god chooses to back off according to his whims. Humans, then, experience the consequences—blessings or curses—of their god-given freedoms. Following this logic, god could have stopped the genocide of the Jews during WW II, the destruction of the Americas' indigenous tribes, the Hutu slaughter of Tutsi in Rwanda, and any and all other evils that have taken place in human history. God could have even stopped the airliners from smashing into the Twin Towers in New York City. Name your personal or collective tragedy: it's an example of the conventional god making decisions to intervene (or not) in our lives.

It is no wonder, then, that a broken-hearted person, an angry disillusioned soul who has faced great loss or trauma, might choose to follow the advice that was given to the prophet Job: simply "curse god and die." Be done with him. Within this theological framework, any thoughtful individual who wrestles with the horrors and absurdities of life might attempt to make sense of the unsensible by rejecting the very idea of god and becoming agnostic or atheist.

Process Theology has room for believing in, as well as questioning or denying, the existence of god. This openness allows one to explore the possibilities of new understandings at all times. Process Theology is always open to new insights, truths, and possibilities.

If there is a god/dess, the ultimate expression and power of this being is, I believe, **love**.

Love—generous, suffering, empathic, joyous, creative love—is this sacred being's way of being. Love is a relational experience of holding all creation within itself. God/dess experiences everything because everything is *within* this being. Suffering, helplessness, joy, grief, and all the other generative and healing energies of the creation. The birth and death of stars, the laughter of babies, and the weepings of death. All these and more are experienced by god/dess. Just as you and I do our best to change the bad into good, this Being too, at infinite levels that stretch before and beyond us, does the same. God/dess invites, lures, persuades, yearns, all in an attempt to move the universe toward beauty, adventure, and healing. This is the most powerful and loving best this being can do—no less and no more.

The creator and the universe are in a swirling, dervish dance of creation. In this understanding of life and creation, there is no *ex nihilo*, there is no *nothingness*. The molecules and particles of our universe experience their own stravage, their own tectonic flow and have always, in some form, existed. If there is goddess and/or god, such a being does not, *cannot* possess unilateral power. This being does, however, possess deep, infinite compassion and love—love that knows no bounds. Instead of possessing the false arbitrary power to intervene into the world at will, this being, infinitely loving, experiences *intimate relationship* with all the creation. God/dess in this understanding, will always work for us, always lures us toward beauty, adventure, expansion, growth, healing, enrichment through experience. God/dess learns from the creation and the creation learns from god/dess. This is the deepest intimacy of all, the creator and the creation enjoying each other, making love, making worlds, experimenting through the intercourse of evolution and re-creation. And how interesting that removing the dash gives us recreation: "god's recreation of the new day." This is the original sacred circle. All is within all and we are within *the all that is*.

The tectonic plates of Earth, and all the beings upon her, including you and me, shift, flow, change, crash, die, resurrect, create, and recreate life and soul. This is a grand stravage, a poetic conversation, a forever relationship, full of joyful, painful, healing, generative dialogue that spins on and on through eternity.

Dr. Royce Fitts

In the Beginning...the Crone

If you feel the call of Iona, then answer that call and make the journey to her.

She is like a very old crone, rocky and barren and eternally loving and gentle and tough and wise. She is very old. She is very holy.

There is no other place on Earth quite like Iona.

Like all Shamballah places, Iona shall always be.

Iona is a Grail-Lit Isle. Iona is deathless.

On Iona one finds the rainbow which bridges Heaven and Earth.

Elinore Detiger
Lifelong Humanitarian & Benefactor

Iona, that tiny piece of Earth's crust floated from somewhere, or many somewheres, upon the vast tectonic plates of our planet to rest where she is now. On Iona, barely three miles in length, you'll find some of the oldest rock on Earth. This three-billion-year-old rock is found almost nowhere else on the planet, and you'd have to travel all the way to Australia to find geologies that are older. Iona has played host to the beginnings of earthly time. She, this old and sensual crone, is a place of genesis.

I was compelled to meet this crone on this most sacred bridge between worlds. I felt her call. I ventured to Iona to

know her, and be known by her, to wonder and converse together. This most ancient of beings, lured, invited me to sail
to her and walk upon her rocky shore, her stony self. We
joined to explore new creations, adventures, directions
through uncharted waters. Together we visited, filled with
the angst and excitement of the unknown. She, this wizened
feminine power wearing the craggy face of this Scottish isle,
dreamed with me and beckoned this shamanic wanderer,
wizard, from the faraway prairie.

It's easy for me to imagine that this place of oldest rock
was one of the places where the goddesses and gods first appeared, metaphorically and perhaps even literally. They
sailed in on holy winds, the *ruach* of god, as the ancient Hebrews called it, and pierced the thin veil between worlds. The
goddesses and gods touched the oldest stones, made passionate, creative love with this crone of the earth, and danced
upon new sacred ground.

The imagery of crone carries beautiful and powerful energies for all of us, but seeing as I am male, I cannot ever
fully understand and experience her multifaceted powers as
women can. I do, however, have the capacity to dream, just
as do you. Among the countless graceful benefits that are
gifted to us through dreaming, dreams teach us empathy for
others. In dreams, the self is fluid. You may dream of yourself as male, female, young or old, as a non-human: a bear,
a puppy, a spirit, a ghost, a tree, an automobile, an ocean, or
a storm. One of the most insightful approaches into the
meanings of dreams comes out of Gestalt psychology which
offers that everything in a dream (every symbol, object,
sound, aroma, and feeling) is a part of you. *Everything.* And

so, if a female appears in your dreams, that represents an aspect of the feminine in you, just as it means the same if a male appears.

Dreams offer us insights and help us build the empathy to understand *the other*, despite our human imperfections. Dreams are designed to feature out-of-the-box logic and transgress waking-life rules. They come to expand the dreamer's vision and awareness beyond the traditional and the conventional. Put simply: if we don't grow, we die. Evolution, as Charles Darwin and others revealed, is necessary to survive and flourish. Dreams always offer to help us grow beyond our boxes—toward more health, wholeness, aliveness. Always.

I recall a recent dream that was full of wonder and power:

I am watching a confusing drama unfold involving male adults and rowdy male teens engaged in some sort of threatening competition in a rural area (later, in my waking state, the area reminded me of the green countryside of England). I see a large, black horse, who is old, yet still tall and elegant. The teens are riding him, but then the humans disappear from the scene. Now, the horse is alone, leaping over large hedgerows, plowing ahead with his feet and legs over and through every barrier that stands before him. Even though he is exhausted, he continues leaping, driven by some necessary and passionate purpose. I admire him so much! Finally, he's finished. He has accomplished his goals. The horse collapses in front of me, lying on his side, breathing heavily, and lathered in sweat. I rush to him but can't find any blankets with which to cover and wipe him down. I know that if I do not massage him and wipe the lather off, he will lose circulation, go into shock, and die. I use my hands to do the work, deeply rub him, not caring about the messy lather or anything else. I intuitively know this will heal him and I feel relieved he will be okay. He will recover. He has much more work to do, more to live for.

In dreams, we shape-shift. In this dream, I am an elegant, tall black steed, exhausted, tired, and passionate. I am shaman, minister, and elder. Sometimes, I'm tired of my many years of service, mistakes, accomplishments, dreams shattered, and dreams fulfilled. Often, I am unaware of my own exhaustion, but even when I feel its weight, I am strong and can feel the power and energy of leaping ahead, over and through the hedgerows of life and its callings. The dream tells me the truth, more than I know (and care to know!) about my aging, exhaustion and, someday, death. And the dream informs me, confirms the truth of my wizardly, creative powers.

On Iona, enthused and exhausted from the journeys of my life, I needed to meet that old sensual crone. I needed to be reminded, inspired, to embrace my own male elderhood. In my over seven decades on Earth, I can deeply acknowledge my wizardly powers that grow and season with my aging. I needed to touch a three-billion-year-old being and feel her eternal energy and know I have my own energies to live with the passions of the ages. Yea, though I'm not an old majestic crone, I am an old powerful steed. The sacred feminine, the sacred masculine meet. We commune, dance, receive, and give gracious blessings. We, unique within our own separate beings, share the gifts of power, healing, empathy, and love.

Within the Realms of Dreams and Beauty

The adventure to that faraway Scottish island, the sacred sauntering toward a far-flung holy land, did come soon after I'd completed the Ridgeway, just as I planned back in Ogbourne St George. Immediately after the hike, I followed my urges and explored nearby Oxford University where I stayed at an elegant college bed and breakfast that looked as if it were fresh out of Harry Potter's Hogwarts School of Witchcraft and Wizardry. From there, I traveled northwest several hours by train to the Scottish coastal town of Oban. The land changed from mild rolling hills to higher, rougher landscapes, and signs along the rails featured the Gaelic language beside the English. When I could tear my gaze from the rugged scenery, from the windswept and misty hills, I would close my eyes and listen, absorbing the musical sounds of my fellow passengers' lilting Scottish voices.

My arrival in Oban was drenched in rain, but the next morning a bright sun and gentle wind warmed the world. True to my improvisational travel style, I'd booked my accommodations in Oban while on the train, just before I arrived. With help from the locals, I called ahead to find a bed and breakfast on Iona. Officially, there are fewer than 180 residents on that three-mile stretch of exposed earth. To get to Iona, I would take a ferry from Oban to the Island of Mull then a long bus ride and, finally, catch another ferry to make the short trip to Iona. Though over a hundred thousand people visit the island each year, only a tiny number stay more than a few hours. Even fewer stay overnight.

A landlubber am I, and sailing the Scottish seas, spotting tiny islands with ancient crumbling castles, simply delighted me. Standing on the deck of our boat, I gasped aloud with astonishment. An elegant elderly woman wrapped in a warm raincoat and wind scarf on her head stood beside. She heard my joy and politely asked, "I wonder where you are from? You have such an interesting accent." Surprised and happy she noticed, I chuckled and said, "From Nebraska and Wyoming, the central U.S." She nodded and smiled, and I asked her where she was from and she replied with a rich and melodic voice, "From London. I have never been here before and want to explore the islands and castles." I forget the area of London she was from, but I imagined it to be as stylish and refined as she. In my daydreams, I imagined that we became friends, and she invited me to her home for a lovely English tea. When we docked on Mull and the scores of people from the ferry disembarked, she moved to join her private tour and disappeared into the crowd. My journey, purposefully solitary and guided by intuition and spirit rather than itinerary and formality, continued in a different direction.

The long bus ride across Mull was hypnotic and I dozed as we traveled along the narrow, winding roads through their version of farm country. The grass, trees, and brush, the steep hilly and rocky pastures, divided by barbed wire fences and small streams felt familiar. It wasn't the geography I recognized, but the routine of the farmers who tended the land and stock. When we finally reached the port, we could see

Iona across a thin strip of sea. A small ferry awaited us, and we boarded for the brief, windy ride to the isle. Gazing at Iona, my heart swelled with pride. *Here I am,* I thought, nearing the end of my sabbatical in the UK, but very much still in the midst of this strange, surreal, healing stravage. Here I am, witnessing the very moment a dream comes true.

The sky was a brilliant deep blue, and the sun, dazzling white in the heavens, bathed Iona and danced joyfully upon the sea. Iona is known for her light. Artists, poets, and mystics have become lost in it, carried into other realms of dreams and beauty. We disembarked and found ourselves on a nearly-treeless island, a great green pasture that hosts sheep, a small herd of adorable shaggy-headed Highland cattle, and a few humans too.

Glancing about, you can't help but wonder why such a nondescript outcropping of sand and stone in the Scottish Inner Hebrides attracts so many soulful seekers. What secret has called so many ancient spiritualities to find a home here, including the Druids, Vikings, and Christians? This place has played host to so many stories and projections. Some who believe that Mary of Magdala was not just a follower of Jesus but also his lover, say that, after his death, she traveled here to give birth to his son. Indeed, Iona invites dreaminess.

My first destination was my bed and breakfast where I could unload my pack. During my one-mile walk, I watched children playing on the rocky, sand-strewn shore as small waves crashed and splashed against the boulders. For all that this was another world, those rolling hills and pastures reminded me of the green grass-covered sandhills of Nebraska in the spring. Iona's few vehicles are confined to the single road that creates an incomplete ribbon around the island.

Mostly, everyone walks. People come to Iona to wonder and wander. While some seemed content to shop at the small scattering of art and souvenir stores, I was drawn to the visitors who were there to do the work of the soul. On the ferry, I'd met a group of Wiccans who were there for an Earth-centered celebration. Then there were the Christians who were on an educational retreat, seeking to understand the cycles of brutal invasion undertaken by Christians and Vikings in times past. Here to contemplate Iona, a place they saw as the cradle of Scottish Christianity, they were willing to look at both the difficult history and the transcendent mysteries of their faith. This group, referred to as the Iona Community, has become an important model of ecumenical and contemplative spirituality the world over.

In my first hours of wandering Iona, I experienced this island to be a timeless cathedral of the soul that encompassed and surpassed all traditions. The stone ruins of Catholic monasteries and convents, and the beautifully restored abbey, contrasted and blended with the land, sea, and sky, which is really its own majestic cathedral. The billions of years of Iona's life and history dwarfs the relatively recent settlements by humans. In fact, the last ice age retreated from Iona only about eleven thousand years ago. It's unclear when the first humans actually showed up, but there is evidence of people living on Iona a thousand years before the birth of Jesus. Most of the records of Iona's human history begins with the landing of the Irish Catholic priest Columba and his monks in the early 500s CE. *What spiritualities,* I wondered, *guided the prehistoric people who lived there prior to Columba?*

Religions and spiritualities are meant to offer peace and

support for the adherents. It's a tragic irony that peace is seldom offered to those outside the faith, those who believe in other deities, or heaven forbid, in no deities at all. Religion is meant to reduce the fears of being alive, to make sense of tragedies, the unpredictabilities of life and nature. At least, that's the intention. One particular belief system may seem to "work" while another may not. That's one reason people make a change and choose to adhere to new and different paths. It's always a spooky thing, however, to give up your god or goddess for another. When a change of faith is a forced conversion, it seems like bloodshed and suffering are just part of a profane equation. Iona has seen the rise and fall of ancient and modern spiritualities across the millennia, and she has seen more than her share of war and slaughter in the midst of all that prayerful grace. Goddesses and gods have been wounded and broken into nothingness on those shores, suffering the whims and projections of humans. On Iona—and indeed everywhere on the Earth—the divine has been made and remade according to the human image. Humans make the gods according to our collective imagination, engaging in the ultimate projective process. Sacred beings are easily discarded when the people no longer need them. A goddess or a god can be replaced the moment a newborn king enters the scene.

Iona, Portal to the Soul

Long before I set foot on her rocky shores, Iona had captured my imagination as a place of unique enlightenment, a place where land and the beings who live upon it, experienced a measure of mystical harmony. The ancient isle floats upon the primordial ocean like a sacred siren, inviting all to notice how thin the veils between the creator and the creation could be. She whispers that it truly *is* possible to access great and unknowable forces of healing, wholeness, and wisdom. The worlds of dreams, of linear waking life, and non-linear spiritual realms, blend seamlessly on Iona, and you can sense the oneness that underlies it all.

Humans, wounded as we've always been by the distortions created by our mighty and terrible brains, have fought to control Iona. But she wisely refused to give herself fully to the spiritual and societal machinations of the people who settled there. Iona has endured, breathing and watching, no matter who has lived, fought, or died on her rocky, nearly-treeless soil. Over the ages of our Earth, she has lured us, wept for us, and called us to transform our human nightmares into dreams of transcendence. Kings, nobles, priests, and commoners have sought sacred burial within Iona's womb. Since the realms of mysterious worlds touch so readily in Iona, this seems the perfect place to drift upon the oceans of eternity. Iona, a portal between the seen and unseen, holds the eternal elements of earth, water, sun, and sky. In the human imagination, being buried within an eternal portal gets us nearer to eternal life.

Because Christians kept written records, we know that the Vikings attacked Iona several times in the late 700s and early 800s CE. They slaughtered many who lived there, especially the monks, and looted many church treasures and artifacts. Despite those atrocities and other nameless tragedies that have surely marked Iona's life, she continued on, a holy beacon offering herself as a place to seek the sacred, no matter what humans chose to name it.

At some preconscious level I must have been carrying an awareness of Iona's struggles, so I was surprised and relieved to see small children playing as I entered the home which served as my bed and breakfast. The delight of a toddler smiling and stumbling through a doorway brought back a sense of normalcy and welcome I hadn't realized I'd needed. After meeting this engaging young family, I settled into simple and private accommodations before setting off once again to take in more of my island surroundings. I walked back to the ferry landing and small businesses located there and ventured into the only cafe I could find. It was closing soon, and I barely had time to order my dinner. The place was nearly empty, and the server seemed a bit annoyed that I wanted to eat. In fact, the bar adjoining the cafe was not opening at all that evening, which seemed strange since a ferry load of tourists had just arrived hours earlier. I ate as quickly as I could and set off to explore the nearby ruins of a convent built about 1200 CE. The crumbling walls of this nunnery were testament to a passionate religious energy that compelled people to build elaborate structures, even here on this small, isolated piece of sparsely-populated earth. When the religious Reformation and anti-Catholicism swept Europe and the British Isles in the 1500s, Iona was affected too. The nuns fled their convent and hid in a cave on a nearby island and the convent fell into disrepair.

I yearned for Iona to be a stravage of personal joy and happiness. I had hoped to get lost within the mystical and historical stories and the serene and dazzling beauty of this place, but even as I landed and took those first steps on her sand and rock, I also experienced unexpected and unexplained emotions: sorrow, anguish, lostness. Involuntarily, I entered a confusing, disturbing, waking dream.

Feelings of isolation and loneliness were not unusual during an endeavor that, from beginning to end, was built to be a solitary experience. On Iona, I was even more aware of the melancholy that always lurked around the edges of my soul. Even in a small gift and coffee shop, I couldn't connect with the barista in any significant way. Having a cup of coffee, often a sacramental act that can invite wonderful conversations, felt unsatisfying. Plus, the coffee was terrible.

Deciding to end the evening early, I wandered back to my bed and breakfast. Walking again on the only road, the sea breeze felt friendly as the small waves splashed playfully along the shore. Briefly, I scoured the shore for little stones and other morsels of beauty to take home as souvenirs. The sky, all blue, orange, and yellow, contrasted with white puffy clouds floating with the breezes. The little cottages along the way didn't have backyards; they had the sea. It all seemed fairytale-like and otherworldly. *Imagine*, I thought, *living on Iona*. Imagine the powerful gales of winter storms blowing fierce and icy cold. Imagine the first wildflowers of spring. Imagine the rotations of the seasons, forever and ever. Iona invited a sensual intrigue of the soul, and an ever-deepening yearning within me.

The *Yin* and *Yang* of Iona

She holds paradoxes, Iona does. She refuses to be anything less than fully authentic, fully real. On Iona, we cannot get away with anything scot-free, so to speak. This holy sliver of Scotland won't let us. Yes, we can sugar-coat theology and history to make them say what we want. We can idealize Iona and make her into a syrupy and sentimental goddess. But if we want authenticity and a fully lived life, then we have to face what Iona faces, and indeed, shows us: In order to be real, we have to own our opposites. We must meet our shadows.

Bits of Iona have been around since the Earth was born. She has always shown us that even pure and unadulterated creative glory will also bear the opposite energy. Iona holds both the *yin* and *yang*, the shadow and the light of life. When we acknowledge that horrible crimes were enacted upon her ancient ground—sometimes in the names of the gods, sometimes for the sake of greed, and sometimes in service to both at once—and that this same ground also hosts dreams of unfolding love, compassion, wisdom, and healing, then we can move toward what is real. Iona is holy/unhallowed, sacred/profane, whole/wounded. She is like all of us. It is earthshaking—island rocking, to be precise—to have our rosy-colored projections destroyed. But, when we make a conscious choice to allow our illusions to break apart and melt away, then we access a truer, deeper form of authenticity. Perhaps this is what Jesus called living life in all its fullness, having an abundant life that includes rather than denies woundedness, and allows it to exist alongside wholeness. Perhaps this is what is true for the Buddhist who recognizes the illusory nature of human reality and welcomes suffering as a teacher of loving kindness. You might see it like the Taoists do and understand that sometimes, in the battle of life, the wise general knows that the first step toward victory is in the mindful retreat.

Humans, and perhaps all living beings, project our unmet needs upon an "other," whether it's a person, island, nation, goddess, or god. These needs, both positive and negative, are the shadows that lurk in the places that are beyond speech-ripe, deep within our unconscious. These are the wounds of our souls, our childhoods, our broken or distorted relationships in our past and present, our awful choices we wish we wouldn't have made, and on and on. We use Iona, and others like her, to hold our projections. We concoct a dreamy dream of her that satisfies our need for a sacred healing space, a place that seems, for lack of a better term, perfect. We want to (understandably!) put these wounds aside, forget about them, suppress them when we turn our eyes upon an idealized object, like Iona. It feels good to imagine we can ignore the darkness within and cast our positive projective energies upon a lovely goddess like her. In this wounded spiritual desperation to idealize another in hopes that she can save us from our own inner demons, we accidentally say prayers that can never be answered and fall into despair and disillusionment.

There is good news, however, and even as it is painful, it is also liberating: Iona refuses to be idealized. She is a *waking* dream, embodying all the beautiful and awful realities of our waking lives. Iona insists on being authentic, real. She is the holder of both light and dark. In a place like Iona, we move toward healing when our illusions fall away, when we recognize our shadows and own our darknesses. Throughout life, we are called to befriend our *yin* and *yang*. It is then that we can, with soul-deep authenticity, finally, wake up.

The Light We Cannot See

She was beautiful. Long brown dreadlocks flowed down her back nearly to her waist. It was my first morning on Iona and I entered the small dining room in my bed and breakfast, hungry for a Scottish feast. My introverted-self held me back and I greeted the only other guest with a mild "good morning." She too, seemed hesitant. Maybe shy. Maybe just careful. I was curious about this interesting-looking soul and what brought her to this isle.

Across the small room, over eggs, sausages, toast, and coffee, we visited. Clumsily, I shared a little of my story of where I was from, the hike in England, and coming here to Iona. Then, in a more confident tone, she revealed she was a Presbyterian minister from Australia who had come to Iona for a personal retreat. Of course, her accent by then had given her away. Happily surprised to discover a mutual spiritual seeker, I mentioned that I too, was a minister, but I didn't belong to any particular denomination anymore, unless you wanted to count my irregular attendance in Unitarian churches.

Quietly, I hoped to myself that this minister-in-dreadlocks was as liberal as her wild hair implied. I hoped that my own white flowing wizardly mane was telling her I was the sort of person who wandered beyond the typical definition of clergy. She said she was overwhelmed by her work and family, and sought, with her church's and family's support, to take some time off to reflect and renew, so she could return once again with healthy direction and purpose.

Evidently, she was older than she looked because she talked about having an adult son who was physically and mentally disabled. She spoke of how grateful she was that her husband, a lovely nurturing man and caregiver for their child, encouraged her to go on this retreat. In a few days, she said, she was going to Edinburgh to meet an old seminary friend she hadn't seen in a long while. In my projective imagination, I envied her. I imagined pastoring a church that would encourage me to take time for renewal. I felt longing for a friendship like she described and mused about what it would feel like if someone was waiting for me in Edinburgh, nurturing, safe, and warm.

Sometimes being an introvert is a pain in the ass. Maybe it was a combination of the swirling contradictions of Iona and the way I was experiencing my own *yin* and *yang* of dazzlement and disillusionment that made me hold back. Or, maybe, deep within me, there was a kind of unconscious cynicism or suspicion of someone like her, a *minister* who would travel across the globe to find renewal on this beautiful, yet contradictory isle. *Holy shit! Here am I, O Goddess, looking into my own mirror!*

What I actually wanted to do, but was afraid to say aloud, was to invite her to hang out and explore this island with me. I wanted to have deep conversations about our different yet similar lives, to share our theologies, to hold nonjudgmental space for each other's spiritual journeys. There was a longing to move beyond any urge to impress her, and to just *be* in this place beside her. It would have been remarkable to share with this fellow seeker my journeys of being a spiritual nomad, a writer of soulful stories, of being lonely and content all at the same time. I wanted to reach out to her, to hear her stories about how in the world she got to where she is in life, how she is able to go through—and maybe even love—the rituals of institutional church life. I wanted to hear about her adult child, how she and her husband navigate such a lovely, willing sacrifice. I wanted to be besties on Iona. I wanted to have memories beyond imagining—to create a surprising, wholehearted, serendipitous friendship that goes beyond the shores of this tiny isle, circles the world, nearly ten thousand miles of a connection that may never end, from oldest rock to oldest rock.

Sometimes, I am an immature man who cannot access, except in retrospect, my yearnings. *What the fuck?* Unable to be fully conscious of what I was yearning for, my shadows held me back and kept me from taking that risk. Old voices of shyness, fears of rejection, protective habits against vulnerability flooded me at some preconscious level and I was partially immobilized. So, I merely offered polite conversation, a little deep, but not too deep. *Besides*, I thought, *she seems shy too.* Maybe she was just professionally reserved, or, in my insecurities, maybe just too married, too enmeshed in careful, conservative ways to have a friendship like I wanted.

It was early October, warm, and the sun, gradually moving toward the south to fulfill the promise of the colder, darker season that was made at the autumn equinox, invited me to take a slow, melodic run to explore Iona. I said goodbye to my new friend, hoped that we would run into each other again later, and left.

Sunlight upon Iona, reflecting off the sea, shines with a brilliance and clarity rarely seen. Shadows are more pronounced, the colors of stone more diverse, the grass, wisping in the breezes, revealed multiple shades of green. The ocean, glorious in its own hues of blues and greens, with small whitecaps appearing then disappearing, filled me again with the sense of disbelief that I was actually there. The wind, chilly and refreshing, flooded with the scents of land and water, swirled about me. I ran first to the north where the paved single-lane road ends. Climbing over the gate, I strolled, sauntered into the field, aware this was a private pasture. The land, grass-covered, was rough and bumpy as it sloped down to the shore. A small farmstead stood off in the distance, a trail road winding its way there. Puzzling over strange flags posted periodically across the uneven pasture, I watched sheep graze on the short, lush grass. Suddenly, I laughed to myself realizing the flags meant the pasture served double duty as a golf course. Scotland, of course, is the birthplace of golf!

How many can say they have run the length of Iona? It was a distinction I was excited to claim. So, with a casual lope, I turned to the opposite direction again and headed back down the paved road toward the tiny village with its dock, businesses, and historical buildings. Perhaps, I hoped, I would run into my new friend and share a visit, exploring life over Scottish tea. Darting in and out of the small businesses and art stores, I made my way to the massive, beautifully restored abbey.

The grand grey stone sanctuary, with its stained-glass windows facing the sea, was filled with natural light, welcoming anyone who entered with warmth and silence. Drifting amongst the empty seats, I touched the hymnals and programs of worship, imagining hymns being sung, the rustle of clothing and voices of congregants as the peace was passed from person to person. I wondered if I would meet the members of the contemplative Iona Community who had come to the abbey for study. I wandered further into the building, exploring the nooks and side rooms. I felt like a ghost moving breathlessly among the stone walls. The inner courtyard with its green grass and sunlight offered relief to the eyes and beckoned me to walk upon it. The cloisters on the edges of the courtyard magnified both the silence and the slightest echoes of my footsteps.

The majesty of the cathedral with all its beauty and purpose was juxtaposed with the irony that it may not have needed to be so...majestic. It felt odd that the religious authorities would have insisted upon the construction of such an ostentatious building. The wisdom of the ancient sand, sea, and stone of Iona was not enough, apparently.

We might like to think of them as the "old ways," but in fact, the old ways are still with us. The thought that a **patriarchal** religious authority would seek to control the masses by creating and propagating a myth that god can only be found in places like the Abbey feels archaic, but things haven't really changed. I'm occasionally crippled by a cynical grief that they—that *we*—still try to box up the gods and goddesses, like a product to be controlled, marketed, and carefully dispensed to the masses.

Perhaps underneath my distrust of religious authority is a brooding disbelief and sorrow. To appreciate the beauty of Iona's religious buildings and, at the same time, feel deeply skeptical about the buildings' necessity, tied me up in a classic double bind. Maybe it's just a sign that old wounds caused by spiritual disappointment at the hands of religious fundamentalism still haunt me. Or maybe it is something more. Maybe I tapped into the grief that Iona feels for how we have wounded both ourselves and her.

The minister-in-dreadlocks appeared again later that evening. We chatted about some of our mutual experiences exploring Iona that day. She was going to the Abbey late that evening for a program of song and meditation and asked if I was going. I did not share my conflicted feelings about the Abbey. Maybe I didn't trust myself to be that open. Perhaps my spirit was too exhausted to try to express my own holy ambivalence. The years of dealing with the contradictions within myself and trying to make peace between rigid theology and lived spirituality had taken a toll on my heart, and I knew it. I felt it acutely. I imagined being with her and enjoying that, but I also imagined being with my dark feelings and not enjoying my own self. I felt sad as I refused the invitation, knowing I would have regrets, yet also knowing I needed to take that risk.

Instead, I walked alone in the starlight with the cold autumn wind blowing off the sea. The light, always dancing, leaped from wave to wave. I talked to the goddesses and gods that evening, to all of them, even to the ones I didn't believe in. The road was lit by the dim starshine, and I gazed at the forms of grey and black boulders that lined the shore and then to the hills of Iona that rose to meet the firmament.

At breakfast the next morning I was heartened to see my friend once again. She said that the music, songs, and meditations were lovely, and it tugged my heart when she shared that she thought of me and wished I had been there. Near midnight, she said, when the service had ended, she walked alone on the dark road to the B&B. She described the stars blazing in the heavens, and how she had worshipped with the wind, the sea, and the land. O Iona, you move in mysterious, beautiful ways.

Sometimes in the months and years since, I have thought about that tender minister-in-dreadlocks from Australia. I don't recall her name, nor the city in which she pastored, but I wondered about the poetic adventures she had traveled and how Iona had affected her. She had sailed through the heavens, covering nearly ten thousand miles from her oldest rock of Australia to the ancient sister rock of Iona. My temporary friend, my friend of this brief holy season, took a sacred detour and the detour became a sacred circle, and the circle became a sacred stravage.

Yes, Iona is a portal: a "thin place" where the worlds meet, a spiritual space where seas, sun, stone, winds, lives, souls, gods, goddesses, and time cross paths. Iona is a detour into the unexpected truth. She is a shocking dream that we can't shake off in the morning light, a dream we carry for days, for years, dazzled and wondering *why*. Iona seeps into our waking worlds, blurring the lines between what we dream and how we live. Iona challenges what we call reality, rousing us to wakefulness even as we walk deeper into the dream. In this place, we encounter that which is not yet seen, only hoped for, and beyond *speech-ripe*. Iona guides us through the darkness of the soul and leads us into the light we cannot see.

What would I be like if I had not heeded Iona's call? I do not know, but I do know that I am more real, more alive, more Royce, and less disillusioned because of Iona. I am forever changed.

Will you sail to Iona? Will you cross your own seven seas of wonder to walk her shores and listen to her sing to you through her winds and the sea birds soaring overhead? Will you feel her tears in the ocean sprays? Will you touch her boulders, walk barefoot on her sands, and in the deepest dark, gaze at her starlight canopy? If you do, you may glimpse the wavering veils between the worlds and get to watch as she and the other goddesses and gods stravage through to dance upon our Earth. If you cannot plot a course to the north Atlantic, you can always venture to her in your dreams and the deepest reaches of your imagination. Read about her. Seek out her stories and her science. Wonder about her oldest rocks and how they carry the beginnings, the genesis, of time itself. She will welcome you however you come. Iona will change you forevermore.

But be prepared. Whether you go to Iona in your dreams or on a ferry that parts the Scottish seas, a part of you shall never return. By your own heart's desire, you will join for-ever the kings, nobles, priests, priestesses, commoners, and sacred beings who came before you.

Chapter Ten
The Flint Beneath My Feet

Before I could take this sacred detour and encounter the mysteries of Iona, I had a trail to walk. Bidding farewell to my Ogbourne St George hosts, the couple who opened up that map and helped me remember my desire to see the holy islands of Scotland, it was time to get back to the Ridgeway.

The sky was overcast and the air cool. The nearby roads had been flooded from a deluge of English autumn rains and yet, despite the muddy trail, I was happy to be on the saunter again. As I walked, the day turned warm and humid, but I hoped the rains were finished. I had fifteen miles of trail ahead of me before I could dream again that night.

The Ridgeway followed busy roads across open country. Hiking for hours on end is often exhausting no matter the terrain, whether it be the enchanted English countryside or the mystical American prairies. Sometimes, the body just doesn't care that you are following an existential mission across land, time, and space. You just get tired. The sights and sounds of rushing automobiles on the main roads and thoroughfares near this section of the Ridgeway drained me even further. For a little while, the land became a boring geography of "anywhere England." Despite my exhaustion, I walked fast and made good time. Up ahead, I saw the distant hills of the Uffington White Horse looming. Suddenly, intrigue replaced boredom.

Have you ever dreamed of animals, of household companions and wild beasts? Have you had dreams of spirit guides that filled you with fear and trembling? Have you ever written your visions and dreams in journal form, or drawn them upon a wall, a rock, canvas, or paper? Join the ancients and try it. Write, draw, sketch, or carve the symbols and feel the powers of your visions and dreams emerge. The White Horse that is carved into the northern face of the Chiltern Hills came to someone as a vision and has lasted for untold centuries. Long before I'd see it, that horse beckoned me onward. I believe the spirit of that horse had been calling to me for years. The powers of visions and dreams are forever.

I had miles to go before I would see that fabled White Horse, however. As the Ridgeway finally veered into more pleasant country and returned me to wooded glens and green pastures, the winds grew stronger, sweeping up dust from the recently harvested and plowed fields. Though the sun attempted to burn away the overcast skies, the southern sky was full of darkening clouds that threatened rain. I stopped by a small embankment made by scrub brush and an old broken fence to rest and escape the wind. Using my pack for a backrest, I munched on apples given to me by my last host. Far down the hill, off in the distance, I watched a single car on the only narrow road in sight. Who were they, all alone? Where were they going? Such random, quirky thoughts would often float through me as I hiked. That particular day, so far from anywhere, the wind and dust were my only companions. I felt even more alone.

In my research of the geology of the Ridgeway, I

learned that much of the land, a former sea, was pushed up-ward a hundred million years ago by the shifts of the tectonic plates. The land is composed of fossils of marine life that formed vast reservoirs of light-colored, mostly white, chalk. Flint, also formed by marine and plant fossils, is encased within the chalk. I've always loved this particular stone and have been fascinated by the early hominids who used flint and other stones, like obsidian and chert, to make sharp, us-able objects. It was wild to imagine that, thousands of years ago, an unknown someone touched a stone, knapped it into a tool, used it in an act of brutality or survival, and then lost or discarded it so I could find it today.

Only a fellow rock hunter could fully understand my passion for these and other stones. It felt like a sacred con-nection to the earth and to the ancient peoples who found so many uses for this simple material. Walking through the open fields of England, some recently harrowed in prepara-tion for planting, I was compelled to look for flint artifacts. In America, I do this compulsively on almost every hike and walk. I've been on the quest for "worked flint" since I was a young boy when my siblings, cousins, friends, and I would scour the prairies hoping to be the first to find an arrowhead.

Sometimes, clearly-shaped stones, like knife points and arrowheads, will be exposed, undamaged and beautiful, their blades still sharp. Modern farm implements, like plows and discs, will often dig up, break, even shatter flintstones that are buried beneath the soil. As I walked, I kept my eyes peeled. Crossing a field and noticing the contrasts between traces of white chalk, the exposed pieces of shiny flint, and the black, rich soil, I suddenly found a small stone about the size of my inner palm. Dark brown, almost black, the flint-stone caught the light of the sun, and in the stone's heart was a translucent streak of amber shaped like a tiger's eye. It glowed with the power of the ages. Part of the stone was smooth, almost like glass. I could feel and see the tiny edges where flakes might have been chipped off by an ancient craftsperson. Hoping the recent rainstorms had uncovered even more pieces, I got down on my hands and knees and dug in the soft soil. I even talked to the earth, passionately searching, but found nothing more. This small stone was enough. Its beauty captured me, and I tucked it into my backpack. Now its' tiger's eye watches over my desk, reminding me of that faraway field in England, that faraway time when the ancestors might once have held it close.

"Even the Stones Shall Sing"

The desert wind blew hard and cold across the Nebraska prairie. It whipped and twisted, casting itself down into the harsh, deep canyons, filling every rocky crevice and brushing the dry blades of grass as it rose and climbed the rugged sandstone cliffs. The wind was alive. Joyously, it plunged downward again to the canyon depths and then upward reaching toward the sky. The faint, early morning sun glinted through the haze of invisible clouds. It was midwinter on the high prairie, and in my soul too. I was depressed, alone, in emotional pain, questioning my heart and my burned-out brain.

I was getting divorced.

The shame and guilt of breaking a vow that had been honored by generations of my family before me was overwhelming. Though my children were adults, I feared for them. I worried over what I had done to their heritage and growing families, to the generations that may follow us.

That day, I was running for my sanity. I had run these hills and canyons for nearly twenty years, in snow, ice, heat, and rain. I ran for my health. I ran to think or to empty my mind, to meditate and pray, to cry and laugh along these old cattle trails, deer traces, and ancient bison tracks. I ran hard that day, up and down the hills, letting the winds blow against me, then with me, flowing along the trails, following my confused heart.

I was going to be okay. The winds said so. I knew it that day, despite the anguish. I was breathing in the wind, the cold, purifying air of the northern snows, the Land of the White Giant. *I was going to be okay.*

Following a turn in the trail, I slowed as I climbed a small hill that I had visited many times. Over the years, I had unconsciously memorized much of the terrain, knowing each tree, sage brush, rock, and dip of the land. Fully in my stride, I nearly passed what I thought was a fallen leaf from a nearby mountain mahogany bush. Something inspired me to pause and bend to touch it. On this trail I had run scores of times, the winds from the White Giant had blown away the sand and revealed a piece of red flint, knapped and chipped into an arrowhead.

The flint was brought to me that day. Or, rather, I was brought to the flint. I felt *chosen* as I handled this artifact from an ancient time. I felt *held* by the spirits of wind, land, and time as I received this gift from the ancient people of the prairie. With this carved flint I accepted grace and affirmation from the ancestors that, no matter my present pain, I was on the path of healing and growth. My dream mentor Jeremy Taylor once said that the ancestors would rush forth, literally or metaphorically, to cheer on our expansion and healing. Despite the growth pains we may experience, those who came before us grow as we grow. They need us. We need them. You don't necessarily need to be on a designated holy isle like Iona to understand that there is only the thinnest veil between the worlds. On both sides, literally or metaphorically, souls yearn for healing, growth, and connection.

Through the lens of Process Theology, as I have already sought to explain, we understand that the universe is alive, yearning, experimenting, and growing toward beauty, growth, healing, and adventure. In fact, the Christian apostle St. Paul alludes to this when he describes that "the whole creation groans with the pangs of childbirth." Our universe is constantly being born. It births new life, from ancient marine life that forms the flint rocks of Earth, to the massive boulders in space we call planets. We are in an eternal creative process.

The practice of searching for ancient flint rocks helps me feel connected to the land, to our mysterious past and our unknown future. One might say that finding a bit of sculpted flint upon a mound of sand that midwinter morn could mean nothing at all, yet I know differently. That morning I accepted the flint beneath my feet as a gift.

Weeks later, a friend who understood the radical life changes I was going through referred me to an esteemed astrologer. At first, my old religious fundamentalism and pretensions of academic "sophistication" caused me to resist, but then I asked myself, *Why the hell not? It could be fun, and I may learn something new.* My birthday was approaching, and I was feeling called to move further out of my boxes of habit, logic, and comfort. At the time, I did not know the word *stravage*, but here I was, straying beyond my old, conventional thinking, defying my incredulity, and booking an appointment.

The astrologer carefully read my star chart, mapping my birth and life across the sky. Sometimes, she'd enter a kind of intuitive trance and describe the influences of the stars and planets upon my being. We discussed my anxieties as I took these huge and painful steps toward change and growth. She noticed I was unconsciously holding the flint arrowhead that I had found on the prairie, rubbing it almost as a worry stone. She suddenly suggested, "I see an old native man, walking beside his pony. He's following you. He's your guide. He's with you."

I chuckled at first, defensive and vulnerable even as I felt the goosebumps on my arms and a chill of recognition running down my spine as I sat in front of this spiritual seer. Quieting my skepticism, I simply held the mysterious vision. A few days later, I awoke from a deep sleep with a start. In the pre-dawn light, I glanced out my bedroom window toward the east, to the canyons and prairies beyond. I saw them. Both the old man and his pony stood there, gazing at me.

Was this a spiritual mirage? Was my unconscious mind playing tricks as I struggled between worlds—between sanity and insanity, shame and healing, imprisonment and freedom? Startled and puzzled, and at the same time, full of calm and understanding, I heard the song of the flint rock lilt through the air. The old guide and his pony were calling to me and singing my soul's song back to me across the landscape.

In his short life, Jesus was often exhorted to silence because he challenged the corrupt religious establishment and secular governments that colluded together to preserve their wealth and power at the expense of the powerless and poor. Jesus heeded an inner call that offered justice, gentleness, and healing to the oppressed and neglected. A reformer, he was compelled to speak truth to power. It didn't go well. One time, after a particularly ugly screed (read "series of tweets") from the powers that be, Jesus retorted that even if he were silenced, his truth was so obvious and necessary that even the rocks and stones would shout it in his place. Some legends say that happened, that the stones did shout, and indeed, even sang.

Do the rocks shout and sing to you? In that *New York Times* travel feature from the fall of 2009, I saw a picture of two human figures standing in silhouette against the horizon, dwarfed by the giant standing stones of Avebury, England. Somehow, the stones called to me. Their dramatic stance against the English sky beckoned, compelled, even shouted that I must come. I had to hike the path of that "oldest road in England and Europe." I needed to be one of those figures standing in the presence of those mighty sentries. I had no choice but to follow the song of the stones, to listen, touch, and wonder.

Callings are strange. Whether you're a geologist, archeologist, or simple tourist, rocks call to be studied, touched, and held in wonder. A shaman places a sacred stone upon the tummy of a sickly child and, fantastically, the child heals.

A stone is placed before a tomb to seal it, and a few days later, that stone rolls away. Massive, oddly-shaped boulders and pinnacles become, in mystical whimsy, the garden of goddesses and gods. All over the earth, the stones seem to shout and sing. Here in England, large stones and boulders, some weighing over forty tons, sang their way to Avebury from scores of miles away. All mined, moved, and erected by the ancients for purposes unknown in our present time. However, in all times, the callings and songs of the stones must be heeded. Listen deeply to your inner being. Ask yourself whether you heed your callings and songs. Do you respond when they beckon you forth? Do you stand out on the ridge of your own life and call your own sacred knowing to you?

A Prairie Monolith

Years before the sacred flintstone and the old native man with his pony had found me, I was hiking far to the east of my home on the prairie. As I sauntered meditatively around the canyons and the flat, rolling lands, I hiked through the adjoining government-owned nature preserve. Following cattle trails across one of many bluffs, I was on a quest to see the valley and river below. Farms and towns spread out to the horizon, and I could see the mile-long coal trains from Wyoming slowly move across the tracks. It was as if I were a hawk soaring through the sky, looking down on a miniature world.

On this public land, walkers were permitted to climb over a barbed-wire pasture fence near a windmill and water tank for cattle and wildlife. I walked past ponderosa pines and junipers, through sage, soap weed, prickly pear cactus, and varieties of prairie grasses. About a half mile north, on the other side of the trees, I halted. In front of me was a large, grassless, sand-covered circle, almost perfectly round. In the center was a pinnacle of sandstone, a single monolith that stood taller than me. The west side of this bare circle was lined by a tall hill with a grove of pines and the southern edge was protected by a smaller hill with a lone ponderosa at its top. The tree's strong roots were exposed, and you could see how it held together the remains of that mound. The other directions were bordered by the rustling grasses and a scattering of other trees. I stared. I was in awe. Could this monolith and its circle be human made? Was this a sacred circle constructed long ago for some unknown purpose?

I looked to the west, to the larger hill, and my logical mind determined that the prevailing westward winds had played a part in naturally constructing this eerie circle. I could feel the western wind blow, from down in the canyons in the west, up over the hill and down again, over the other side. The air would form a tiny tornadic dance, twisting the sand and rock to form the monolith and the large grassless circle.

There is a geography of air. With all its invisibility and fluidness, air forms canyons and mountaintops. It plays with the flat plains of silence and stillness until it storms up, up and away to unknown heights. Then, air dives back and crashes into the earth, into caves and oceans, deserts and forests, reshaping, with eons of patience, all it strikes and caresses. Air is the true shapeshifter, and yet, we humans love to craft stories around the mystery of the elements. Whether it was a sand statue I encountered unexpectedly or the way the snow was blown from the branches of a particular tree during a winter walk, I would see the work of these unseen hands and declare, "Canyon spirits are playing today."

The ancient ones had names for the winds, identifying them according to the four sacred directions. Perhaps we formed the goddesses and gods by casting our own mystical projections upon the wind and sand. Or, you might say that the air and earth are the medium through which the gods reveal themselves. In the great mystery, both are true. Humans mimic the goddess called nature. Humans seek to follow the winds, the calls and songs of rocks and stones to be close to the gods, whether on the ancient prairie or on the meadows of England.

Strangers in Their Own Land

After I completed my doctorate in the early 1990s, my family and I moved home to Nebraska from Indiana, and I opened my psychotherapy practice. Sometimes, in the old tradition of the country doctor, I did home visits with families and clients who lived on the vast stretches of north-western Nebraska. This was and is a land of low population, with a few scattered ranches and dying prairie towns. During this period of my practice, I was working with a ten-year-old Lakota boy and his family. The Lakota are a people who have lived on this land for at least a thousand years. Since the imperial invasions of Anglo-Europeans over the last five centuries, much of the history of the indigenous people in

America has been lost. Because I was one of the few qualified and licensed family therapists in that region, I was asked
by a government agency to work with some economically
and emotionally impoverished native families. I was grateful
for the opportunity and made it my goal to help my clients
achieve some form of emotional well-being within a world
of systemic racism and poverty that forced them to become
strangers in their own land. I did not see myself as some kind
of "white savior" or a "great white father" coming to guide
and help assimilate native families into the oppressive over-
culture. I yearned to help families rediscover and affirm their
ancient systems of native family life. Of course, at best I
would only be effective in the most microscopic ways because of my own blindness and unconscious racism, which
was compounded by centuries of white supremacy, and
would always, somehow, be at play.

One day, my ten-year-old client and I took a walk in his
neighborhood. Words were not forthcoming. This isn't unusual for any child who is assigned to talk to an adult who is
unknown to him. I assumed he was introverted and intimidated. Introverted, perhaps by culture, and intimidated by
being with me, a representative of an aggressive people who
dominate his world. We walked around a vacant lot covered
by grass, weeds, and sand. This session wasn't his idea, so I
did my best to not be any more intrusive than I already was.
Silently, we walked, and I did what I always do: I scanned
the ground for flint pieces. I asked him if he ever looked for
arrowheads or other artifacts. He barely answered with a
shake of his head. I wanted to encourage him to search the
earth with me, hoping this could represent a connection and
a sense of pride in his heritage. That's when I spied a flake

of flintstone, a remnant of a larger piece that might have been worked by this boy's ancestors, long ago. I bent down to pick up the piece and showed him, trying to encourage him to see the piece as a symbol of his own heritage.

I had hoped the flint piece might be a bridge for him and me, but he wasn't interested, at least not as far as I could tell. Had all the creative spirit been sucked out of him and his family after generations of living in powerless poverty? Or perhaps he needed to hide his responses from this white stranger who he did not believe he could trust. I felt helpless and sad when our counseling relationship came to a quiet end soon thereafter. I would never know what went on in his mind as I held out that piece of ancient, storied stone.

In his book *Centennial*, the white American novelist James Michener tries to write from the perspective of an Arapahoe man. The character, consoling a grief-stricken child, says, "Only the rocks live forever." Like the author, I project into the stones a kind of life, a kind of living energy, an organicity of the earth and, indeed, the universe. Whether they stand in Avebury for over five thousand years, hide in a secret sand circle above the canyons, or appear as a tiny chip in a vacant lot, only the rocks live forever.

On the Ridgeway, I wondered about my own English ancestors and how they shaped and used the stone that they found and mined. Beneath their differences of language, skin color, and belief systems, cultures bear remarkable similarities. It all comes down to simply finding a way to survive with the help of the materials available. Inanimate substances—chalk, obsidian, flint—somehow shouted and sang to humans. Not only that, but the stones sang us into growth and new life. Once again and for the first time, I felt as if I were sauntering upon sacred ground, that the flint beneath my feet held me as it held all of creation.

Were the artists of long ago who dreamed up and carved the mysterious being now called the White Horse compelled by the same sort of song? The white chalk beneath the earth, the remains of that vanished sea, was mined and resurrected to new life to form a creature that would run across the English hills for millennia. In an age that must have been so preoccupied with survival, why would they have spent so much time and effort creating such a thing? We cannot know. Perhaps I must ask that old native man and his pony, those unexpected friends who appeared to me in that pre-dawn light back when I was transitioning from my other life.

Stravaging is Praying

To walk across the Earth is to have an intimate conversation with the land and the people who once lived upon it. It may, in the beginning, be like an awkward first date, a stumbly getting-to-know-another-person kind of experience, taking the wrong steps, stubbing your toe, being embarrassed, and feeling goofy. Hopefully, as you become more confident and at ease on the trail, you move into a flow of mutual respect and maybe, grace and loving relationship.

Some years ago, I was introduced to minimalist running shoes. Minimalist shoes have little or no cushion in the soles and no heel incline. They are as close to moccasins, the original human-made shoe, as possible. Minimalist shoes allow me to feel the trail, to get to know the bumps, lumps, and shapes of the earth. Indeed, this form of hiking is similar to exploring all intimate relationships, human or earth-based. The sharp edges, natural blades of flint along the Ridgeway, could easily slice into the soles of my running shoes as I walked the English fields. This is not unlike the soul pain that we sometimes experience in human intimacy. Sometimes it was painful to feel the edge of a rock protruding into the sole of my shoe. My surefootedness increased with each step, however, as I grew to anticipate the roll and scape of the land. It was like conversing with the land intimately, freely, unhindered, including curses, jokes, pleasantries, tears, and vulnerabilities. Over time, a first date with the land matures into a seasoned relationship.

To stravage across the landscape is to engage in deep, sensuous prayer. You may find yourself called to an earthy, off-the-trail stray from convention in which you say, "Yes, I'm willing to risk disapproval for the sake of authenticity, in order to be real." It is being aware of that which is immediately beneath your feet, noticing the soil, rocks, the ground that holds and supports you. It is simultaneously being aware of what surrounds you, including what is behind, above, and ahead. Stravaging as prayer means you breathe through your entire being as you move, step by step. It is feeling the sensations in your feet and legs, the currents of air wisping by, your hair blowing, and your sweat rising. It is being aware of your breath, in and out, gasping sometimes, inhaling deeply, expelling air in a great purge. You seek balance in life, the *yin* and *yang*, as you stravage. You are aware of the backpack's weight upon your shoulders, and you consciously shift yourself and the weight you bear, seeking greater balance in every moment, across every stretch of earth. Stravaging is coming to understand we all walk upon sacred land and that we are called to listen to the stones as they sing. Walk lightly. Find attunement with the earth. Trust the tiger's eye that guides us all.

Chapter Eleven
Only the Shadow Knows

Wisps of rain began to swirl in the wind as the day ebbed and I neared the hills of the White Horse. The sun was hidden by grey clouds, and I was concerned about the impending downpour. Dreading the possibility of a soaked backpack, soaked clothes, and a soaked computer, I draped my oversized waterproof windbreaker over my body and pack and pulled my broad-brimmed hat more tightly over my head. I must have looked like the Hunchback of Notre Dame, but I had no way of knowing that this strange costume was quite appropriate for the strange scene I was about to enter.

Wayland's Smithy, the next landmark on the Ridgeway, is a graveyard that dates back five thousand years. It was built in at least two phases, the latter featuring more elaborate and expansive burial chambers. As far as I could determine, this well-preserved Neolithic-age memorial included less than twenty graves. The origins of the people who first used this place are obscure. Centuries later, strangers would name it after Wolund, the Germanic god of horse care. Legend has it that if you leave your unshod horse on the grounds overnight, you'll awaken the next morning to find fresh shoes on your steed.

The ancients had first constructed an earthen mound to shelter the graves, using timbers to hold up the structure, but they decayed and eroded with time. Later-peoples used large stones to form more sturdy, elaborate tombs to shelter the burial plots. The graveyard seems to have been built and re-built several times over the eons, probably altered by each new clan as it came into power. In recent years, the barrow was carefully reconstructed so that most of the eight-foot boulders that supported the structure stand tall once again. These massive stones are positioned at the mouth of the bur-ial chamber like sentinels. Beside them are a set of stone steps that lead you up to the thick grass that grows atop the barrow.

After walking alone for so long, I was surprised to see a few people around the graveyard when I arrived. I knew I wasn't far from the famous White Horse of Uffington, so it made sense that a few tourists would explore this ancient burial ground too. Soon, however, the coils of mist pushed them back to their warm, dry cars, and I assumed I was alone. The site is large, covering several acres and surrounded by a thick border of trees. I wondered what it would have been like to experience the tombs and chambers in the original primeval forests, instead of today's open pastures, fields, and the occasional coppice of trees. We can assume that the orig-inal graveyard might have been nearly invisible to early Ridgeway travelers.

The mystery that hung about Wayland's Smithy deep-ened. All full of mist and solitude, this place had a strange beauty all its own. The energy of the dead and departed in-vited contemplation. A sense of melancholy settled into my walking meditation as I crossed this holy ground. At Ave-bury, I had walked into the tombs at West Kennet Long Bar-row, but this experience couldn't have been more different. That site was open and exposed, set high on a hill surrounded by grass and cropland. Wayland's Smithy was secluded within its small grove of trees and those guardians loomed over every visitor and seemed protective of the space. This gloomy weather altered this experience, of course. The changes that I had undergone through my days of walking made this all feel very different too.

Feeling this contrast acutely, I did not choose to follow the old stone steps to the top of the grass-covered tombs. An easy climb, it is often done by visitors, but it would have felt disrespectful at that moment. Neither did I walk into the small, narrow passageway that led into the inner crypts, though it was open to me. The symbolism of building tombs for the dead and using boulders and earth to honor those who have gone before always invited me to wonder about the people of the past and what spirits might have accompanied them in life. This seemed especially true for me in that moment as I walked all along the Ridgeway and imagined those ancient ones who traversed, lived, and died on this road. This place, now called Wayland's Smithy, was selected as a final, sacred destination for some. Who were these people and what drew them to honor their loved ones on this specific patch of land? Walking into their tombs felt like a violation. It felt downright nosy. Later, I read that one archaeological excavation here unearthed a child's body. One can only assume that the grief of people who lost a tiny and vulnerable member of their clan thousands of years ago would have been much like our own.

When I emerged from my reverie, still standing frozen just a few feet from those great stone sentinels that guarded the tomb, I realized the wind had quieted and the mist had partially lifted. Seeing the site with fresh eyes, I entered a whispered conversation with myself and with the spirits of this place. I considered the changing beliefs that occurred over the centuries. How had the gods changed? Who were the goddesses to whom these ancestors prayed? Had the gods died, along with these people, and been forgotten? Was this a graveyard that served not only an ancient people, but held the immortal bones of their deities too?

The Men in the Mist

Suddenly, I noticed another person quietly walking around the tombs. The tall, lean man with dark hair and a full beard looked to be in his late twenties. He wore a long, dark trench coat. I attempted eye contact so I could say hello, but he acted as if I was not there. His face was expressionless. At one point, I was less than thirty feet away and I called out to him, but again, no response. He simply moved to the other side of the mound. Intent on surveying each angle of the yard, he moved from one edge to another, always returning to the place beneath the tree from where he had started.

He was dark. In his presence, I began to feel dark too. It seemed odd that he purposefully avoided contact with me. Was he in deep thought, in meditation about this place? Earlier, I described our mental projections as movies, both simple and complicated, that constantly run through our heads. This scene took on the significance of not just a waking dream, but something tinged with the nightmarish. It began to feel like more than just a random, anonymous encounter.

Like everyone, I carry around an internal film crew all the time. As Jeremy Taylor would playfully remind his dream students, we serve as creator, producer, director, and we issue casting calls for nearly everyone we have ever met, seen, or heard of (and those we haven't too). We create and compel everyone to join us in our dream dramas. In the lifting mist, I started to narrate and direct the situation inside my head without making a conscious choice to do so. I was trying to make meaning of what I was seeing and figure out my role in this strange plot twist.

In my academic and counseling education programs, we studied Freudian, Jungian, Existential, and Systemic theories of human behavior, among other approaches. We explored transference and countertransference processes. I came to understand that those terms are basically equivalent to "projection." Eventually, I adopted the term *projection* because it seemed more flexible, usable, and relevant as I delved into the study of dreams. A lifetime of conscious and unconscious memories shape and produce our projections as well as our waking and nighttime dreams. Some of these memories are positive, nurturing, and healing and some may be tragic and forever wounding. All of these projections will influence how we relate to others and the world. As I have said before, we can't *not* project. Our goal, then, is to become aware of *when* and *how* we project, then we can move into more conscious choices of how we act.

Projection, for better or worse, is how we learn to live. It is a tool that has evolved from the beginnings of time itself. Speculation is a form of projection. Guessing is too. Questions are motivated by our projections, though the projections are often unconscious and unspoken. This is a natural, crucial part of our sense of learning and wonder. We use our own filters, perspectives, and stories to get to know another and to get to know the world. And, unconsciously, I called on the power of projection to help me navigate those uncertain moments at Wayland's Smithy.

What part of me was reflected in this stranger? What part of this man was reflecting me? This place we were in, this once-upon-a-time forest graveyard contained centuries of forgotten stories, tragedies, and triumphs. Now, my musings about the past and concerns about the present moment were swirling in my mind like the wind that had ceased a few moments before. There was this tall, bearded being in the long, dark trench coat. There was I with the long, white flowing hair, appearing as a humpback in a windbreaker and wide-brimmed hat. Wasn't I odd too? This man and I, weren't we just mirroring a part of each other?

You might easily think, *There were two strange men in the graveyard that day.* Yes! Correct you are! I couldn't help but speculate about him and, as mysterious as he was, I hazard a guess that he too, had his speculations about me. My clinical skills came to the fore and began to color my projections. I started to wonder: *Is this man acting standoffish and withdrawn because he has a mental health condition? Maybe he simply can't respond to social cues like 'normal' people do.* But then, my own defensive mechanisms began to emerge, as they often do when I feel anxious, insecure, or threatened and want to find a way to control my environment. I began to wonder if this man might be dangerous. Would he threaten me, physically or emotionally, if I accidentally forced a connection with him? We were alone in this desolate place in backcountry England, and it was starting to feel like anything could happen. His dress and demeanor fit into my own scary movie projections: a tall, lean man wandered alone into an ancient graveyard in the gray English autumn rain, plotting crazy, dangerous things, and then he met another tall, lean man... Ironically, in the course of later research, I came across a 1970s British movie that actually featured a late-night murder on this *very* ground. Obviously, I am not the only one who engages in crazy projections, particularly here. Some people get paid handsomely to make movies out of their own creative nightmares.

We Are What We Fight

I have darkness within. We all do. Some of the darkness I know. Some darkness, maybe lots of it, I don't. It's impossible to fully discern because most of our darkness remains in the unconscious. In Jungian psychoanalytic terms this is called the *shadow*. We push the shadow away because we do not want to admit, know, or own such aspects of the self. Fearing the shadow side, we do our best to lock these shadow fears into closets of unconsciousness. To some extent we live in fear of being exposed, worrying that people would consider us crazy, immoral, unacceptable, or dangerous if they ever knew the extent of our inner darkness.

In the internal movie I created when I met the stranger, I was consciously and unconsciously creating a story about him. In that process, I was revealing my own story. I was revealing my own fears about myself. I have a streak of mild (or maybe not so mild) paranoia. I feel people are out to get me. Once in a while, I'm right. Mostly, I'm not. Deep within me, there is a primal raging energy that could rob, attack, or even murder someone. I don't want to admit it because, somehow, I believe that if I admit to possessing such darkness, I might enact it. In this waking dream at Wayland's Smithy, I was confronted with this potentially crazy, dangerous side of myself.

One of my most beloved psychotherapy clients, (who has given me permission to share his story) someone I worked with on and off for over two decades, was wounded by abandonment and racism. A person of color, his beloved grandparents adopted him after his father and mother left him behind. Growing up as a minority person on the western prairie is often tough. Systemic racism permeates the culture, some of it visible and much of it invisible. In this case, family pain went back for generations. Survival was cruelly complicated. This particular man became alcohol and drug dependent as he grew up. He also became a feared and violent gang member. Several years before I met him, he had entered substance abuse treatment and got clean. He came to me because he was seeking guidance on how to approach his new life. He had a girlfriend and a baby and wanted to be a good partner and parent. Turns out, he was one of the most effective, *imperfect*, and loving fathers I have ever met. Over the years of our counseling relationship, he would tell me how he sometimes felt he "just needed to fight someone to feel better." In his past, he would cruise the bars just looking to start a brawl and draw some blood. I never wanted to know how far the violence went. I didn't want to know if he had ever killed someone in his violent past. It wasn't that I was judging his behavior. Instead, my reticence was about *my own fear*—about what I feared about myself. Deep down, I know I have the potential to kill.

We are all fucked up. Jung, Freud, Jesus, the Buddha,

you, me, and your wisest aunt have always known this: At some level we are all the same in our brokenness. Sometimes, we are so blind to our needs that we can easily point out the sliver in the eye of another and never see the log piercing our own. Aware as I am of my woundedness, it is hard to be hopeful about myself and, indeed, about the human race. And yet, I yearn to live in a state of hope anyway. One of my most treasured sources of hope comes from the Jesus story. Specifically, I'm inspired by *where* Jesus was born. Whether I believe in the literalness of that story is not as important as the metaphorical beauty and truth of his birth: He was born in a *manger*. He was born in a dusty, smelly, shitty lean-to of a barn. Not in some inn or safe, hospitable home in Bethlehem. This is really good news for you and me because *we* are that lean-to, that sorry excuse for a barn. Again, where did this beautiful, vulnerable baby born of hope and healing first appear? Where we need hope and healing the most: in the dark, dusty, smelly, shitty place within the human soul. This is also where we are most vulnerable, raw, and real. Go figure. Hope and healing are born in our most shadowy, ugly places. Imagine that!

The purpose of the healing journey is to explore the deepest parts of ourselves in order to bring healing light into the areas that we do not want to see, to the stuff that we do not *want* to know about ourselves. Ironically, when we allow light to pierce our internal darkness, we actually begin to make friends with the shadow. When we find the grace to bring consciousness to the parts of the self that were once unconscious, we're able to make choices with more healthy awareness and to live more freely, authentically, in the world. We begin to take more responsibility for our own lives. We heal as we become more curious about who we really are and about the contents of the most authentic self.

Maybe, when all was said and done, that tall, strange-to-me bearded man wearing the long, dark trench coat wandering this mysterious place named for Wolund, the ancient god of smiths, simply wanted to be left alone to carry out his personal mission, nothing more or less. The other strange man, the white-haired Humpback of the Ridgeway—me!—was, perhaps, intruding upon his meditations in that sacred place. With a gratitude I didn't quite expect, I bid a silent farewell to my accidental companion, my mirror in the mist, and melted away into the wind.

Chapter Twelve
The Bedrock of Life,
of Death, of Dreams

I hiked the Ridgeway eastward and could not help but notice that I moved across the ridges of history as I moved across the ridges of land. The trail began with Avebury's standing stones and hills once constructed to mark the star paths and Earthly seasons. Now, I was moving toward castles and monuments built to protect territory, project authority, and memorialize the dead. The trail that left Wayland's Smithy was lined with wild shrubs, thick hedgerows, and tall trees, giving the illusion I was walking in a forest. In a matter of strides, the vegetation thinned, and I began the steep climb toward the magnificent White Horse of Uffington. Here on the Ridgeway, you stravage the thin veil between worlds where imagination yields to something that feels like magical power. Travelers on this glacier-sculpted ridge, which is its own version of *earth art*, are guided between seen and unseen realms.

The mist swirled around me, first heavy, then light, and then impenetrable. I kept walking, hat tied down and rain jacket billowing like a sail behind me. I nearly stumbled backwards as I took the full brunt of the weather. The walk into the wind was unprotected, raw, and tiring.

Above me, despite the brutal weather, I saw people milling about the trail heading toward the White Horse. As I got closer, I could see a family wandering around without jackets. Many wore short sleeves. None of them were prepared for the damp, but the parents and their small children were laughing, yelling to each other to be heard above the wild wind. Their joy was contagious, especially after my dark shadow journey in the graveyard below. The father, a huge muscular man with long curly black hair blowing in the wind, smiled at me. Without words, I felt invited to join their welcoming, playful energy. A spontaneous team, we opened and closed the gates in the fences to leave the Ridgeway and follow a winding path that would take us to gaze down at the three-thousand-year-old earth sculpture. We soon parted and spread out over the vast hillsides, all following different paths to try to find the best spot to see the great shape below us.

This elegant steed seems to fly across the steep grassy hill. I had seen aerial photographs of the Uffington White Horse and had long looked forward to seeing this mysterious and ancient sculpture-in-the-earth. If you can't see it from the air, it's best to see it from the hills or highways opposite the carving. Those hills, far off and steep to climb, were a walk of two or more miles away. After waiting so long to experience its majesty in person, I had to imagine the vastness and artistry that existed directly below me. Though they say it's best to see art in its original form, I found myself substituting memories of the images for the real viewing experience. It had to be enough to simply catch glimpses of a few white chalky segments as I wandered around the top of the hill.

The damp, cold wind that still howled around me discouraged me from pushing on to find a better vantage point. This quest to witness the White Horse ended up being a lot of work! It also inspired even more appreciation for the ancients who dreamed and then carved a design of such magnitude. Creating such earth art would be a great undertaking today, but back then it must have been a near incomprehensible enterprise. The abstract, four-legged flying beast—tradition says it is a horse, but it could be any creature, really—is cut deep into the soil and rock. It was shaped by an imagination that could conceive what the design would look like from afar, rather than up close, where I was. Deep trenches were dug into the turf and then filled with the white chalk from nearby quarries. I imagined the many thousands of baskets of crushed stone that had to be lugged up the slope, then poured into the great curving forms. Perhaps the original artist, or artists, sat on the faraway hills and gazed back to where I now stood, imagining the shapes to come.

What sacred power did this figure represent? It has an eternal, spellbinding power that captures the human imagination and, three thousand years later, still does not let go. The great white beast, whimsical yet so serious, flies beyond the grass, soaring, stravaging toward the blue skies for eons. It could have been lost by erosion and new growth, but it has always been preserved by the various peoples who happened to live upon the lands. There are accounts of lusty mid-summer equinox festivals in the 1600s complete with flower-laden tents, foods, drink, music, acrobats, and other performers, all there to celebrate the soaring beast. At the conclusion of the yearly festivities, the party folk would scour the shape of the beast back into perfection, adding new crushed chalk to freshen the art. During World War II, the sculpture was covered with brush to prevent German bombers from using it as a geographic landmark. After the war, it was uncovered, scoured, and refreshed so the beast, which never stopped soaring into the earth, could once again move beneath the human gaze.

The Earth was likely the first canvas for the first artist of the first hominid clan who decided to engage in the intentional expression of a message. We can only guess about the mysteries and experiences that would have captivated the ancients and compelled them to pick up a tool and try to depict concepts that defied common understanding. I can imagine ancient people seeking to draw power from the earth, from lightning, storms, and winds. It's easy to picture how they might have sought to draw protection and prosperity from common beasts in their bid to survive in a dangerous and unpredictable world. We moderns seek to manage and control a world that makes us feel helpless and vulnerable by building soaring temples, churches, and other religious-inspired art. We seek to "divinely" impress each other as we endeavor to impress the gods we worship.

Perhaps the original artist of the White Horse saw a beautiful hillside and it simply became a gigantic green canvas for the simple sake of whimsy. If that be true, it's good to note that the playful word "whimsy" may have come from those Nordic invaders and settlers of England, *hvima*, meaning "to let the eyes wander." And why not? How appropriate that "the eyes" are blessed to have their own stravage, to wander, in both beauty and defiance. Created in harmony with the geography of the land, perhaps as a spiritual expression to honor the gods and goddesses or out of simple beauty and playfulness (or both!), it is a testament of human imagination.

How *does* one imagine? What is that ability called *imagination* that causes a person to gaze upon a hillside or a cave wall and see (or, you might say, *project)* images that are then rendered into recognizable shapes? Where does imagination come from?

Artists, architects, poets, wordsmiths, shamans, ironworkers, farmers, and so many more all depend upon what we call imagination when they set upon the work of seemingly creating something out of nothing. Nothingness, of course, doesn't exist. There is always something, visible or not, that precedes the idea, the art, or whatever it is that's being created. The traditional Judeo-Christian belief that god created the universe out of nothingness, the *ex-nihilo*, doesn't bode well in Process Theology, as I have stated before. There is always, according to process understanding, *something*, seen or not, that exists previously and serves as a primordial, inspirational stew when the mysterious impulse to create happens.

So, what might be that mysterious *something* that exists before imagination and precedes the impulse to create? Dreams. Yes, those inexplicable, mysterious, jarring, illogical, unconscious movies of the night just might be the spoon that stirs the primordial imaginal stew. Evolutionary biologists ask whether bees dream because, it seems, they learn while sleeping. And don't we all learn and grow as we sleep? Dreams may be the deepest instinctual, creative impulse that rewires the brain and body both biologically and spiritually. Dreams may inspire humans (and, perhaps, other life forms) to live, evolve, and create beauty and compassion. Dreams, stirring within the unconscious, may emerge in the waking life and shape the conscious imagination. Imagination is, for all practical purposes, "awake dreaming" and out of this phenomenon comes the impulse to create and make something new.

Standing on the hill, buffeted by the creative powers of the universe and by the wild winds of the flying beast, I held hard onto my hiking hat. I realized I wasn't going to be able to see the full figure of the White Horse. I felt discouraged because part of me hungered to gaze into its eyes and walk its entire outline in a meditative saunter. I was disappointed, not by the art, but by how the practicalities of time, exhaustion from the wind, and the limits of my own determination stopped me. I realized I couldn't truly observe this magnificent earth sculpture without taking a serious detour. And today, sadly, was not the day for a serious, sacred detour. I envied the "car people" who could simply park far below and gaze hillward and imagine the great white beast flying into the beyond. But the ebbing day had its own voice, and it chanted "Miles to go before I sleep." My promised bed at a place called Down Barn Farm pulled me on. My style of sauntering and stravaging the paths of life, tracing the geography of the soul, also made me vulnerable to disappointments. The clouds, weather, and the need for rest became more compelling than my desire to commune with this particular ancient dream. Saddened, I pushed on, walking away into the green hills.

Dr. Royce Fitts

A Cup of Cold Water

O, England, you, as everywhere and everyone on Earth, have moods of weather and wind. One moment, the gales whip and slash across the earth and soul. Then, suddenly, your calm and warmth gently caress all that is, bidding peace and joy to all creation.

As soon as I was blown away from the White Horse, a strange and beautiful quietness settled upon my saunter. The mists receded, the winds calmed, and the golden sun flooded the trail again. The return to mild weather calmed and re-energized me. The land flattened and the trail relaxed, becoming straight and open.

The map indicated that there was a hiker's water source just ahead. A bench with a small, engraved sign was tucked between a farm fence and a simple water faucet. The sign indicated that the faucet was a gift for the Ridgeway walkers, given in memory of a young man, a teen, who had loved the trail. Though it was not clear from the engraving, there was an implication that this young soul yearned to hike, but for unexplained reasons could not, so he devoted himself to imagining the adventures of the trail. I envisioned how this child of the Ridgeway, this imaginative child who lived in the realm of waking dreams, would wait by the fence to greet the saunterers. Perhaps he would offer to fill the hikers' bottles and gave encouragement to all who passed. In my daddy-heart, the deepest part of me that nurtures a child, I could see him asking questions of hikers in hopes of uncovering tales of the trail he loved so much. The answers would help him picture his own journey along these ancient ridges of time. I stared at the engraving for a long, long time and then gazed at the faraway farmhouse that served as host for this delicate and tender memory. In meditation, I filled my water bottles, drank deeply, and filled them again. I held compassion for the boy who had died and those he'd left behind. With a heavy heart, I wondered about his parents.

I have not experienced the death of a child and I can only imagine the waking-life nightmare, the wrenching, never-ending grief that follows such a loss. I have counseled clients, ministered to parishioners, and served as a chaplain in hospitals, supporting parents as they experienced the anguish of losing one of their own. A sort of solidarity in the face of helplessness is sometimes all we can offer as we seek to be present with those who have experienced the unthinkable. I felt the helplessness of the Mommy and Daddy, who would have gladly traded places with their son, giving him life. They would strike wild, impossible bargains in the face of the unfairnesses of life. There, at this humble memorial, I prayed a quiet prayer. It was a prayer that did not heal and could not heal, but a prayer that offered to be with the anguish of those who carry the deepest darkness of all.

The shadows of grief, the sunshine bursting through clouds and water, so fresh and vital, offered in memory of one who was gone, these are the contrasts of life. This brief stop on the Ridgeway revealed again the eternal struggle, against all odds, to heal that which may never heal. So, what do we do in the face of life's inevitable companion—loss, and grief? We can *be with*. Being with another, being fully present and noticing the awful awkwardness, the mutual helplessness that holds and traps you both. Sometimes, that is the best you can ever offer. Your presence is healing. Not the talking, nor the acts of service. You offer silence, and, maybe, a cup of water. Maybe the person who is mourning will offer you the cup instead, and the circle of compassion is complete. Woundedness is often the compassionate teacher of healing empathy.

We are healers who are wounded. Wounded, we are healers.

There is a beauty in this simple water faucet along the side of the trail. It is a stark beauty that insists that we pick up the awful pieces of life in order to cope, soulfully and compassionately. It is a painful beauty that moves us toward healing and offers us the courage to keep hiking. These grieving parents who farmed along the Ridgeway offered me, someone who does not know the terrible pain of losing a child, a graceful rest from the painful winds of life and a replenishing cup of cold water. These moments of simple transcendence are not asking us to deny the pain but are instead a call to stumble forth into the next step of life, to do our best, even within tragedy, to try to create meaning, hope, and beauty *anyway*. It was what Jesus meant when he encouraged his friends to look for the small acts that would bring relief and healing to the "least of these...by offering a cup of cold water."

In gratitude, I drank.

Chapter Thirteen
Life Is But A Dream

Tired and windburned, I neared Down Barn Farm just before sunset. After the exhausting, windy ordeal at the White Horse, the emotional moments of prayer at the water stop, and the long walk that followed, I looked forward to my overnight stay on a genuine English farm. In my eager weariness, I passed by the grass-covered lane that led down a hill to the farm and found myself on a nameless country road. Confused, I stood at the crossroads, such as they were, hoping to get my bearings, turning in every direction. I spied a small stand of trees up the way and considered walking there. I tried to conjure up a quaint cottage in that shaded grove. Frustrated and anxious, but also a dreamer occasionally prone to magical thinking, I even imagined the kindly residents in the cottage who would help me get my bearings and perhaps offer a nice cup of tea. But my logical brain won out, and I knew I couldn't dream such a sanctuary into existence. I checked the map in my Ridgeway Trail book over and over. Nothing made sense. I was, once again, lost.

Suddenly, I could hear a faint sound familiar to my childhood: a tractor coming from a field on the other side of a distant hill. I could not yet see it, but it was growing louder. Man and tractor soon appeared, a swirl of dust around them. Bald head uncovered, eyes settled into a squint, he was focused strictly on the business at hand. He drove rapidly and directly onto the Ridgeway, and even though I was just a few feet away, hardly gave me a glance. The machine he pulled behind him was called a disc, which consisted of a series of twelve-inch rounded steel blades that could be elevated and lowered by hydraulics. It was autumn and it was time to turn the soil. This tool was designed to rip up the top layer of soil as well as the dying or dead crops and turn it all over, grinding and slashing the vegetation into tiny pieces. This practice allowed the summer's leftover bounty to decay into fertilizer over the winter and enabled the soil to rest in preparation for next spring's planting. I managed to get his attention before he began work on the next field, and, apologizing for the interruption, I approached the idling tractor and asked how I might find Down Barn Farm. He was puzzled for a moment. I mentioned that the bed and breakfast was somewhat near the Ridgeway and couldn't be far. Realization dawned. "Oh! You mean Penny! Yes, about a mile the way you came. You'll see a lane on your left. Take the lane and follow it. You'll be there." I thanked him and, in the blink of an eye, he lowered the disc, ramped up the tractor engine, and was gone in a cloud of dust.

Relieved and happy, I turned around. Backtracking a mile, I found the lane that was nearly invisible in the tall grass, and resolutely took the left. Now I could saunter again as I made my way down the hill, the sun still hovering and creating a peaceful early evening in England. The lane merged with another, and I found myself on a well-traveled track that easily guided me into the farmyard. Soon, I met the welcoming committee. A friendly herd of large hogs approached me, scratching and rubbing their huge bodies against their pasture fence, emitting satisfied grunts and gruffs that sounded a bit like "hello." I would learn that the hogs were a source of great pride. This particular breed boasted ancient English ancestry and the farmer was on a mission to preserve them.

I met my host, Penny, and after I had settled in my room, we walked the farm together as the light faded from the sky. She explained that the name of Down Barn Farm was inspired by the lay of the land. The hill slopes from the crest of the Ridgeway down to the house, the pastures, and the barns, and then continues beyond—spreading out—forming a lush, rolling meadow. Again, I greeted her beloved hogs, observed the free-range chickens, ate a ripe pear from the organic orchard, and gazed at the setting sun far to the west as it silhouetted the hedgerows, trees, cattle, and Arabian horses grazing in the meadows.

The world is small. I discovered that Penny spent some of her self-described "hippy days," her 1960s college years, as a horse wrangler near Sheridan, Wyoming, less than a day's drive from my own western Nebraska homeland. It was out in the American west that Penny became passionate about endurance horse racing, which is a safe, carefully regulated form of racing that puts horse and rider to the test across miles of open range. Penny, herself an endurance rider in her younger days, is still a leading advocate for endurance horse racing in the UK. She shared these stories and others as I enjoyed an enormous meal with her extended family who lived in a converted horse barn just across the yard. After the day's challenges, the all-organic spread of roast lamb, baked potatoes, greens, salads, wine, and a luscious dessert soothed my tired, wind-chapped soul. Penny's light-hearted son-in-law had prepared the meal, and with a twinkle in his eyes, leaned toward her and nudged her with the question, "Mum, have you had the 'Trump talk' with

Royce yet?" The 2016 U.S. presidential election was coming soon. Everyone laughed and rolled their eyes. I shook my head and asked for more wine, a lot more.

The next morning dawned cool and sunny, and Penny served a breakfast of eggs provided by her flock. She offered a large carafe of French press coffee, exhorting, "You Americans must have your coffee!" Gratefully, I gulped it down. Restored, I bid farewell to that hippy of the farm and her family. Sacredly sauntering up the grassy lane toward the Ridgeway, my shoes already soaked in the early morning dew, I passed that ancient breed of snorting hogs that shall, if Penny has her way, always grace this earth.

The day warmed and the trail continued straight. Around midday there were more walkers, families riding bicycles, teens out for an afternoon hike, and to my surprise, an older couple slowly driving their car on one of the few segments of the trail that allowed automobiles. Noticing my backpack, they waved and greeted me warmly, and when they heard my American accent, stopped and beckoned me over to their car for a visit. They mentioned they had been attending a regional agricultural event nearby, something like an American county fair. They asked where I was from and when I said, "Nebraska, the central U.S.," their eyes lit up with delight. I discovered they were cattle farmers who hailed from Cornwall, an area to the distant southwest of England. They surprised me with tales of their travels to western Nebraska some twenty-five years before when they visited numerous farms and ranches in the region to learn about raising cattle on the open prairie. Their travels took them just a few miles from where I was raised! I reflected that within the span of just a few hours, I had met folks who had traveled halfway across the world to get to know my particular part of America. Again, this Ridgeway, following the ridges between worlds, revealed the interconnected web of trails, tales, and time that weaves us all together.

The River of Dreams

The Ridgeway began to slope gently downward. I was headed toward Goring-on-Thames, another historical village that, early in its history, served as a mill town in service to England's once mighty forests. This beautiful community also sits near the rise of hills called the Chilterns, which I would be climbing the next day. Soon, I'd see that ancient, life-giving water artery, that mature heartbeat of a river called the Thames. Not even ten days before, I had walked on a bridge across this same elegant river, surrounded by the cars, buses, thousands of tourists, and ornate buildings of London. Here, I would walk the river's boggy, countryside banks and contemplate its whispering grasses and quiet hedgerows. Again, it was as if I were walking in a dream, a waking dream that I once feared might never come true.

The Thames is as alive and eternal as the land through which it flows, carrying nourishment to all it touches. Over the eons, the river has been worshiped as a goddess or god, depending on the era. This acknowledgment of its sacred nature reflects the power of water and how it brings life or death to everything in its path. Now, I see the Thames like an old sage that constantly communicates the wisdom of its life's journey in its eternal flow. Seeing the river far off into the distance, I once again could not help but wonder at the mysteries that brought me there. Being here could have been a random desire, which, like so many other desires and ideas, could have simply floated up and then flowed away. How and why did this desire to stravage the Ridgeway stick? We all have so many inklings and callings that, due to the what-evers of life, are barely taken seriously. And yet, in the span of a short seven weeks, I would walk through so many long-held dreams: hiking in England, sailing to Scotland's Iona, then various wanderings and saunterings through Europe. Visions beyond imagining became incarnated into flesh and blood. Oh, the risks. Oh, the eternal joys.

The ego is a tricky beast. In its honorable efforts to help us survive potentially dangerous situations, it risks becoming a dictator of the soul. The ego, in its unbridled thirst to protect you, can become like the English oppressors of old Scotland. In an arrogant bid to bring "peace," the invading autocrats attempted to suppress a wildly independent people by trying to outlaw, of all things, free-range walking. The Scots, defeated by armies on their own soil, would never be defeated in the soul. They wandered defiantly onward, challenging the ultimate egomaniacs, the British ruling class. Breaking out of their spiritual prison cells despite military defeat, they refused safety and conventional survival for a life of soulful *stravaging*.

Sometimes, we fantasize that living a dream is gentle and feels like riding a peaceful rolling river, as the Thames flows through Goring and eventually into the North Sea. We sing the old song, "Merrily, merrily, merrily, life is but a dream," but we forget that rivers, like dreams, sometimes explode their banks. Rivers and dreams roar as they are birthed, shaping, being shaped, by the spiritual and physical geography of their origins, remaking the world.

Thousands of years ago there was a massive ice and earth dam that held back the North Sea waters. The Thames flowed over that land that once existed between what is now England and Europe. In the distant past, it flowed on and on and fed Europe's longest river, the Rhine. Then one day, like a frightening nightmare that insists on recreating our world, the Thames, combined with the water of melting glaciers, erupted through the dam. The land between England and Europe disappeared and the English Channel was born. A nightmare grabs our attention and challenges us to change and expand. "Bad dreams" actually come in service to our health, healing, and wholeness. The nightmarish explosion of that frozen earthen dam eventually birthed a lush, green, new island that holds England, Scotland, Cornwall, and Wales. Out of death, rebirth and resurrection.

Now, walking and looking ahead across the broad valley toward Goring, it was easy to see the lines of trees and pasture lands that followed the winds and turns of this slow-moving sage of a river. The Chilterns' forested hills beckoned beyond. Soon, I would cross this river again, not with horns bleating or crowds rushing through a circus atmosphere, but simply, quietly sauntering over this sleepy, gentle, serene waterway.

Massive willows grew along the banks when I reached the village, shading homes and an expensive-looking boutique hotel and spa. I leaned on the bridge rail and spied on the people having midafternoon drinks on the deck. I yearned to splurge and rest at that elegant place, eat on the deck at the water's edge, ignore my judgmental projections for the rich and powerful, and soak in the ambiance of luxury on the Thames. But, alas, the price of that luxury was beyond my budget, and I moved on.

The fresh, clear signage about the Ridgeway Trail along the entry to Goring spoke of how this village took pride in the trail, giving visitors a sense of a welcoming city park. In the small business district, I hunted for an affordable meal and found a bakery that had just made fresh sausage rolls— hot, flaky, and steaming. I devoured them, feeling the grounding of fresh food and nourishment from my long day's walk.

The baker directed me to a pub just a few blocks away when I asked about local bed and breakfast options. Fortunately, they had a room open, and a hot breakfast was included the next day. The pub, named the John Barleycorn, intrigued me. It was old and I had to hunch through the doors and nearly bumped my head on the low ceilings. The walls and tables were made of the same heavy dark wood. The small dining and bar rooms were crowded with people, yet it was surprisingly quiet. The bartender, in his tiny station surrounded by high walls, had to lean down to see his customers unless they were sitting at the high stools directly in front of the bar.

I found a table in a corner by a small window and set up my computer to write. The light was soulfully dim, and with a warm beer by my side, I began to record the day's walk. I drank in my surroundings. It was early evening, the sun slowly fading outside, and I gazed out on a small street and the riverbank of the Thames. Two men, one quite elderly, walked in. The older man wore a formal suit and tie and looked professional. I projected my little story upon him, imagining that he was a local judge or solicitor. He was elegant—white-haired, quiet-spoken, and kind looking. His friend was a younger, nondescript man without a tie. They visited in low tones and sipped scotch. I wrote in my journal, typed in my blog, and gently eavesdropped. It sounded like they were discussing some cases, possibly sorting out the dynamics of a difficult situation. But more than that, more than the problem solving or debriefing they may have been doing, it was clear that they were friends. I liked that. The elegant old man seemed a wise sage. He sipped and shared words I could not hear, but I felt them, words with perspectives forged with the wisdom of ages. They finished their drinks, and with quiet consultations, ordered another. I had the sense that this gathering of men took place regularly—even daily, as the sun set—in this old pub sitting alongside another sage, that wise River Thames. I felt comfort in these men; friends and colleagues.

The Cloudy and Dark

The next morning, the Ridgeway trail would carry me along the river's edge. The trail was paved and narrow for a short time as it wound and followed the bank of the river and through the neighborhoods of Goring-on-Thames. Trees and bushes lined the trail and people were out for their early morning walks. One man stopped me, seeing my proverbial backpack, and wanted to visit.

He asked where I had stayed the evening, and when I mentioned the John Barleycorn, he responded with a spontaneous foot shuffle and a rendition of an old rock song of the same name. His singing wasn't half-bad, and it helped me remember the British rock group of the early 1970s, Traffic. I later puzzled over the song, doing google searches to discover its meanings and history. I wrote a blog post about John Barleycorn, and I began to see its significance when I shared it with a Wiccan friend from Colorado. She helped me understand the beauty of this subversive poem with its deep meanings related to the circle of life and death for the pre-Christian peoples of these ancient islands. The poem honored the hard work of grain harvests, the making of fermented drinks, and the celebration of fertility rituals that followed. The Christian church outright stole these stories, poems, and songs. Making acrobatic leaps, they bended and twisted the John Barleycorn legend into a distorted symbol of the resurrection. Jesus, I think, be not proud.

Further along the trail, I spied a thatcher re-roofing a large old home. Centuries of skill culminated in the hands of a living craftsman as he carefully replaced the old thatch with new straw. The John Barleycorn legends were being woven into the structure and the sacred grain stalks became a roof. This ritual of using the empty grain stalks for shelter after the grains had been harvested for food and drink, mingled the elements of human survival, nourishment, and pleasure. It all added greater breadth and resonance to that circle of life and death.

The trail moved closer to the river's edge, and I walked just a few feet from the water. The path was damp, muddy, boggy at times, and the warm air humid. Tiny flies hovered in the still air, and I had to walk through their clouds. Although the autumn of my hike was one of the warmest and driest in the region in recent memory—which made for lovely weather for my trek—in times of heavy rains, the river would easily rise over these banks and flood the trail, pasture lands, and fields on both sides of the river. Boats both large and small floated past in the dark, green water. I had met a couple the night before in the pub and they had told me that they were on holiday, cruising in a small yacht on the Thames. I wondered where they were this quiet morning. Children played in the tall grasses, splashing in the water. Much of the land was now pasture and a few cattle grazed nearby. Thousands of years of life flowed here, and for this brief moment in time, I was part of the story of the Thames.

I was curious about the meaning of the word *Thames*. Where did the name come from? I had asked a few folks, but no one seemed to know. It seemed they were content, as we humans so often are, to remain ignorant about the wonders right outside their door. Sometimes it takes an outsider to pose the question. The name does not seem to come from these isles, but instead originates in faraway India. The word Thames may be a derivative of the Sanskrit word meaning "cloudy and dark" and may have been co-opted by the Romans to describe this river. Those Romans, who were so adept at borrowing stories and stealing the essence of the cultures they conquered, forever left an imprint upon the consciousness of this land. I wondered what other names were applied to this mighty river by the forgotten ancients who came before.

The mystery of names and naming reflects our human need to express control and meaning. We're wrapped in the fantasy that naming something gives us a sense of control over it. We can define that person, place, or object. A name diminishes the mystery.

The ancient Habiru people, the likely predecessors of the Hebrews, roamed the Middle Eastern deserts. Much like the Vikings, they invaded and pillaged the land and property of neighboring tribes. They were not alone in such behavior. As the Habiru community grew more established and they yearned for their own identity and sense of meaning, a figure of mythological proportions emerged: Moses. He had an earth and soul-shaking encounter with a mysterious deity he could not name. In fact, the deity refused to allow Moses to use a name, telling Moses, simply and profoundly, to tell his people that the deity is the "I am." Yahweh, the "I am who I am," the one who cannot be named, defined, or controlled. The River Thames has doubtless been called many things, and yet, its essence refuses to be reduced by the bounds of human language. Here, the nameless mystery flows end-lessly from earth to sea.

Chapter Fourteen
The Shepherd of Swyncombe

Tiny settlements appeared and the trail left the river to veer toward a cluster of homes. I had felt the foreverness of the river. It's so gentle, and yet at many times in its life, these waters had been a wide-ranging, raging force that created this valley and carved out so many other landscapes. Of course, if called upon by the gods of rain and flood, this old river would again burst its banks and dramatically change this pastoral idyll. This day, however, I sauntered through as beautiful and as quiet a scene as you'd wish to imagine. It saddened me to wander away from the gentle wilds of the water, but I was here to walk the entirety of the Ridgeway. First, the trail took me behind the homes and back gardens bordering near the banks and, true to the casual British treatment of walkers, I was hardly noticed by the occupants. Then, abruptly, the trail took a sharp turn and I found myself walking between the side door of a home and a small, dilapidated garage. Caught off guard, I felt invasive and unintentionally sneaky as I approached the residents who were sitting outside on their back steps having a smoke within a few feet of me. I nodded a greeting, and they responded in kind. I was on the official trail, I knew, but sometimes, this freedom to roam law was weird. The trail circled the house, bent again, and then took me down a street.

While the Thames continued on toward London and further on into the North Sea, the Ridgeway and I angled away toward the Chilterns. This range of tall hills was born millions of years ago when the tectonic plates pushed the earth upward and the shallow sea drained away. Now, remnants of ocean life, including great deposits of flint and chalk, lingered in land that is currently blanketed by forests, pastures, and farms.

Ambling along what was a still relatively flat path, I was making good time and passing by small shops and intriguing churches when I spied a bakery that advertised pastries and espresso. Though I was always tempted by fresh, tasty English sausage rolls and scones that drooled with melted butter and honey, as a diabetic, I had to resist many a beguiling carbohydrate. This morning, that conflict was resolved for me. The shop was closed, and my belly was still full of the John Barleycorn Pub breakfast from just a few short hours before. Grateful, I curbed my lust, left the small chain of villages, and fled toward the hills.

The climb through the Chilterns was more rigorous than any of the hills I'd encountered thus far on the Ridgeway. It was refreshing to merge into the forests. The spirits of god and goddess, the Green Man and the Green Lady, revealed themselves and hovered in the trees. The forests built a wall and sealed away the sounds of the towns left behind. Enveloped in the silence of the old, stately trees, I walked a path shrouded with mystical shadows and streaks of yellow sunlight. Everywhere there was a glowing, holy ambiance.

The path crossed small, narrow country roadways that were seldom traveled. Everything was covered by the dry leaves that had fallen in the first breath of autumn. The roadways were fenced on both sides, and I soon lost count of the gates that had to be opened and closed as I walked. The Ridgeway didn't follow a straight line, so I had to stay vigilant, searching out trail markers as I crossed each lane. No matter, as the woodsy trail was refreshing, inviting, and gave me the energy to walk on, even as the climb became steeper. Immersed in awe of the naturescape, my walking meditation was interrupted by a hard-driving mountain biker. Dressed in his Lycra garb, protective gloves, and helmet, he hurtled downhill toward me. Presumably, he was frustrated with another gate that forced him to stop and lift his bike over the fence. Standing at the gate, I smiled, greeted him, and held open the gate so he could cross more easily. Impatient, he grunted a thanks, lept on his light-metal steed, and sped on. I met several more of those mountain bikers that day and guessed there was a competition happening. The racers, a serious lot, seldom said hello. The contrast between my forest saunter and those men on a mission who raced against time and one another struck me as rather funny. I strolled in sunshine and bright shadows, and they could hardly notice anything beyond the next stretch of trail.

Could the mountain bikers see what I saw? Maybe they had been on that trail scores of times and familiarity erased the beauty and mystery of the land. As a first-timer, my spiritual and physical eyes were child-like and open wide. And yet, I too had run and hiked upon land that I knew as well as the bottom of my soles. I am proud to say that I still held that oft-trod land with eternal wonder. In all lands, familiar or not, there is mystery—if only we are willing to see it. This mystery draws us to explore, sail, hike, walk into the unknown. It may be our human curiosity that draws us to take those journeys, dangerous as they may be. Or it may be greed or survival, a desire for beauty or adventure, or a combination of all of these, that drives us into that which we do not know. Such is true in this land we now call England. The first humans who were drawn here came with the stories of their own homelands, but they were soon influenced by this very particular bit of earth. There is that unavoidable relationship, that irresistible conversation, that develops between the land and the people who walk upon it. Traversing rock and soil opens you to find new routes to self-knowledge. We discover ourselves as we discover the land upon which we walk. This is a natural outgrowth of any saunter, any wandering, any stravage.

The old conversations between the land and people along the Ridgeway resulted in the placement of the standing stones of Avebury over five thousand years ago. The dance between humanity and nature inspired the abstract earth sculpture called the White Horse of Uffington over three thousand years ago. Such exchanges inspired others to dig a vast network of broad, deep trenches at about the same time, approximately 1000 BCE. This mystery, which I was about to enter, is called Grim's Ditch.

This unpoetic name describes a fascinating series of human-made landmarks that, at first glance, one might call crude and clumsy. Calling these earthworks a "ditch" makes them sound simplistic and boring. This vast system of trenches, both deep and wide and often miles long, are not connected to each other, but they spread out across the region. Were these long, strange trenches actually a series of roads and intersections that had been carved into the earth by a people wandering, exploring, dominating, settling, and protecting their homes and land? Theories abound. The name we use now, Grim, may come from Scandinavian settlers who could have built these earthworks in honor of Odin (known also as Woden and Grimr), the Norse god of magic and war. Of course, to us moderns, the word "grim" connotes some version of a gritty, miserable, even ugly image. Long ago, the Church went further and declared these earthworks as the work of satan. Oh, again, the ways we humans project our own darkness upon the unknown!

These high berms and deep ditches, mysterious earthworks, ancient and unknown, invite us to wonder and craft stories about their purpose. They compel us to do something we find utterly irresistible: apply our projections and make guesses in hopes of figuring out what these constructions *mean*. How were they built? The thought of using Iron Age tools to dig into this rocky, forest-covered, deeply-rooted land is daunting. What kind of crew did it take to perform this work? What was their purpose? The miles and miles of disconnected earthworks in this expansive region of southern England does not make sense to the modern, logical mind. The time it took, the perseverance it required, winter after winter, storm after storm, harvest after harvest, war after war, to build these strange deep cuts into the earth. Why?

They probably were not highways to assist travelers. It's unlikely they were trenches to channel water to settlements and crops. Nor were they built as boundaries to mark land ownership. They were not fortifications built to repel intruders. These earthworks, perhaps, another form of earth art, were just...built. These trenches, earth *art*-ifacts carved into the ground, are now held in wonder alongside the other mysteries of the Ridgeway. What conversations between people and land elicited these wonders? Only the Earth knows.

I walked these earthworks for hours and miles through beautiful forests and fields. Rarely seeing another human, I moved in the silence created by the sacred sounds of nature:

breezes blowing, leaves rustling, birds singing. The carpet of dead leaves that had washed and drifted down into the center of the wide trenches, and now that held moisture and mud from previous rains, added to the beauty of the walk. The berms, with the walls above me and the path in the center of the trench, gave me the awareness of walking *below* the forest, walking *within* the cathedral of the Earth.

And then, the earthworks were gone. The trail traced a new direction and the forests eventually yielded to rolling hills of open pastures complete with sheep and cattle. Along this stretch, the Ridgeway had its own fenced-in walking path in between the pastures. Curious sheep drifted near the fence, hoping, I assumed, for a morsel or two. It was a good moment, simply stopping in these clearings to dwell upon the gentle scenery and converse in low tones with my wooly friends.

Vampires of the Soil

The open pasture sloped steeply upwards, and then the forests took primacy with their beginnings of autumn colors, contrasting against the majesty of the eternal blue sky. The trail led to the hill's crest, and I walked amidst the line of trees that I had seen from below. Turning to look back at the pasture and the places from which I had come, I saw off in the distance another walker far behind. He ambled slowly, and even from that distance, I could tell he had no backpack. I stared and wondered, and then realized he had cameras slung around his neck. He was photographing the naturescape. He stopped where I had stopped to gaze at the sheep, pasture, trees, and sky. *He will capture the beauty and colors of it all*, I thought. I silently envied the treasures he was collecting, especially when compared to what my small phone camera could capture. Imagining our meeting and conversing along this scenic path, I felt a kind of oneness with him. He clearly appreciated the sensuous beauty of these steep rolling lands under azure skies as he calmly communed with this hallowed terrain. I couldn't help but compare his meditative stroll with those rushing mountain bikers just a few miles back. Bidding him a silent farewell, I turned and began the downward trek into the forest, following the trail map toward a country road.

This hill country, so rural and farm-oriented, felt comfortable and home-like as I walked. I felt an understanding of the land and fields, similar to what I'd felt while walking softly through the friendly herd of dairy cows. A warmth filled my heart. For a farm boy like me who was always eager to see something new, yet always on the search for echoes of familiarity, this was a thrilling experience.

Coming down the hill, the trail took me down a long private lane of a large farm. Unsure I was following the correct trail markers, I backtracked several times to make sure I was still on the Ridgeway. Taking a breath, I remembered (and hoped) that the freedom to roam laws still applied, even on this vast country estate. The lane was tree-lined on one side, and a small pasture containing a series of corrals and buildings lined with feed bunks for the horses and cattle, spread along the other. This was, I knew, a big agricultural enterprise, a huge corporate farm. The big house was surrounded by tall privacy hedgerows. A gated walk led to the hidden front door. It was intimidating to walk nonchalantly down the lane toward the owner's mansion and to peer at all those large outbuildings and barns.

The farmyard buzzed with employees who were focused on loading feed wagons and driving tractors. I was hardly noticed as I dodged vehicles and other equipment during my stroll through the yards. Despite the all-business attitude, I decided I was going to try to be engaging and friendly and hoped to stop for a brief visit if I could get someone's attention. I knew farms and farm-talk, so this would be interesting for me and them, I thought. Walking within inches of some farmhands and repair workers, I tried to make eye contact and offer a hello, but not one person stopped doing whatever they were doing to even acknowledge my greetings. A man on a large tractor raced in front of me, the loader carrying a large round bale of hay. He drove into one of the outbuildings and deposited the bale. He backed up and off he went to pick up another, without a single glance in my direction, not even to tell me to get the hell out of the way.

Moving through the main yard, I continued to follow the line of trees. There were no trail signs here, but the path took a sharp turn and took me down a slope behind the barns. There I saw a young man, maybe in his late teens, washing a sporty car. He looked at me curiously and I offered a friendly hello. He was the only one on the farm who waved to me and returned a warm smile.

The young man's friendliness, as fleeting as it was, contrasted sharply with what I'd experienced just a few yards away. It was odd, I thought, after walking for so long and often being the only human for miles, that I could cross this busy farm without receiving even a basic hello. It almost felt personal. It seemed to be a policy of arrogance shared by those who lived or worked on this large estate: Thou shalt not waste energy on the acknowledgement of anyone who is not of your own kind or who cannot be used to better the bottom line. Perhaps they perceived me as a wandering, landless, long-haired American peasant intruding upon their domain. But this, I thought, was a farm! On farms, people work hard and close together, depend on each other for help. A simple hello would have been easy. These farmworkers and their relentless purposefulness were no different than the relentless bicyclist who seemed to begrudge my presence even as I assisted him on the trail. What a puzzle. Would those ancient diggers of what we now call Grim's Ditch have treated a wanderer with a similar indifference?

The trail continued downhill, maybe a half mile or so, and entered another long lane beside more pastures and fencerows. Tall trees offered their shade and cooled the air, inviting me to relax as I left the estate behind. It was suddenly quiet again, just the sounds of nature and my own footsteps. I reflected again on how, despite its beauty, that grand estate with its laser focus on profit and production, was so cold and impersonal. It reminded me of large American farms and ranches. The profit margins for agricultural products are narrow, oftentimes non-existent. In that kind of risky, unjust economy, only the largest facilities are able to stay afloat. The big have to get bigger and the family farm disappears, and everything is replaced by gigantic corporations. These days, the owners are often not farmers or ranchers themselves. The people in charge may never have touched a shovel or a tractor and they have no idea what it means to get their feet covered with the rich, springtime manure of farm life. Instead, these mega farms produce at a nearly unimaginable scale in hopes that the world markets, which are controlled by other mega corporations and governments, will occasionally tilt in the direction of profit for the large farm and ranch corporations to survive another year. Different owners and investors cycle in and out, and for many, farming, ranching, and land ownership is simply a write-off for those who *want* to have financial losses to reduce their taxes.

Though the landscape may be stunning when you drive through the rural areas that blanket our nation, there's a century of tragedy tilled into every acre of soil. The small family farm, with few exceptions, is dead. I was raised on a ninety-acre farm in western Nebraska. Ninety acres. It was not prosperous, although some years were better than others due to the fluctuations of weather and market prices. The acreage of our farm nearly doubled while I was in high school, yet the profit margins became even thinner. Most farms in the arid plains regions are not able to grow garden vegetables and fruit crops and take them to market in nearby towns and cities because such large population centers don't exist and transporting such a harvest is nearly impossible for the small independent family farmer. So, like many others, we turned to the "cash crops" that could be sold in bulk for the huge food manufacturers, sold on the international markets, or served as food for livestock.

Sugar beets, potatoes, grains, dry beans, soybeans, corn, alfalfa, and other crops dominate the mid-western and high plains regions of our nation. The land is now mostly depleted of natural nutrients so large infusions of nitrogen and other fertilizers are literally injected into the soil to feed the crops. The stalks and roots of the plants are simply held up by the nearly-dead soil while the crops are fed with artificial foods. It is junk food for the food, and it is a ruthless way to farm. The farmer gives up being a respectful, environmental steward of the land out of simple desperation to survive. Those massive corporate agricultural empires are vampires of the soil, sucking the life out of the Earth and her people. Small farmers who do exist and might want to do things differently have little choice but to mimic those brutal practices. The courageous, determined small, sustainable and organic farms are relegated to the economic sidelines, especially by the U.S. Department of Agriculture which is, for all practical purposes, owned by the industrial farms and food corporations.

Now, farms in the Midwest and West must span thousands of acres. No ninety-acre farms exist unless they're a fortunate person's hobby. The farms on the Eastern Seaboard, whether the disappearing dairy farms in New York or peach orchards in the Garden State of New Jersey, are no luckier unless those farmers can cater to nearby urban areas. These days, due to tragic necessity, there is little time to focus on the romance of land sustainability and ecology that farm families were known for.

I could be writing about any small, family-owned business, not just farms and ranches. Corporate power brokers, supported by hand-picked officials who are elected thanks to funding from these same corporate dynasties, masquerade as defenders of free trade, but they're often the only ones who seem to benefit. Master manipulators, they employ strategies that allow them to tap into and take advantage of the instinctual fears and anxieties of the voting public. Often their tactics, by design, discourage many people from voting at all. It is disheartening to see much of our nation unable to detect how these super wealthy, capitalistic, greedy entities manipulate, use, deceive, and control the collective consciousness of a vast number of voters. As part of their power trip, they have found ways to manufacture cheap, nutrient-deficient food that seduces the masses into blind, ever-hungry consumption. So, the small farms die, the family businesses die, and the people, at least in spirit, soon follow.

A mystic and a dreamer, am I. Or, as Saint Paul would say about those who believe in something as outrageous as loving sacrifice and compassion: "I am a fool for Christ." Despite my deep pessimism and my inability to believe that the U.S. will change its economy for the good, I believe all is not lost. Though they're close to extinction, I need to hope that family farms, ranches, and other small businesses will endure. Despite the awful injustices perpetrated in an endless war economy that's rife with racism, sexism, and homophobia, I need to hold on to hope. There is an energy between energies that will not die. In so many ways, and in the spirit of Saint Paul's words, we may be seduced and controlled by these evil *principalities and powers*, but the ever-yearning particles of compassion, empathy, beauty, wonder, and the pursuit of justice endure in the midst of it all. Even within the long history of oppression, concentration camps, lynchings, witch burnings, the decimation of native cultures, and other forms of slaughter, the dreams of healing endure within these waking nightmares and hope will *not* die.

There never has been and never will be any guarantee that compassion, beauty, and justice will triumph. Still, those eternal creative dreams that invite new possibilities of wholeness and healing persist. We have the chance to turn those visions into waking-life dreams-come-true. It deeply pains me to say this, but in America, in my beloved America, the nightmare of fascism and the wounded, selfish side of capitalism is a waking life reality. Perhaps forever. Perhaps not. The spirits and dreams, however, of compassion, empathy, beauty, and wonder are at our core and within our cells. These spirits and dreams—literally or metaphorically—emanate also from the loving goddesses and gods who join us, yearn with us, eternally inviting the human heart and all creation to ever pulsate with hope and healing. The ancient songs of the sweat lodges sung for the sake of the tribes, the rapture of gospel music that lifts the oppressed soul to soar into freedom, or the tender, bold song of the meadowlark nesting within the tall grasses of the prairie after a violent springtime storm, these are the energies that compel us to lovingly stravage through the painful paradoxes of life, with compassion, tears, joy, even unto death. These spirits and dreams will never perish.

The Good Shepherd

The land on which I was now hiking in modern-day England was no different, not any more open, just, or free than the farms and ranchlands in America. This heavily forested and scenic region I walked through that day was called Swyncombe, or the Valley of Wild Boar. In 1086 it was the exclusive hunting domain of royalty. If you were hungry and poor, you were forbidden to hunt there. To do so was to risk the penalty of death. The royals and nobility, the agricultural monopolies and corporate farmers of that time, fancied themselves predestined by god and the Church. They were the power hungry "elites," and in the patterns of history, the same energies now occupy the upper echelons of my modern America.

Lost in these painful, sobering thoughts, I sauntered slowly down the pasture lane as it followed the edges of a steep hill. The tall trees on the side of the lane reminded me of the prairie's rugged, elegant cottonwoods that often lined the boundaries of gravel country roads and offered inviting shade from the hot sun. Suddenly, an old, beat-up pickup truck appeared right beside me. The driver, a white-haired man smoking a cigarette, had his arm draped out over his window. I gasped in surprise and saw he was smiling and waving his arm in a kind of apology. "Sorry!" he quietly said, "I saw you walking and didn't want to frighten you by coming up quickly behind you. So, I turned off my engine and coasted." Calmed by his obvious friendliness, I noticed his small, beautiful sheepdog silently prancing and dancing in the back of the truck. "I am going to move my sheep from one pasture to the next and will be using this lane. I didn't want you to be caught in the middle of the herd."

What a contrast! My thoughts had been mired in such gloom, but here was a genuinely friendly, sensitive soul. Gathering myself quickly, I sensed a new adventure. "Can I watch?" I asked. "Sure," he said, "It'll take a bit to get set up." I followed him to where one lane intersected with an-other, and I saw a couple of large, metal livestock gates used to separate the lanes from the pastures.

He came over to where I was standing and, as I intro-duced myself, thanked him for the chance to watch a sheep drive. "I'm Graham," he said, and we shook hands. He explained that he was a shepherd. I was so caught off guard by his sudden appearance and excited by his openness, especially after my experience at that brutal machine of a corporate farm I'd just left, I didn't even think to ask whether he was affiliated with that operation. He certainly seemed the antithesis of that cold, closed place. As he began to prepare to move the sheep and arrange the gates, I asked if I could take a video of him and his dog separating the sheep. Graham easily agreed, but laughed as he warned me, "I may use some colorful words as my dog, Jesse, and I do the sorting and herding." *No problem there*, I thought. I had been part of a lot of sorting of hogs and cattle on the farm and knew firsthand the intensity and yelling that came with the process.

It was a marvel. Graham stood back, perhaps a hundred feet or so from the herd, and directed Jesse with hand signs and one-word commands to go forward or back, left or right, according to the movements of the sheep. The sheep, familiar with Jesse, allowed her to run amongst them, even crawling beneath them, to get them to move in the right direction. It took less than twenty minutes, and the sheep were headed happily toward a pasture full of fresh, tall grass.

Graham came back over to the gate where I was standing. He told me he has been a shepherd for many years and was one of the few remaining shepherds in the region. "I love my work!" he exclaimed. "Some people have to go to their town office every day and..." he gestured his arm toward his old, beat-up pickup, and then to the land, "this! This is my office!" I explained my hike and told him that Swyncombe was one of the most beautiful areas I have seen. He grinned as I showed him some of my recent pictures. He said,

"Royce, you should come back in early spring. The wild-flowers cover the land, up and down the meadows. I will email you some pictures." In a day or so, he did. Oh, to see the hills and forest floors covered with unimaginably thick carpets of wildflowers.

"Have you been to St. Botolph's Church?" Graham asked, pointing to a small stone church shrouded in a deeply-wooded area just outside the pasture gates. "It has been here for over fifteen hundred years," he said, as he cocked a knowing eyebrow and sucked deeply on his cigarette. I had previously read about this church in my Ridgeway hiking guide and told him I planned to explore it in a few minutes. He and I gazed at the building, and I commented that it was surprising that this church was still active. Something in his demeanor made me smile and I already knew the answer when I asked if he was part of the congregation. With a wry grin and a twinkle in his grey-blue eyes, he took another puff of his cigarette and again waved his arm, this time in a giant circle. "This is my church!" he cried. I laughed and ex-claimed, "Good for you, Graham, good for you!"

We said our goodbyes and I was left to contemplate the shepherds of the Bible and how New Testament stories show us the bold, subversive compassion of the shepherd called Jesus. He took great risks to watch over his flock. This shep-herd called Graham, this man of this quiet English forest and the exploding spring wildflowers, guided this smart, gentle dog and watched over sheep who knew they could trust him as mother, father, lover of their souls. This shepherd of Swyncombe is no less a priest than the one who serves the formal church just a few yards away. Graham lives with this land and the land lives with him, a natural and sacred trust.

Dr. Royce Fitts

Nightmares of the Sheep

I am writing about shepherding and the offering of compassionate, healthy care for the vulnerable in a moment when the universal church, the universal human family, and the universal systems of humanity—be they governments, schools, professions, faith groups, military or police forces, prisons, or any entity that purports to serve others—are being laid bare for the violations of their vulnerable ones, of their sheep. To borrow the wounded language of the Church, these institutions are being exposed for their sins. Of course, the systems of humanity are and have always been wounded. Greed and abuse have always run rampant. Now, however, at least some of these violations are finally being exposed. The sins are not new. The cover ups are not new either. What is new, however, is the light. One wave and particle of light at a time, the light is penetrating and revealing these crimes and transgressions. Abuse is being revealed and disclosed. The vulnerable are mobilizing, casting light, calling for our attention, and demanding justice.

Whether it was a thousand years ago or yesterday, it is always a tragedy when a shepherd of any order betrays a member of a flock. In family systems theory in psychotherapy, we often note that the effects of past trauma upon a single person will traumatize current relationships, as well as multiple generations to follow. Whether it is a priest, minister, rabbi, coach, king, president, judge, boss, parent, officer, or teacher, any time a person in power violates the rights and trust of someone in their care the abuse causes deep, often irreparable, wounds that continue to echo through families and communities across time.

My thoughts drifted. I was no longer beside a church in the wildwood in the English forest, but on the prairie. I remembered a woman who used to ask to have her therapy sessions in the small gazebo outside the office building that held my counseling practice. It was quiet, serene, and safe out there. The soft breezes brushed through the grasses and nearby pine trees. Sunlight streamed and highlighted sharp, prickly yucca plants, and revealed a narrow path that led down to a neighborhood lake. In this safe place, she told secrets: of her deceased father, a "pillar in the community" in a town faraway. One day, when she was about six, she was out picking wildflowers on the prairie. Her father, evidently stalking her, came out of nowhere and ripped her panties off. She didn't remember the rest. Often, she went to Mass along with her family. One day, the priest, a trusted family friend, got her alone. He molested her. This priest was charming, powerful, and threatening. One day he moved far away, promoted to a new position in the diocese because, evidently, he was good at what he did. Very good.

The story is not new, nor is it the only one.

The myriad tragedies of the abuse of children by people in power, whether by pastors in Protestant churches or Catholic priests in parishes anywhere on Earth, or the abuse and murder of indigenous children in church or government-sponsored boarding schools, violates trust in unimaginable ways. The victims often suffer throughout their lifetime. The cover ups, whether orchestrated by the church or enabled by systemwide denial, convinces the victims that their voices do not matter, and that justice and healing are not meant for them. The perpetrators can proceed with their rampage while the institutions' public relations campaigns and damage control efforts are more important than the lives of the victims. These are the terrifying waking nightmares of the sheep.

For four long years, America was a nation without a shepherd. Instead of having a leader who fiercely advocated for the vulnerable and unprotected, thanks to the 2016 election, we had a president who assaulted our basic values, demeaned, insulted, and bullied anyone who challenged him. He did not get there alone.

In office, Trump was a lightning rod for the distorted and wounded side of humanity (*our* distorted and wounded side) that refuses to show genuine compassion and insight for the downtrodden. One can only assume he'll adopt a similar role in private life. He accepts the admiration and support of racist groups. With the blessings of the businesses that reap the benefits and profits, he supports the most selfish side of capitalism that rapes our environment and reduces taxes for the super wealthy like himself. Evidently, he was good at what he did. Very good.

Trump's abusive power and energy was and is fed by the conservative religious, economic, and political power brokers in our nation (indeed the world) who flocked to his side. We watched as the self-righteous coalition that supported this man and his policies raised funds and made political hay to ostensibly protect babies from abortions. These same leaders prayed and waved their Bibles on their temple steps, exalting themselves for their righteousness and purity, while pointing with disgust to the vulnerable. These postmodern Pharisees, in their zeal to escape their definition of sin and their passion to preserve the almighty dollar, look down upon the downtrodden of modern-day America, the undocumented immigrants, and the welfare mothers. They refuse to provide the full and just economic support to nourish that child they claim to have "saved" from abortion. What a crock of holy shit.

This brings to mind another shepherd, from long ago and faraway, who watched unspeakable tragedies with piercing eyes. He saw the religious, political, economic, and military coalitions, with their insatiable narcissism and hunger for power consume the vulnerable, the poor, the young, the human sheep who had no shepherd. Amos, that ancient Hebrew shepherd-of-the-desert, personally confronted the kings of Israel and Judah, as well as the religious establishment that aligned with them and profited from their actions. He accused them of, among other atrocities, selling "the bodies of the pure in heart for silver and the needy for a pair of shoes...and trampling on the heads of the poor, grinding them into the dust of the earth, ignoring the sick and afflicted." He outraged the principalities and powers to such a degree that a riot broke out in the temple, and he was arrested. It was said the high priest intervened temporarily, but Amos disappeared soon thereafter. The tyrants and the Trumpsters of his day silenced him, and for a time, appeared to have won.

My mind returned to that woman in the prairie gazebo and the girl she had been. I thought of all the unnamed victims through history who tried to put their lives back together after abuse, trauma, and neglect at the hands of those charged with caring for them. I thought of the brave survivors, some who lived to tell their tales, and the great multitudes who, for so many reasons, could not thrive or speak after what they had gone through. Legend has it that the prophet Amos was murdered by the high priest's son because of his efforts to save the neediest from the greediest. *Graham, I thought, we need a Graham.* We need authenticity. We need an earthy, vulnerable, humble, cigarette smoking, cussing, kind, honest, joyous, good shepherd.

Dazed and disheartened, I drifted off the trail, headed toward the quiet, forest-shrouded road that led to the small church. A peaceful, hidden, sacred place it was. The late afternoon sun cast long shadows over the building and its yard. I followed a short path through the small graveyard that spread before the church. The grave markers told their own stories of ancient Swyncombe. Not caring to linger there, I approached the old wooden doors. Unlocked. *A welcoming message all by itself,* I thought. There was no narthex, no lobby, so I suddenly found myself standing at the rear of the sanctuary. Alone, I surveyed the room. Hovering in the dry, musty air was the mystical awareness that this little church in the wildwoods of Swyncombe, alongside the even more ancient Ridgeway Trail, has been here for over fifteen hundred years. I wondered who the present priest was. I wondered what it would be like to be the priest of this ancient, forever parish.

Smiling quietly to myself, I gazed at this room that served as a place for fellowship, feasts, rituals, and an assortment of ancient symbols and stories. It all felt homey and inviting. I didn't know what to expect exactly, but I noticed it had a lived-in feel, maybe a bit untidy, but in a good kind of way. This helped me understand this church as something like a family place, not pretentious, just real and offering a come-as-you-are feel. Immediately, I thought the upkeep likely fell upon church volunteers. As a former pastor, I knew what it was like to depend on parishioners who had busy lives outside the church. As I wondered about the up-keep, I remembered that the Ridgeway Trail guidebook promised that this church always provided fresh water, coffee, tea, and snacks to hikers. Off to the side, I spied a small table, complete with an electric kettle. An old, handwritten note tacked to the wall declared that visitors were indeed invited to partake in this modest feast. Bold instant coffee, along with a little snack, served as my communion in the little church in the wildwood. I left a small offering of change in appreciation.

I peeked around the modest sanctuary, walked up the aisle, touched the pews, glanced at the hymnals and old programs of worship stored in the pew racks. The kneeling benches were old, scuffed, and well used. Many churches in England are dying because of shifting belief patterns; people do not believe in or value the traditional worship of old. As elderly parishioners die, there is no one to replace them in the pews. Built along what would have been a major thoroughfare a thousand years ago, this place must have been bustling with life at some point. What was life like, then, five hundred years ago, or a thousand, when the Ridgeway was active, busy with the commerce of life? The stained-glass windows captured my eyes, and I watched the sun stream through, illuminating some of the stories of old and the great sweep of history—of this church, of this country, of this god they worship, both now and then.

I wondered about the commoners who had flocked here. I wondered if the nobles and the royals had ever stopped and worshiped in this place before or after they purged the forests of precious game. I imagined what stories the old pews could tell, stories both recent and from so long ago. The pews reminded me of going to church as a child, sometimes three or more times a week, and trying to endure those hard, straight-back wooden benches. One day, when I was about five years old, I wore my new bright red leather cowboy boots to church. I laid down on the pew and tossed my legs high into the air to show off these magnificent leather boots to the friendly adults seated behind me. They laughed warmly, and gently shushed me to not interrupt the service.

Finishing my coffee, I strolled outside and circled the sturdy stone walls of the church. The walls glistened in the rays of sunlight, and I gazed upon more of my holy flint rock. I marveled at this small parish, a community living together in some form for over one and a half millennia. Inside the building, I had seen some upcoming announcements of a yearly festival and other events on the bulletin board. A part of me yearned to come back someday and attend, wearing red cowboy boots. I yearned to see what it felt like to be with a story, a long, long story, both good and bad, ancient and modern, and be with the people who are still creating it.

Chapter Fifteen
Being Lost is Being Found

As much as England loves walkers and walking, this country prefers its walkers to stick to designated paths and steer clear of the edges of their narrow motorways. After leaving the peaceful presence of the shepherd and his flock, I promptly lost my way as I tried to find the village of Watlington. Though the Ridgeway is generally well-marked, the signs were either missing or I'd somehow missed them. Consequently, I spent the late afternoon walking as the crow flies, crossing overland in the direction of the little village. I used the main roads as my guide, and as the sun began to set and the evening rush hour commenced, I found myself clinging to the narrow verge along the pavement. The nettles were high, stinging my legs and the oncoming traffic was relentless, fast, and dangerous.

Plus, my hiking strategy of securing lodging in an inn or a pub the day before arrival did not work in Watlington. I had called numerous places, but to no avail. Finally, just before I arrived in the village, the local pub manager returned my call. Through his kind graces and his network of local bed and breakfast hosts, I had a place to stay. Unfortunately, even though it was a small village, my good fortune didn't extend to making it easy to find my lodgings once I arrived. I found a small park in which some elderly women were playing fetch with a small dog. The dog ran up to me with his ball, dropped it in front of me and, tongue and tail wagging, expected me to toss it. I laughed and did as commanded. The kindly owner took note of my backpack and my American accent, took pity on my plight, and offered to walk with me to the address I'd been given. But even she couldn't find it. Finally, she cornered a young daddy pushing a stroller and he used his cell phone to map the location. The home was on a hidden cul-de-sac, quite invisible to these locals who had lived in the village for years.

My pilgrim's desire to be spontaneous, "to follow the spirits of the trail" and not plan ahead for lodging had its risks, and yet, the risks were all worthwhile. I was on a stravage after all, straying and seeking spiritual attunement with the trail, wandering and wondering aimlessly, discovering and being discovered. I ended up staying in Watlington for two days, writing stories and journaling. As ever, I was gratified by my commitment to unexpected serendipities along the trail that bid me to be open to people and places, including a meeting with a strangely interesting thirteen-year-old boy.

Being Thirteen Again

I was thirteen once, and I testify, that we thirteen-year-old boys are indeed strangely interesting. We know so little of life. At least, that's true for those like me who grew up in a relatively safe cocoon. All too many boys cope with awful things: war, death, abuse, and other scarring traumas. Even "normal," safe childhoods are full of disruption, depression, wounding insecurities, and the weirdness of teen angst. We are stretching into the unknown, often with fear and a great deal of anxiety about whether we will ever grow hair in all the right places. The young boy-wonder I met in Watlington was probably no exception.

During a stroll through the village, I discovered a newly-opened coffee and tea shop. The building was old but well cared for, featuring quaint creaky floors and walls of aged, polished wood. The shop had Wi-Fi, tea for the long writing haul, and light lunches. The friendly barista did not mind that I camped out for hours. I found a perfect spot with a window on the quiet village street so I could gaze out and offer my eyes relief from the computer screen.

After I had been there a while, a slim, black-haired boy popped out of the kitchen and began assisting with customers. He spied me, came over, sat down, and with barely an introduction, began to tell me about his plans for world domination through his future software programs that had something to do with statistics and banking. He told me he worked part time for a bank, getting school credit and learning new ideas that he believed would make him wealthy someday. He bubbled about his favorite video games, described his own ideas for new games and plans to create the software. He was the son of the owner of the shop, but he told me he didn't get to see his father much because he was busy with the family's numerous businesses. He said his mother flies to California often, every six weeks or so, for yoga training. She ran her own yoga studio, which I assumed was somewhere in the village.

The boy kept talking and I kept listening. This spontaneous exchange was something I could not and would not cease. The boy was annoying, endearing and, I projected, lonely. If this were my childhood, I imagined I would be lonely and may not know it, for loneliness would be normal to me. I too, would get lost in video games. I would imagine new games and new ideas to fill my emptiness, seeking something to distract and soothe me, something like money that could fill the black hole within. In my imagination, my parents would be loving but emotionally far away, unable to understand my hyperactive burbles about wealth and fame because they were racing after their own distractions. I am being judgmental, I know, about this boy's parents, since I had no idea who they were or what they were like. There is nothing innately wrong with wealth and fame, owning numerous businesses, or traveling far and wide for one's edification and fulfillment.

This boy didn't know me either. And yet, he assumed, with the hungry sense of entitlement that only a thirteen-year-old could muster, that I would be his mirror. He needed to be seen, heard at a level way deeper than his surface imaginations of wealth, knowledge, and material success revealed. I felt myself being drained and exhausted as he went on and on. I knew those familiar signs. It meant, in part, that his neediness was probably exhausting for him. I was simply, intuitively, feeling his feelings. I had choices because I was an adult. I could stop him and protect myself from being drained if I wanted. Unlike this boy, I could make adult choices about what my family life would be like, how I would form and be influenced by my intimate world. I had the power to make choices about the world in which I lived, and still I sat there and made the choice to listen.

In the world of dream work, spiritual counseling, and relationship psychotherapy, I need to constantly monitor myself. I must be aware of what I am feeling in the presence of others with whom I have been invited to work. Sometimes, I feel anger, grief, sorrow, joy, and other feelings while working with a client. Those are not my feelings alone, but my response to an intuitive, unconscious invitation from a person who wanted me to experience their world. They needed a witness into their world. They needed to be seen and heard.

In psychotherapy training and supervision programs, students are coached to be curious and attuned to our internal emotional responses to whatever the client was sharing. We all have issues, experiences of trauma, grief, heartache—the awful and yet very normal experiences of life. We need to be aware of our own inner workings, and this is why the best counseling training programs require students to be in their own therapy during the duration of their training and beyond. Therapy for the therapist is often a career-long, if not a lifelong, necessity (including, but not limited to, continuing education programs, workshops, and personal retreats). If a therapist doesn't honor this personal commitment, and has not, as the saying goes, "done their own work," there's a great risk that they could do therapeutic damage to their clients. Being a therapist means holding compassionate space for the other, deeply listening to individual stories for the sake of the client's health and wholeness. In fact, the term *psychotherapy* comes from the Greek and means "listening to the soul" or "healing the soul."

When I am in a counseling session with someone, I seek to always hold the awareness that every thought and wonder I have, every question I ask, every feeling I experience while with that person, comes out of my *own* personal, mostly unconscious, projections. We all carry a library of life experiences and memories within, and we draw upon this vast library to make sense of and guess at what is happening before us at any one time. That fact, by itself, is not bad. It is natural and unavoidable. It is when I am unaware or unwilling to acknowledge my projections that I am at risk of injuring the client and the therapeutic process. Instead, it's actually possible to tune into a projection and follow it to a helpful, healing insight. A person may feel deeply seen, understood, and use such a moment of connection to move closer to their more authentic self. Projection can be a beautiful bridge between souls that leads to shared wisdom and the kind of healing that changes lives.

I'll say it once again: We can't *not* project. That's true in everyday life and in a therapeutic relationship. That said, it's not necessary to start every counseling session with the declaration that I'm going to do some projecting during our time together. Though it may be important to name the process of projection, the client's needs are priority. The focus is on their feelings and experiences, not on my reactions. I must, however, *notice* when "my stuff" is being activated within me as I sit with my client. Later, I'll work on my stuff and sort through my projections. That is why it is crucial that I—and all therapists and healers—have places for personal psychotherapy and healing.

My teacher and mentor, Jeremy Taylor, consistently and passionately held up the belief that everything we say, do, think, ask, or imagine is nothing less—or more—than projection. Everything. Sadly, he'd chuckle about the resistance he would meet from his theological and psychological colleagues. His experiences prove how hard it is for professionals to give up our thrones of expertise and become something other than high priests who exist only to judge and interpret others. We all want to believe we have access to the ultimate truth, but I think we need to embrace a concept I learned from the theologians: We are called to be part of "the priesthood of all believers." This approach serves as a caution to all of us "experts." It's a reminder that all responsible humans are capable of being our own best authority. We don't need the ordained ministers and the doctors of philosophy to tell us how to pray, love, vote, or move through the world. We are our own best priests.

I often tell clients that I seek to be a mirror—albeit a cracked, imperfect mirror. My goal is to reflect the client's real, growing-self, back to them. I would do a disservice to them—cause harm, in fact—if I unconsciously "took" their story and imposed my life experiences, opinions, successes, failures, attractions, and preferences upon it. I do my best to be aware of my internal responses and, at the same time, put aside my stuff so as to not accidentally spill "me" onto the client and "make" the other into my own image. It's vital that I hold space for their viewpoints, not push them to live their life according to mine. It's complicated. Very complicated.

Of course, I was not formally invited to act as therapist for this endearing, annoying boy. I was, however, spiritually invited to be his adult mirror and friend. This was part of my stravage, to be open to the synchronistic droplets of discovery wherever they might land. It meant that I too, was invited to remember and explore my own thirteen-year-old world.

I was raised in a form of poverty that was, for the most part, invisible to the outside world. We grew enough food to eat and always had clothes to wear. And still, we lived on a perpetual economic knife-edge, at the whim of the rise and crash of crop and cattle prices. Farmers and ranchers never control the prices of their products or labor. Agricultural unions have never been successful because you cannot strike against yourself when you are both a laborer and producer of products. Prices are set by outside forces, like corporations, government policies, and the ever-changing geopolitical scene. Farms are vulnerable to weather, whether it's drought, flash floods, or those unbelievably destructive hailstorms that could wipe out a summer's crop in seconds.

From year to year, we often lived with deep anxiety of the bank foreclosing our farm loans, which would force the sale of all assets including farm equipment and land. If we even owned the land we farmed, that is. For much of the time, we rented it and had to pay thirty to forty percent of any income to the landlord. Some years, we feared that the bank would not even lend my parents money they needed to begin the spring farming season.

Unasked questions were always in the air: *What would we do if we did not live on the farm? Where would we live?* This terrifying anxiety hung over us all. Unemployment in any situation is always a crisis and I do not minimize that awful fact for anyone. Unemployment for a farmer is a unique tragedy because it includes the loss of identity and heritage. You lose the farm, the land you had tended for years, maybe generations, and watch as it is gobbled up by enterprising neighbors or faceless corporations. You walk away with nothing except shame, defeat, and awful debt. It is a waking nightmare of your own death. Many defeated farmers accept the nightmare of death literally and commit suicide. Being tied so closely to the land, Mother Earth, and having her ripped away, is similar to the experiences of many of our native tribes who are still in despair centuries after their lands were stolen.

Poverty is relative, and it is hard to compare our situation to those outside the farming community, especially those in urban spaces or in other countries. Sometimes, one's own suffering is all one can understand. We were never homeless. My mom went to the grocery store as needed, probably using farm loan money to purchase the goods. In fact, it is difficult to even claim the word "poverty" when you compare my experiences to those who risk death from malnutrition, disease, or exposure. All the same, we lived in a form of constant peril, and this took an emotional toll on all of us, parents and children alike.

As kids, we looked upon the "city kids" with envy. To us, they were rich because they seemed to always have enough, even more than enough, of whatever material goods we wished we had for ourselves. I couldn't figure out why some other farms seemed to be doing better than ours. I watched expensive, prestigious grain-storage silos built on neighboring farms while we had none. I remember praying numerous times for financial relief so that we would not lose the farm. I prayed for rain to break a drought, then for it to stop when too much rain came and flooded the land, washing out the irrigation ditches, melting the sandy loam and sweeping away the crops. I watched my dad staring out the window of our home as wind and hail ripped leaves off trees and stripped crops, so they were little more than broken dying stems. Then came the overwhelming smell of alfalfa, corn, beans, and sugar beet leaves ground to a pulp and rotting into the earth. My father, in the grief and terror only a farmer knows, looked at my mother and said over and over, "We're losing it all, we're losing it all…" My mom stood tall, stoic with all the power of her Scandinavian pioneer blood and ranch-woman fortitude. She absorbed those fears, praying silently. Crises like these did not make us cry and hug each other with warmth and nurturing compassion. We couldn't show each other that we were deeply and richly loved no matter what economic shit hit the fan. Instead, we were just scared and scarred, alone, each of us in the living room. We didn't know how to be safely vulnerable and tender with each other. We were all together, alone.

Shame-based religious and family training sent us into guilt-ridden anguish over what should have been normal childhood curiosities. I endured the chronic anxieties of parents and family members who carried spoken and unspoken fears of economic and personal destitution, as well as deep religious fears of condemnation. I saw and felt our wounded father's violent outbursts that resulted from personal demons and economic despair. I witnessed our mother's unspoken traumas as the oldest child in a ranch family who had to buffer the violent, sociopathic sickness of her own cowboy father. I still grieve these personal and systemic family memories.

As a deeply lonely thirteen-year-old boy, I lost myself in wounding, guilt-ridden religion. I also turned to fantasies of early teen love and dreams of being my comic book hero, Superman. Depression, anxiety, and illness were as close to me as my breath. Asthma was a constant companion in my early life. School was torturous, especially when it came to anything that resembled chemistry, math, or physical activities. Though I often had failing or near-failing grades, I tried to look fine and act okay. If I showed the truth, I feared public shame would force me to feel more lost than I already was. Obviously, I could not hide the low grades, so I hid the feelings. I smiled, tried to look cool and smart, and avoided being vulnerable and authentic with people around me. I could not drop my guard. I didn't even know I had a guard. All I knew is that if I did not act okay, life would be even more emotionally dangerous. I would be even more lonely. I moved through life in a kind of invisible despair.

In the church and church activities, like Bible school, youth camps, and revivals, I found refuge in becoming a born-again Christian, *very* born-again, meaning that every time I "sinned" I needed to be resaved, resulting in numerous trips to the altar (or some variation of this) to repent again and ask Jesus for forgiveness. The frequency of our visits to the altar eventually became a source of dark humor between my friends and me. Once we got older and had the strength and perspective to understand our teenaged fears, we would tease each other about who made the most trips to the front of the church! It was a strange badge of honor.

Religion was both a curse and a blessing, a source of fear and assurance. I had deep fears of going to hell unless I was saved and had Jesus in my heart and soul. I yearned to be approved by the only place I felt some connection, my church. Yet, unless I diligently sought to be "sinless and sanctified," I would be lost forever. That made me even more lonely because I couldn't cuss or masturbate without believing I had committed some unpardonable sin. But that didn't stop me, thank god! It just added more layers to the wounds.

I hope you will understand this crazy-making double bind, and, even more, have a gentle smile of recognition as you think about your own awful and wondrous journey of adolescence. I am amazed, frankly, and proud in the here and now, that I survived.

Not all was awful in my childhood and my religious experiences and upbringing. Painful as much of it was, I am grateful for the entire journey because I don't think I would have become as loving, capable, thoughtful, and philosophical about life without walking such a rocky religious trail. Numerous friends from those years are still my brothers and sisters of the heart. Some were deeply wounded by the oppressive religiosity and do not attend any form of church now. Some remained in the church, resigned to accept the faith and fate that they were given. Others boldly created healthier expressions of faith and belief that became safe and nourishing for them.

As a child, and later as a college student, I had a few life-changing relationships with pastors and their families. In fact, those relationships played a big part in reforming and re-envisioning what spirituality and justice in the world looked like for me. Without knowing it, they helped give me the room and courage to question the rigidness of "that old-time religion," to experience grace, and break free.

Never would I believe that "everything happens for a reason." Nor do I think, as some people do, that we "choose" to be born into our family and life situations in order to learn and expand our souls for future lives, like some version of reincarnation. I do, however, know that I am enriched by all of my life's sorrows, joys, regrets, mistakes, creative adventures, and bold dreams. I am a rich and expansive soul. I am grateful, in anguish and joy, to live what Jesus described: an abundant, fulfilled life. I shall do my best to create meaning, healing, beauty, purpose, compassion, and adventure until I die. I entered into the ministry, discovered Process Theology, became educated and proficient in psychotherapy, fell in love with the wisdom and healing of our dream worlds—all because of my life experiences. Being an atheist, agnostic, believer, and dreamer gracefully frees me to become all that I am and be fully and gloriously authentic. I could not ask for more.

I could never have been as bold as the boy-wonder of Watlington, to venture and strike up a conversation with some random adult who might have felt compassion for me, who wanted to listen, and could see me and allow me to be myself. As a boy, I internalized my pain. I saved those conversations for god, Jesus, hoping "he" would hear my cries and not condemn me to eternal fire. The pursuit of the god-thing, with all the fear and judgmentalness that implied, was the best I could do at thirteen.

What might it have been like if a kind man ambled long ago onto our farm and safely and compassionately sought to understand and listen to my endearing, annoying self?

The Enchanted Forest

I left Watlington the next day, carried by the warmth of the autumn sun as I followed the Ridgeway's path through the fields and along the fences. The first miles of trail ran close to the sights and sounds of traffic, but I found relief for my eyes and ears in the solace of the trees and hedgerows.

Eventually, I passed within sight of an airport, which I assumed was a Royal Air Force base because of the numerous helicopters that flew overhead.

My path took a turn, and I began to move to higher, tree-covered ground that was cool in the heat of the day. The beech trees dominated with their height, width, and breadth. The first autumn leaves had descended to the forest floor while others, in various shades of red, orange, and green still clung to their trees high above. The contrast was dramatic. The warm sunlight found ways to play and sparkle through the trees, sometimes breaking through the canopy and splashing upon the forest floor.

I felt I was being watched. Not by humans, but by trees, beams of sunlight, holly bushes with bright red berries, ground cover plants, and by the path itself. They all held me and watched me as I hiked. Insulated from the buzz of faraway traffic and noisy farm equipment that marks the beginning of autumn harvest, the forest was free of human sound. The songs of birds, high and far away, gave a sense of majesty to the tall trees. The chirping and rattle of insects sang of the end of summer; some sang an end to their brief lives. Invisible forest animals, scampering under leaves and rustling to be ready for an English winter, brought soft words from me. I whispered to the Earth and its creatures, talked with it, as if this forest were my friend. An invisible blanket of warmth and nourishment held *us*, all forest beings. Quietly grazing on the undergrowth not far from me was what looked like a tiny deer. It was actually a muntjac, a non-native species originally introduced from China. I felt like I was in an enchanted forest. Indeed, I was.

I came upon trail signs without words. The simple arrows were pointing in slightly different directions, and I wondered which was the Ridgeway. I grabbed the map and sought out the path descriptions in the guidebook. Evidently, another trail intersected with the Ridgeway in this forest, but it wasn't clear which trail was which as both arrows looked like they would lead in essentially the same direction. I experimented with one trail and came back and tried the other. There was no discernible difference. There was a higher path that led over the top of this forested hill, while the other, going in basically the same direction, stayed low. I chose the higher.

After a while, I met a couple, arm in arm, walking toward me. Having no packs, I assumed they were day-hikers. They looked about my age and we smiled at each other and said hello. In my projection, they looked like new lovers cooing to one another. I thought about asking them for directions but, at the moment, I was confident of my choice and didn't feel I needed to confirm that I was headed the right way. I ventured up the hill into the forest. After a long while, I took a turn on the path, and it seemed to end abruptly. I backtracked and tried again. I searched the landscape all around me for hints of a path that I had missed. There were none. I followed a slight depression through the trees, hoping that I was on a portion of the trail that had been covered by early autumn leaves. I pushed on. Gazing around, I stopped often, looking for arrows or signs on trees, trying to make logical sense of the trail's disappearance. I tried to consult Google maps, but there was no phone signal. The sun would set soon. My worry was rising, and I imagined what it would be like to spend the night in this forest. It would be uncomfortable, but doable. It would be particularly unsettling to miss my stay at the next bed and breakfast. I walked on with a firmness and determination.

Somewhat later, I rounded a turn, stopped, and uttered a low gasp. Everything was familiar. Suddenly, I realized I had walked in a giant circle. I saw again the same arrows posted on the trees. I felt foolish and disappointed. Then, I saw the couple again! I had no joy this time, only embarrassment. They were going in their own direction, following a completely different path, in the direction back to Watlington, I assumed. Was I imagining, or did they snicker at me? I am not proud of myself to admit that I did not pursue a conversation with them. I didn't ask where the hell I was or how to find the Ridgeway, but of course, I should have. Angry at myself, I felt frustrated, embarrassed, and made a crazy, reactive, reptilian decision and ignored them. *I'll stay in the forest if I have to and find my way out tomorrow*, I thought. This kind of stravaging, maintaining a defiant attitude despite my own best interests was exactly what a thirteen-year-old boy would do.

I was in an enchanted forest, on an enchanted trail, on an enchanted mission to heal my soul. The reappearance of the couple, the way I got lost and walked in giant circles, unconsciously retracing my footsteps, can be understood in retrospect, through the lens of a waking dream. In the dream world, when we have recurring dreams that have similar themes or dreams that are repeated over and over again, we need to ask ourselves, "What is it that I'm not getting? What messages have to keep being repeated over and over until I understand?"

My reactions to the couple illuminated something in me that I had been avoiding. I am an introvert, but I am also kind and friendly. It was not typical of me, in the middle of English Nowhere Land, to simply pass by an opportunity to meet some locals, have a conversation, and ask directions. Why did I avoid visiting with them, not once, but *twice?* What was this recurring waking dream trying to tell me? What did the dream want me to awaken to and reckon with?

Barely two years before I took the Ridgeway saunter, I had been divorced. As I have described, I was disoriented and unclear about the direction my life would take on the other side of my marriage. I was lost, immobilized, walking in circles, and trying to find my way, all at the same time. Here in England on this sunny autumn afternoon, in a sacred, quiet, and enchanted forest, I met a pair of lovers who looked like my contemporaries. Was this a flash backwards into time, into my unresolved life and marriage? Was I re-living memories of love, tenderness, and sensuality, as well as the conflicts, pain, and sorrow that could *not* be overcome? Or was this couple, somehow, a picture of my future self, in a new, cooing communion? What if I was not mourning what was lost but was instead frightened about what might be possible?

If you were to say "both," you'd be correct. The waking dream in that faraway English forest was graciously showing me both the pains of my past *and* what might lie ahead. When I saw that loving couple, arm in arm, being tender and touching each other awkwardly as they walked, I projected "newness" upon them. Unconsciously, they bothered me. They seemed so gooey with each other. In my childhood family, we weren't free to hug, cry, and support each other through life's seasons. We were, as I've said, *together, alone*. This sauntering couple reminded me of one of my deepest struggles in my psyche—the simultaneous fear of and deep yearning for intimacy with another. In other words, I didn't know how to be close and safe without losing my own identity. This dilemma existed in my marriage too.

Lord knows we tried, my wife and I, we really tried. Over the years, we spent time in therapy doing our best to renegotiate our relationship and form it into something that served both our needs. Sometimes, we almost made it and got close enough to keep trying time and again. But I believe in the end, it came down to us being mismatched in our core selves. That seems easy to say but hard to understand and harder to explain. Still struggling with my own childhood experiences, my core self couldn't relax and trust that I would be safe and whole in our relationship. She felt I was pushing her to be someone she was not. I felt I was being pressured to form myself into what she needed and wanted. All this tapped into my vulnerabilities, conscious and unconscious, to appease, hide, placate, and accommodate her at the expense of my real self.

We had both yearned for openhearted, unguarded intimacy with the other. But in the end, it was not possible. After the overwhelming flood of shame and failure subsided, we realized, each in our own way, that no one would die from our decision to divorce—not our family, not our beloved friends, not us. In time, we both arrived at a sense of peace, perhaps, as St. Paul would describe, "that passeth understanding…"

Now, the unhealthy demands we placed on the other have ceased. I can only speak for my journey: I know I am richer and healthier for having been married and I am grateful for all I learned along the way. I am less likely to project my unconscious, unmet needs upon another. I am more able to see my brokenness, take ownership of it, and release the unconscious expectations that another should heal me. When I can own my brokenness, I am made more whole. Doing so may not make me any more pretty but allowing myself to be broken *does* make me more real, authentic, healthy, and congruent.

These days, my former wife and I work to do our best to be kind and helpful to each other when we're called to do so. We work to heal the wounds of the forever disruption of our respective family systems, to be loving parents to our adult children without dragging them into our shit. We share grandchildren whom we admire and love dearly, and we shall always bless them as they unfold and create their lives.

The enchanted forest that I walked within on that English autumn day cast a spell upon me that I did not consciously seek yet needed and secretly yearned for as I stravaged to form a new life.

You might say that this innocent, beautiful couple, so clearly in love as they sauntered carefree along their path, were unconsciously terrifying to me. At the same time, as only a dream can do, they gave me a gift, a glimpse of a new life, a new trail to follow. It is possible for me to be vulnerable, deeply close to another. It is possible for me to be with another and breathe, fully and freely. I can change those old patterns. This waking dream didn't come to cast judgment. Instead, it was inspiring me to forge new paths of fulfillment so I might see myself with joy, wholeheartedness, and unguarded free-wheeling expression. The experience revealed my past and potential future. Ultimately, this dream says we can't ignore the signs and arrows posted before us. If we do, we run the risk of walking in circles, repeating old patterns in our waking lives. When we refuse to heed the signs, we just might miss the healing, renewing messages that offer to change our lives...forever.

Enchanted forests, enchanted trails, enchanted waking dreams.

Chapter Sixteen
Keep Calm & Saunter On

Enchanting as this forest was, I still needed to get out of it. I studied the arrows on the Ridgeway path again and cursed. It was not logical that I could not find my way out of this place. I determined I would simply walk in as straight a line as I could, keeping the sun at my back. If I refused to take turns, I figured at some point the forest ended on some other side. After what may have been several hours, I proved myself right. I came down the hill and saw a country road. Relieved and victorious, I ventured out into the road and the welcoming sunlight. Now out of the woods, I tried to connect with Google maps again, but to no avail.

Suddenly, I saw a daddy pushing his toddler in a stroller toward me down this empty rural road. Relieved, I bantered with him and his little one. I asked for directions for the bed and breakfast at which I was to stay that night. He had never heard of it, but he offered to google the name, the Ridgeway Lodge. Though his cell phone worked, the place still didn't show up. I simply thanked him, said goodbye to the little one, and headed down the country road in what I hoped was the right direction since I was no longer on the official Ridgeway path. The dimming sunlight enhanced the greenery of the small fields. Mature nettles and patches of other wild plants grew alongside the road, sometimes clustered around the wooden electrical poles. Clumps of trees and shrubs lay further ahead indicating farmyards and homes. I came to an intersection and, after a long time of indecision debating whether or not to knock on a nearby door of a home to ask for directions, I decided to simply keep walking in a straight line. Straight was better than changing directions. I knew I was not far, maybe four or five miles, from a village and, if nothing else, I would seek a room in a local pub. I walked for a couple more miles and, quite unbelievably, with a rush of relief that could have only come from the kindness of the forest spirits, I found myself standing in the driveway of the Ridgeway Lodge.

In the shade of a grove of trees that sheltered the road, I stared and stared at the bold letters spelling out the welcoming words on the wooden gates. I gazed down the graveled lane toward the lodge. Suddenly reaching what you might call "the grail" after my frustrating, desperate, take-no-turns quest, left me in a bit of a daze. This grand, modern bed and breakfast where I had reservations for the night was surrounded by a vast manicured lawn dotted with fruit and shade trees. Hot, sweaty, exhausted, and lugging a backpack fit for the trail not for the parlor, I felt a bit intimidated by the formal landscaping and beauty of the lodge. Wondering if my scruffy appearance might cause me to be viewed as a highwayman, that old fashioned term for a robber, I slowly sauntered down the lane.

The Ridgeway Lodge, the only bed and breakfast actually sitting directly on the trail, was devoid of hikers, except for me. The lodge is found in all the trail guides and is billed as a haven for the weary walker, but its clientele generally seem to arrive by car or small tour bus. Many are seeking a countryside refuge after paying a visit to the nearby historic town of Princes Risborough, a place of quaint restaurants and markets dating prior to 1086 CE. The cozy guest rooms, to my relief, were not as fancy as I had feared. The hosts were gracious and one of them allowed me to video interview her about the B&B, and this part of the English countryside. She simply asked that I not record anything she had to say about Brexit. Brexit, like Trump's America First movement, is jarring and divisive for the UK. Venturing an opinion, she implied, would invariably offend someone.

The next day's walk took me through open fields and pastures and bypassed the town. I was leaving behind the forests of England. The area was more populated, and the trail led directly through the yard of a quaint pub, the only pub located directly on the Ridgeway path. I was sorely tempted to stop and enjoy a pint, but time was short that day. I strolled through the yard. Some guests eating on tables in the gazebo-covered yard saw my pack and ventured a quick hello. The smell of freshly cooked pub grub that wafted through the air was tough to resist, but onward I hiked.

Later, I would enjoy a great feast of my own, more rich and enjoyable than the restaurant filled with humans could offer. I sprawled out in a glorious, sun-covered hillside pasture. I consumed yet another protein bar, as well as some fruit and nuts, and then napped next to a fallen tree. Just a few feet away a herd of angus cattle grazed, barely curious about this man in their midst. I was in sacred communion with them and felt at home.

Following the trail up a hill, I spied a fellow hiker with his own broad-brimmed hat eating a sandwich on the steps of a gate between pastures. We greeted each other and I stopped to visit. The man welcomed me in a relaxed, inviting manner. His friendly energy made me feel relaxed too, and I felt drawn to him. This retired physician explained that he takes a train out of London to this region every week and spends the entire day walking. I envied the ease with which the English can do that, take a train from their biggest city and go for a day's saunter. As he explained his weekly ritual, he turned his gaze beyond me, contentedly looking up at the land and hills. This day, he accidentally got off at the wrong train stop, but when he realized where he was, he said to himself that it didn't really matter where he started to walk. All this land is beautiful, and he couldn't go wrong.

He was delighted to hear my American accent and shared that he spent one of his medical residencies in a hospital in Philadelphia. He had been invited to remain there and begin his practice, but he was drawn home to London. He liked his country's health care program, alluding to the controversies that surround both the UK's National Health Service and America's chaotic, capitalistic medical mess.

When he found out I was a psychotherapist, he said he was married to a psychiatric nurse and, chuckling, commented, "She knows a lot about other people's diagnoses but misses obvious issues of her own." He wasn't unkind as he reported this, and I did not press the point on this quiet, welcoming man in this quiet, welcoming pasture. Though I said nothing, I was aware of my natural and intuitive therapeutic nudges and began to wonder about his marriage. He kind of slammed his wife with those words. I began thinking about my own struggles in a marriage that often left me feeling helpless in the face of what were, ultimately, unresolvable conflicts. In my projection, he pushed his conflicts aside (maybe too often, as did I) and had given up hope that those conflicts would diminish over time. Perhaps he was satisfied enough in his marriage. Maybe there were other, more meaningful bonds with his wife that overrode those deficits. Plus, he was older than I, and fully retired. He was going to die this way. His marriage worked despite the unresolved stuff, for better or worse. He appeared content, after all, and who am I to challenge that? Hiking, I mused, had multiple benefits: not only improved health and self-care, but also a break from a partner and relief from unhealed relationship wounds. I know well that "taking a hike" into the countryside is often motivated, in part, by a need to avoid conflicts and pain.

The physician then pointed to the south to my next destination and reminded me that the trail goes through the fields and yard of the country home of the Prime Minister of the UK. Even though I had read about how the trail passed by that government estate, which goes by the quaint name of Chequers, I wasn't prepared for what I experienced.

There were more walkers on this section of the trail, especially as I drew close to the official summer residence. I expected the path to be fenced off from the vast property. Instead, the well-worn path simply followed a wobbly, knee-high, single cabled fence designating the boundaries of the place. The mansion, shaded in tall trees, was easily visible about a quarter of a mile from the trail. The land between the trail and the home alternated between being a sheep pasture and a soybean field.

I am from Fortress America, where private land is often gated and where the "retreat" for U.S. presidents, Camp David, is walled off with the highest security possible, including sensors, military personnel, and weaponry that would stop a small invading army. The lack of visible security for the national leader's country residence was startling. I expected visible armed guards patrolling the fence lines. I imagined cameras in the forest, posted high in the trees watching each movement of each hiker and sensors hidden in the ground detecting vibrations from the steps of intruders if they walked toward the home.

Perhaps the British, with their history of James Bond and all, are exceptional at modes of covert surveillance and more. Perhaps not, and what I saw is what I got. I was observing an elegant country mansion in the autumn in England. The American brand of anxiety and paranoia is not experienced as much here in this ancient land that has been fought over, conquered, and bombed for centuries. *Here I am*, I thought, *stravaging upon a five-thousand-year-old path that traverses through the summer estate of the Prime Minister of England.* The freedom to roam law never felt so good.

The trail led through a soybean field that was being combined by a farmer who worked this government estate. He barely noticed me as I took videos of his work while the dry dust of the bean field drifted in the sunlit autumn air. It could have been Iowa or Indiana at harvest time. The trail then led across the long tree-lined driveway that connected the house to the nearby highway. The cool shade of the trees was welcome on this hot afternoon. Again, I couldn't help myself as I looked up into the trees and wondered if there were hidden cameras watching my every move. The only obvious security that I saw was at the gate and the gatehouse where there were guards. The irony was that I was *behind* the secured gates and on the *inside* of the estate. *What invasion*, I thought, *would risk going through the armed gates while a much more effective plan would be to simply use the Ridgeway Trail and invade from within?*

The United Kingdom has been the victim of war and terrorism, both recently and in times far past. The UK has its own history of inflicting similar misery on other people and nations as they cruelly built and maintained their own self-serving empire. It's ironic that a nation so accustomed to receiving and inflicting anguish has the physical and spiritual room within its identity to calmly allow a tiny hiking trail and its free roamers to walk mere feet from its prime minister, one of the most politically and militarily powerful people on Earth.

Broken Heroes

Not far from Chequers, a monument looms above the Ridgeway. The tall spire stands high on Coombe Hill, dominating the nearly treeless landscape. It commemorates the local soldiers who died in what the British empire calls the Boer War. This war was fought in South Africa in the late 19th and early 20th centuries against the rebel Dutch and German forces who sought independence from the British Empire. Of course, this battle of Euro-Africans was waged on land that had been stolen centuries before from the original African peoples. The human cost was immense, and in the awfulness of this imperialistic war, the slaughter of thousands of native Africans was not even acknowledged. Plus, the land itself suffered and paid dearly, a commodity to be carved and exploited. This was, as all wars are, brutal, cruel, and devastating.

I stood and gazed at the monument. Clouds had rolled in, and the air was cold now as a brisk breeze blew through. I didn't care to linger. The chill of the air matched my sorrowful mood as I thought of the exploitation of a people for the cause of land and gold and diamonds. These sins were not unlike those committed by my own Anglo-European ancestors who stole from the first Americans for the sake of land and gold.

I get that soldiers died in the Boer War, under orders, often heroically, to protect fellow soldiers and their vast empire. I get that they left loved ones behind, and the anguish of loss runs deep for generations. This was also the war that led to the capture and imprisonment of a young Winston Churchill, not a soldier at that time (he had been a soldier in India prior to this), but a newspaper war correspondent thirsty for adventure and glory. The story has it that he fought like a warrior before he and his companions were captured. Churchill loved the thrill of war and later, dramatically escaped. He became a hero back home in England. In my imagination, he became the passionate hero because he needed to compensate for his own life-long insecurities, depressive episodes, and wounded ego. Churchill, for good or ill, believed in the righteousness of the British empire and monarchy. Our heroes are flawed, as all humans are. Despite Churchill's blind sins in service of personal and national glory, he later saved us—all of us—through his courageous leadership nearly fifty years later.

Tired, with the wind blowing melancholy through me, I moved on. I hiked on toward my next stop: Wendover. As I drifted downhill toward town, the sun came out and the wind lessened. I met other people out for a late afternoon walk who seemed extra friendly, and that gave me comfort and lifted my spirits. I wandered the busy village streets, ate an early supper, and called my bed and breakfast host who came to collect me and take me to his home. I was now less than fifteen miles from my final destination: the end of the Ridgeway National Trail.

My Friend, Melancholy

The next morning, I joined the trail in downtown Wendover and followed the signs that pointed me southward along a small creek. The path then began a gentle climb into the hills, pastures, and wooded fields and wound east toward Ivinghoe Beacon, the official end point of what has been preserved of the Ridgeway National Trail. As I described before, the Ridgeway once continued onward for hundreds of miles, far to the east, even crossing the former land bridge that existed between the British Isles and Europe millennia ago.

This hike, this chosen and sacred saunter, was nearing an end. I was excited, and I was lonely. I had no one with me to share these moments. I knew I needed this aloneness and its accompanying loneliness. My stravage was a strange wandering, a painful mix of happy and sad, of fulfillment and continued longing. My mind returned to the couple in the enchanted forest. I thought of companionship with a mix of hope and sorrow. Alone now, with the trail upon which I walked as my only companion, it became my mother and father confessor, accepting all of my sins and victories. This land knew me best, held me in grace, witnessed my authentic self, acknowledged the painful discrepancies of my past, and the growing, imperfect hopes of my future. This trail led me into the shadows and lights of my soul.

Step by step, I surveyed my geography. I surveyed from where I had come, felt the delights of the work I had accomplished thus far in my life, all the ways I attempted to offer a healing presence to those in need. I surveyed, with each step, how I have loved—wounds and all, regrets and all—and that, as I crossed this blessed landscape, I was creating a new future.

In my mid-twenties I had an elderly mentor, a clinical chaplaincy educator who guided me through my pastoral care training at a hospital in New Orleans. During one of our group discussions, this wise sage remarked that depression and melancholy always seemed to linger just under the surface of my being. He quietly observed that I had access to a "bank" of not-okay-feelings within me. It was easy for me to make withdrawals from my internal emotional savings account and, as a result, I was gripped by a chronic lack of self-confidence. He gently laughed and mused about this savings account analogy, not as a judgment upon me, but as an awareness of something I needed to manage. He then quoted an obscure Old Testament scripture from Proverbs about "a friend that sticketh closer than a brother." He suggested that I have an intimate friend called *Melancholy*. Though I felt vulnerable, even naked with that small group of chaplaincy trainees, his words made sense. At last, I had a label for those "always there" feelings that I naturally carried.

Melancholy, my friend who *is* pain. Melancholy, who leads me into deep introspection, sometimes into loss and despair. Melancholy, who offers deep insights into my own humanness. Melancholy, the force of loving curiosity, who leads me into the world of nighttime dreams and onto paths of healing. Melancholy, the teacher of empathy, who leads me into the soul journeys of others. Melancholy, my friend, who sticketh closer than a brother. Melancholy who nudged me—*compelled* me—to take this stravage into the mystical English countryside and into the geography of my humanity and the landscape of my being.

My divorce was less than two years old. Of all the things I needed, one thing I did *not* need was a relationship outside of myself. I longed for an intimate relationship, a lover, maybe a wife. This forever friend, this loving, awful Melancholy, stopped me, insisted that I must, no matter what, marry *myself* first. I sigh as I write. I have no words to explain this wisdom, the wisdom of *that which is not yet speech ripe,* but this knowing is held within my weary soul.

My friend Melancholy holds my unexplained anxieties and sufferings, that which I describe as loneliness and emotional disorientation. Many of us have filled our modern world with intentional distractions to help us avoid our pain and ultimate aloneness. Oftentimes we don't want to take responsibility to create meaning and purpose. We want to delegate it to another. It's hard to search the soul and find the authentic self. Sometimes it's easier to get lost in screen time or plead with a doctor for meds to relieve that existential pain. Though we've been taught to avoid her, perhaps Melancholy is the friend you most need. You might know her as the witch, the hag who haunts you in your nightmares. She sits on your chest and you gasp, horrified, unable to breathe until you learn to embrace her, kiss her, take her into yourself. Then you will awaken to see your wounded, tattered, and, oh-so-beautiful self. She will encourage you to stay with your "not knowing." She will support your struggle toward "that which is not yet speech ripe," and hold space for that cursed and loving emptiness. But of course, our culture wants to burn that witch at the stake and do away with the messenger that stirs within our dark shadows and chants, *Double, double toil and trouble, fire burn and cauldron bubble.*

Yet, in the stirrings of our darkness, in the dreams that wake us with terror, in our deepest cauldrons and most profound melancholic moments, we see what we need to learn in order to fill our souls with wisdom and lead more authentic lives. Then, it's possible to sip from the cup of living water, from that freshwater faucet that appeared days and dazed ago on the Ridgeway. Friends at last with Melancholy, you find that long-sought place of refreshment along your stravage, that place that defiantly conspires to turn your storms of darkness into healing beauty.

These are the authentic spiritual voyages, the saunterers—*a la sainte terre!*—that lead to empathy, compassion, healing, strength and courage. Though filled with fear and trembling (and with some wailing and gnashing of teeth) I want to continue to learn from this muse called Melancholy.

"O Taste and See..."

The day warmed and the English breeze gusted as hard as my beloved Nebraska prairie wind. The closer I got to Ivinghoe Beacon, the further away that final Ridgeway hilltop seemed. It was Sunday and I spied a full car park that revealed this to be a popular destination for day hikers. They emerged, I assumed, from the nearby cities and towns to spend the sunny day doing what the Brits do best, walk the countryside. A snack and ice cream truck was stationed under a distant shade tree and children, along with their compliant adults, were enjoying a post-walk treat. That moment of watching them enjoying togetherness, licking delectable ice cream, made me both happy and sad as I missed my family and friends. My Melancholy whispered again, reminding me of my aloneness on this last stretch.

More and more people were sharing the trail as we walked through the pastures that stretched before the last hills of the Ridgeway. Small herds of cattle lazily ambled alongside small herds of people, neither paying much attention to the other, and I smiled at this little expression of earthly harmony. As I walked, I found I wasn't able to judge distances accurately because of the openness of the landscape and its lack of landmarks. The illusion of space distorted my perspective, and I kept hoping the next hill was the last. But then the next hill just wouldn't end. I marched on and on in a kind of giddy exhaustion.

Toddlers scrambled up the steep slopes behind watchful parents. Pre-teens awkwardly raced one another up and down the hills. Many adults seemed ill-accustomed to rugged terrain, but they refused to give in to gravity or fatigue and kept pushing on. The last two miles of the Ridgeway, it seemed, were the ideal place for the locals to celebrate an afternoon together. Everyone had a different favorite path to climb, ignoring the marked trails, and simply trudging up the hills that seemed most inviting. The hillsides didn't care. They welcomed anyone to find an old trail or blaze a new one. "Just come," the hillsides said, "just come."

Up and down the grassy draws we walked. Sometimes, I was alone, then a moment later I was within a family pack or strolling beside a couple who nodded and murmured a hello. I kept staring far ahead, seeing the end of the trail, and then looking down and around, glancing behind, seeing the distant car park below and how far I had come. This was not just a series of hills we were walking I realized, but more like one long, long hill marked by an assortment of banks, knolls, and small mounds. We would go up, then down, and up again, all the while, step by step, slowly gaining elevation.

I realized the trails were converging, funneling everyone into one narrower area as we headed toward the top. The sun hid behind large drifting clouds, adding to the coolness of the air as the wind blew. Now there were no more ups and downs, just a long, straight upward shot to the crest of Ivinghoe Beacon.

Soon, the hill flattened onto a small plateau. In the distance, I could see two granite markers, one low lying and broad and the other a taller pinnacle. There were walkers milling, gazing at the markers, and surveying the vast lands below. I caught my breath, hesitated, knowing I was now nearing the end of the Ridgeway. Walking more slowly now, beginning to feel the magnitude of what I had accomplished, I headed toward the markers.

The wind whipped and swirled, drowning out the laughter of children and the conversations of adults and all other sounds. This was a strange kind of solitude, being able to see but not hear anything except the wind. In this privacy, I began to reflect upon what I had accomplished in this sacred saunter, this dream come true. I wasn't just thinking about this near one-hundred-mile hike, but about my life, healing, breaking free, breathing free. "The spirit that is like the wind" compelled me to remember a recurring, terrifying dream.

The dream, with some variations in plot and location, has recurred over and over since I hit middle age. Its main themes are always the same: I am imprisoned and am afraid of brutal punishment, torture, and death.

I am in a stainless steel, spotless prison. I don't know why I am imprisoned. I'm full of shame, guilt, humiliation, like everyone knows what I have done or am accused of having done. I feel vulnerable, emotionally naked, exposed. There are others in the prison, but further away, indistinct, not very visible. There are guards who threaten punishment and torture. I'm trapped. I have made a vague attempt to consult with an attorney, someone who will advocate for me, protect me, maybe get me out. But the attorney is not visible, and I am not getting help. I am sitting at a spotless, stainless-steel table, like a large cafeteria table, bolted and chained to the floor.

Every time I have had this dream, I suddenly wake up, gasping in terror, heart hammering. It is a "so real dream," and it takes long moments to realize it was just a dream.

You are already interpreting and projecting upon my dream, as you should and are welcome to do. Instinctively, you cannot help but do this. A dream always comes to us at the moment it's needed, either as a dream while sleeping, or into waking life as a memory of a dream we have had. As I walked the last steps of my stravage, the dream resurfaced, unbidden but necessary.

My mentor Jeremy Taylor and I had worked on this recurring dream. While the individual can do good work by deeply reflecting upon our own dreams by ourselves, we also need the connection with an "Other." We need someone outside ourselves who can lovingly and non-judgmentally reflect with us, challenge and stretch us into new and different perspectives.

Jeremy helped me to ask many of the therapeutic questions that I myself would often explore with a client: How do I imprison myself? What does it mean I am having this dream again, *now*, even though I've changed, have had much healing in my life over my years of maturation and growth? What do the objects in the dream mean—a spotless prison, everything made of stainless steel? What about the people, that unreachable attorney, the looming prison guards? What of the feelings of terror, shame, humiliation, vulnerability, being exposed, expecting torture or death?

Together, we explored further projections, like what part of *me* is symbolized by each of the elements and objects in the dream. What part of me is like a metal window bar in a prison, a floor and a table of stainless steel? What part of me is "spotless?" What part is like an attorney or a prison guard? You may go on and on in these wonders, as did he and I, as we attempted to decipher the what, the why, and the unique timing of this dream.

This dream, of course, as some dreams do, screamed *real*. My ancient brainstem with all the power of my rattlesnake cousins didn't know I was dreaming and was ready to strike or flee. Why did the dream feel so palpable? Was this a kind of "traumatic memory dream," a self-torturing dream that calls upon memories of our waking world, like accidents, abuse, war experiences, and other traumatic stress events, and only serves to re-traumatize us? Some experts in the helping professions believe these kinds of "memory dreams" just reflect harmful experiences and treatment means that the dream must be reduced or discarded with medications, hypnotism, and other techniques to take them away. Again, I must remind us, every dream comes with a purpose to heal and move us in the direction of health, wholeness, and wisdom. Every dream, no matter the dream, comes in friendship.

Why did this dream come repetitively through my life, and *why* did the conscious memory of this dream come *now* as I was nearing the end of one of the most glorious journeys in my life, during a moment of such personal freedom and success?

Some recurring dreams (and conscious recollections of dreams, in this case) serve as markers of our lives. They point to where we have been, are now, and to where we are going. This dream, and the memory of the dream as I walked the last steps of the Ridgeway, painfully and beautifully, marked my path. It showed me my scars of living, the pain and progress of being in and breaking out of an existential prison where I was trapped by my anxieties of perfectionisms, by my wounded religious incarceration. The dream reflected the anxieties and shame of generations of my family should anyone dare to be visible, stand out, and embrace a new, bold, adventurous living. It reminded me of how much

I would have missed and how much I would have had to endure if I had been unable and unwilling to break the rules of my life and strike out on my own stravage. If I had not, I would still be in my nightmare, trapped, waiting to die.

This dream is also a truth of my age and my aging. We don't know when death will come. The dream is a calling to seize the day, to live this moment as fully as is possible. It is the dream world's own *carpe diem* for life's sake. The dream pushed me—it was not gentle!—to make me face that my life will end and I must ask tough questions: Will I imprison myself, lock myself up in order to stay safe, to remain "pure and undefiled, spotless" like my "risk-free" old-time religion demanded? No. The day must be seized—it is the only day you or I ever have—and we must take the sacred risks, imperfect as we are, to contribute to the adventure and beauty of our lives, to the creation. The gods cheer us on, in fact, join us, as we seek to be the companions of compassion, willing sacrifice, and the boldness to make meaning, beauty, adventure, and purpose as best we can, *no matter our age.*

My thoughts turned to that beloved teenaged boy memorialized with the water stop near the White Horse. He never had a chance to hike his beloved Ridgeway before he died. I grieve for him and those who mourn him. I am, for lack of a better, more accurate term, simply *lucky.* Assuming I continue living, I know I am much closer to death than I ever have been. How do I want to say I have lived? How do I want to meet death? We all ask these questions, though mostly we do so unconsciously. This dream, in its loving, even terrifying mission, refuses to allow me to be unconscious about my eventual death. I must take responsibility to unlock the prison gates, to be conscious and liberated. I have the power, the dream says; I don't need any attorney to advocate for me or to rescue me. No matter my age, I must embrace my responsibility to live and die, as best as I can, *unlocked and free.*

The wind tore at my shirt sleeves. If my broad-brimmed hiking hat hadn't been cinched under my chin it would have blown far away down the steep slopes on the other side of the ridge. For about fifteen days, I had hiked. It was important that I didn't count exactly the number of days. I wandered, got lost numerous times, stayed longer in some locations than others, defied the conventional rules of the trail to make lodging reservations well in advance, and did just fine, thank you.

Chilly and warm at the same time, I watched as the sun was blanketed by large wispy clouds. I drew close to the monuments marking the end of the trail. Ivinghoe Beacon stood above an immeasurable expanse of land, a valley below dotted with towns, villages, highways, groves of trees, farms, and a railway. I stood aghast, speechless, praying wordlessly. I was there, at the end of the Ridgeway.

Under the limitless sky, I stood amongst thousands of years of memories. Imagining the ice sheets that pushed, carved, and sculpted the earth, and then melted and receded so the prehistoric beasts and beings could move along these rocky ridges. I bowed in their honor. Back at Avebury at the genesis of my hike, I had turned to the four sacred directions on that small mound called Windmill Hill and thanked all who brought me to that beginning. I did the same here, walking in a slow, wide circle on Ivinghoe Beacon and offering gratitude to all who brought me to this end.

My soul was celebrating this moment. I yearned for connection with someone, anyone. I longed to visit about these hills, the Ridgeway, and about my triumph. But it was like I was invisible. I said hello and smiled to several people and received only the barest of greetings. It was as if I were in a dream, disassociating, standing separate and watching the scene play out around me. Melancholy surfaced again, and I felt the full weight of my solitariness.

The weather turned, and the sun disappeared behind a large dark cloud and the wind picked up even more. In the strangeness of that moment, almost everyone disappeared. Suddenly, I remembered I wanted someone to take my picture here at the end of the Ridgeway. I turned and saw a couple who had just arrived on top and quickly asked them to take a picture before they too left. In a kind of perfunctory politeness, they agreed. Then, probably trying to get out of the chill and wind, they were gone. I was alone, fully alone, at the far end of the Ridgeway.

It would have been easy to feel imprisoned by loneliness in this moment and to feel as if my entire journey was tinged with a sort of lonely melancholy, but I returned to the soul of my stravage, this desire to live unlocked and free. I hadn't come this far to merely "glance and go." I was determined to immerse myself into this sacred place that called me so many years before. Again, I turned toward the west, the far away west, toward the direction of my birthplace, the Nebraska prairie. The darkest cloud passed, and the late afternoon sun hung low and bright in the cloudy western sky. Even though I was alone, I felt grateful that this day was now. I was proud, fulfilled, determined.

Wanting to linger and savor the moment a little longer,

I decided to splurge on a series of international calls. Huddled behind the low-lying monument that topped the hill, I called my loved ones. Most of all, I wanted to speak with my mom and dad to celebrate this moment. They would never understand why I was called to do what I had just done. But no matter. I understood my mission and I simply needed to reach out to them. My mom, in her Scandinavian, prairie-pioneer stoicism, expressed her own pride for my accomplishment, reflecting my own sense of pride back to me. My father was simply relieved that I was safe from the highwaymen who might still roam along the English trail.

Even in my Melancholy, in my lonely and wise soul, I felt an energy growing within and beyond me, an energy of the ages. It was a sacred knowing that, though I am by myself, I was *not* alone. I knew that, *felt* that. I *knew,* beyond logic and speech-ripeness that, in this celebrative, mystical moment, I was going to be surprised.

Huddled and happy behind the small monument, I finished my calls and saw another dream unfolding before me. My eyes grew wide, and I couldn't help but smile. Out of nowhere, people emerged from the far side of the hill. They must have climbed up a trail from the valley that stretched beyond the end of the Ridgeway. They were like rising angels, garments blowing in the wind. They crossed in front of me and gathered around the other pinnacle-shaped monument that stood just a few feet away. This group of a dozen souls were talking and laughing, and so glad to be in one another's company. And they were carrying a large, thickly frosted cake. I *knew* it was for me.

Okay, it was not for me, and yet, it *was.* I jumped up, ready to be playful with these new visitors who appeared out of everywhere. Their voices rose above the wild winds, and they sang "Happy Birthday" to each other. I started to laugh aloud. Seeing me, they laughed too. Interrupting them, I asked, "Who's birthday is it and why are you celebrating here?" They all started talking at once, explaining that they were a local walking club and they have been together for fifteen years, meeting twice a month to saunter across this land they loved. I gushed, laughing more, and declared that I, *just now*, am completing *my* Ridgeway hike. Oohs and ahhs erupted and all at once they exclaimed, "Please, eat cake with us! You deserve it!" A sudden community of friends, who knew one another and understood this holy moment, was formed.

There is a tiny phrase from a biblical song. Written thousands of years ago, it speaks of melancholy and longing, of hiding and being found, of being nourished when one needed it most. As I ate the delicious, sugary cake, the line sang in my heart, *O taste and see what our beloved Creator has done.*

And, of course, I did.

6 Basic Hints for Dream Work

One: All dreams speak a universal language and come in the service of health and wholeness. There is no such thing as a "bad dream"—only dreams that sometimes take a dramatically negative form in order to grab our attention.

Two: Only the dreamer can say with any certainty what meanings his or her dream may have. This certainty usually comes in the form of a wordless "aha!" of recognition. This "aha" is a function of memory and is the only reliable touchstone of dream work.

Three: There is no such thing as a dream with only one meaning. All dreams and dream images are "over-determined" and have multiple meanings and layers of significance.

Four: No dreams come just to tell you what you already know. All dreams break new ground and invite you to new understandings and insights.

Five: When talking to others about their dreams, it is both wise and polite to preface your remarks with words to the effect of, "If it were my dream…" and to keep this commentary in the first person as much as possible. This means that even relatively challenging comments can be made in such a way that the dreamer may actually be able to hear and internalize them. It also can become a profound psycho-spiritual discipline—"walking a mile in your neighbor's moccasins."

Six: All dream group participants should agree at the outset to maintain anonymity in all discussions of dream work. In the absence of any specific request for confidentiality, group members should be free to discuss their experiences openly outside the group, provided no other dreamer is identifiable in their stories. However, whenever any group member requests confidentiality, all members should agree to be bound automatically by such a request.

Acknowledgments

How does one acknowledge *the all that is* that has gone into the creation of a work? The mystery of all that has gone into each word, memory, dream, sorrow, joy and story is limitless. This is the gestalt of life…the whole is indeed greater than the sum of the parts. Some parts are visible, easily identifiable while others—most others, in fact—are invisible, infinite, molecular, and yet are as vital as the most visible of *the all that is*. Ahh…these are the particles; this is the dust of life and creation.

I am grateful for…

Jeremy Taylor, my priest of dreams. You, who would often don your shamanic hat with humor and joy when we met for our appointments for those many years as we explored my dreams in sacred projective fashion. I am forever grateful. You died without my permission. This version of the world could not hold you. So, you went on, leaving behind your sacred particles, your stardust of wisdom and love, for us to heal through our dreams of life. I still dream of you. I think, in the great weirdness of the unknown of "after life," you know that.

Laura Deal, who, soon after my hike into ancient England, was willing to be a reader and early editor of my soulful trek. I got lost (again and again) as I was writing this walk. I froze up, as only a writer can understand, for at least a year or two or three. Thank you for your gentle, wise grace.

I met Marisa Goudy at a retreat for writers and healers, in the Catskills of New York, the day after I completed another symbolic hike, an existential and fearful walk into the shadows of our U.S.

military. Nothing about that journey is congruent and is only barely explainable in this book. However, out of that fearsome and eventually loving journey into my shadow, Marisa became my editor and book coach for this, and *all* of these sacred saunters described. Many times, I froze, melted, froze again and again, and melted. Through the fires of determination, passion, and patience from both of us, I wrote this book. Her fiery Irish wisdom conjured with my soul, and I am releasing this lovely testament to fly. So, with my hand over my heart, I bow to you.

Oh, my clients, former and present, what shall I say? Do you know your contributions to the healing of our world? You breathe meaning into the world's soul. Not because you fully heal, nor because you live "problem free" because of that damn "solution-focused, evidence-based therapy" that capitalism and wounded insurance companies insist you receive, but because you are real, authentic, vulnerable, and so bold and brave to saunter into this painful world. Your geography of your soul offers gifts to all of us, to me. The stravage of your chaotic and beautiful dreams and stories heal us all. Please continue to teach me, teach us all.

I'm often a client too. I work on my own dreams and my own therapy struggles. I want you to know that. Authenticity heals. Therapists need therapists. All of my past professors, supervisors, formal and informal therapists, spiritual counselors, and deep soulful friends have held me, helped me move in the direction of healing. To you, thank you.

Writers expect rejection. I may hold the record of being ignored, rejected, looked over or dismissed by god/goddess knows how many agents and publishers. When I would read about how many times some of my favorite authors were rejected, that would inspire me (sometimes). Be afraid. Be very afraid as a writer. But, also, don't give a shit about getting approval to get your story out

288

there. Don't stop. But of course you will, because you're human. I often did. And then, as the Bible says, I girded my loins, and ran that race again. One hot summer Sunday, Thea from Flint Hills Publishing, sent me inspiration and excitement in an email. She loved my book! She got it, the message, the soulful stravage! I couldn't believe it. Still don't. Thank you, Thea, for this part of a waking dream come true.

I know I have missed the mark in not mentioning you. But you are in my heart, all of you who have not been named. My brain is not big enough to remember. Perhaps too, I am not bold or brave enough to name you. But you are a part of the gracious *all that is*.

Thank you.

About the Author

Dr. Royce Fitts is a Licensed Marriage and Family Therapist in five U.S. states, an ordained minister, and lover of Process Theology. He holds a Doctor of Ministry in pastoral counseling. Royce is a certified Spiritual Care Professional in The American Association for Clinical and Pastoral Education and a Clinical Fellow in The American Association for Marriage and Family Therapy. He currently serves on assignment as a Military and Family Life Counselor for active U.S. military members and families. Royce also has an online practice dedicated to open-hearted, spiritual counseling and dream work.

Royce enjoys slow running and hiking everywhere from his beloved Nebraska prairie to crowded urban centers.

Above all, he is a lover of dreams, even the dreams that shake, confound, and terrify. They are, he believes, an ancient inner compass, perhaps one of our deepest instinctual energies, that will always guide us—and our world—into healing, wholeness, and beauty.

To learn how you can connect with Royce about his spiritual counseling and dreamwork:

www.RoyceFitts.com.

Printed in the USA
CPSIA information can be obtained
at www.ICGtesting.com
LVHW092310141123
763980LV00016B/68/J